Confessions of Faith and the Books of Discipline of the Church of Scotland; of Date Anterior to the Westminster Confession, to Which Are Prefixed, A Historical View of the Church of Scotland ... and a Historical Preface ...

THE
CONFESSIONS OF FAITH AND THE
BOOKS OF DISCIPLINE

OF THE

CHURCH OF SCOTLAND,

OF DATE

ANTERIOR TO THE WESTMINSTER CONFESSION.

TO WHICH ARE PREFIXED,

A

𝕳𝖎𝖘𝖙𝖔𝖗𝖎𝖈𝖆𝖑 𝖁𝖎𝖊𝖜 𝖔𝖋 𝖙𝖍𝖊 𝕮𝖍𝖚𝖗𝖈𝖍 𝖔𝖋 𝕾𝖈𝖔𝖙𝖑𝖆𝖓𝖉

FROM THE EARLIEST PERIOD TO THE TIME
OF THE REFORMATION,
AND A

HISTORICAL PREFACE, WITH REMARKS.

BY THE

REV. EDWARD IRVING, M.A.

MINISTER OF THE NATIONAL SCOTCH CHURCH, AND
AUTHOR OF " THE ORTHODOX AND CATHOLIC DOCTRINE OF
OUR LORD'S HUMAN NATURE."

LONDON:

Printed by Ellerton and Henderson,
Gough Square,

FOR BALDWIN AND CRADOCK,

PATERNOSTER-ROW.

MDCCCXXXI.

CONTENTS.

THE LESSON.

2 Chron. xxxiv. 14—31.

And when they brought out the money that was brought into the house of the Lord, Hilkiah the priest found a book of the law of the Lord given by Moses. And Hilkiah answered and said to Shaphan the scribe, I have found the book of the law in the house of the Lord. And Hilkiah delivered the book to Shaphan. And Shaphan carried the book to the king, and brought the king word back again, saying, All that was committed to thy servants, they do it. And they have gathered together the money that was found in the house of the Lord, and have delivered it into the hand of the overseers, and to the hand of the workmen. Then Shaphan the scribe told the king, saying, Hilkiah the priest hath given me a book. And Shaphan read it before the king. And it came to pass, when the king had heard the words of the law, that he rent his clothes. And the king commanded Hilkiah, and Ahikam the son of Shaphan, and Abdon the son of Micah, and Shaphan the scribe, and Asaiah a servant of the king's, saying, Go, inquire of the Lord for me, and for them that are left in Israel and in Judah, concerning the words of the book that is found: for great is the wrath of the Lord that is poured out upon us, because our fathers have not kept the word of the Lord, to do after all that is written in this book. And Hilkiah, and they that the king had appointed, went to Huldah the prophetess, the wife of Shallum the son of Tikvath, the son of Hasrah, keeper of the wardrobe; (now she dwelt in Jerusalem in the college:) and they spake to her to that effect. And she answered them, Thus saith the Lord God of Israel, Tell ye the man that sent you to me, Thus saith the Lord, Behold, I will bring evil upon this place, and upon the inhabitants thereof, even all the curses that are written in the book which they have read before the king of Judah: because

A 2

THE LESSON.

they have forsaken me, and have burned incense unto other gods, that they might provoke me to anger with all the works of their hands; therefore my wrath shall be poured out upon this place, and shall not be quenched. And as for the king of Judah, who sent you to inquire of the Lord, so shall ye say unto him, Thus saith the Lord God of Israel concerning the words which thou hast heard; Because thine heart was tender, and thou didst humble thyself before God, when thou heardest his words against this place, and against the inhabitants thereof, and humbledst thyself before me, and didst rend thy clothes, and weep before me; I have even heard thee also, saith the Lord. Behold, I will gather thee to thy fathers, and thou shalt be gathered to thy grave in peace, neither shall thine eyes see all the evil that I will bring upon this place, and upon the inhabitants of the same. So they brought the king word again. Then the king sent and gathered together all the elders of Judah and Jerusalem. And the king went up into the house of the Lord, and all the men of Judah, and the inhabitants of Jerusalem, and the priests, and the Levites, and all the people, great and small: and he read in their ears all the words of the book of the covenant that was found in the house of the Lord. And the king stood in his place, and made a covenant before the Lord, to walk after the Lord, and to keep his commandments, and his testimonies, and his statutes, with all his heart, and with all his soul, to perform the words of the covenant which are written in this book.

A SHORT HISTORICAL VIEW

CHURCH OF SCOTLAND.

In republishing to the church the symbols of doctrine and discipline which the Church of Scotland adopted at the Reformation, I feel moved by a strong sense of duty to set forth God's dealings with my mother church and native land, in such a way as may consist with the limits of an Introductory Discourse ;· reserving the full and exact account of these high matters to some future opportunity, which I pray the Lord to grant me in his good providence. The slighter undertaking to which I now address myself, in the strength of Divine grace, will be best performed by endeavouring, in the first place, to shew the origin and progress and prosperity of the Christian church in the region of Caledonia ; which, inhabited by the Scots on the West, and the Picts on the East and North, maintained its national independency for more than three centuries, against the continual efforts of Rome, triumphant over the southern parts of the island ; and afterwards arose into the small, but formidable, kingdom of Scotland, now happily united, with equal rights and privileges, to the realm of England. After having thus exhibited the form and fashion which the Church of Scotland assumed, and the

b

ıabours which it underwent in propagating the faith of
Christ, it will be proper to open, in the second place, the
steady resistance which for many centuries it presented
to the spirit of Antichrist, embodied in the wicked
hierarch of Rome; until at length darkness covered our
land, and gross darkness the people. And, lastly, we
will record the blessed work of·Reformation, and the
chief of those trials which the church hath since had to
endure unto this day.

PART I.

The early Plantation, Progress, and Prosperity of the Church in the Realm of Scotland.

The Christian religion spread itself in the first ages
with such amazing rapidity over the world; that the
Apostle Paul could say, in his Epistle to the Romans,
" Have they not heard? Yea, verily, their sound went
into all the earth, and their words unto the world's end."
This was spoken only twenty-eight years ·from the day
of Pentecost, when the Gospel began to be preached to
the Jews; and eighteen from the time it began to·be
disseminated amongst the Gentiles. The very choice of
the day of Pentecost, when people from all the world
were gathered to Jerusalem, with all the circumstances
therewith connected, the arresting of the eunuch on his
way to Ethiopia, the whole history of the Acts of the
Apostles for the space of thirty-two years, as well as
the unanimous traditions concerning the labours of the
twelve Apostles and the seventy Disciples, do all com-
bine to shew that it was the purpose of God without

delay to proclaim the Gospel far and wide over the earth, as a witness unto the nations. We are not therefore to be surprised at, or to suspect as fabulous, the constant declarations of our earliest historians, that it was preached in Britain by men of the apostolical age; yea, and by the Apostles themselves. Witness Paul, who declareth that it was his purpose to preach the Gospel in Spain also; witness Eusebius, an ecclesiastical historian of the fourth century, who, as proof of the Divine commission of the Apostles, declareth that they had preached the Gospel " to the Romans, Persians, Armenians, Parthians, Indians, Scythians, and to those which are called the British Islands;" and Theodoret, a bishop of the Greek church, surpassed by none in learning and authority, who lived in the fifth age, thus beareth his witness, " These our fishermen, publicans, and tent-makers persuaded not only the Romans and their subjects, but also the Scythians, Sauromatæ, Indians, Persians, Seræ, Hyrcanians, Britons, Cimmerians, and Germans to embrace the religion of Him who had been crucified." And to this effect Gildas, the most ancient of our native historians, writing of the insurrection and revolt which drew on the destruction of the Druids, the ancient priests of this island, doth thus declare the introduction of the Gospel to have been coeval with that event:—
" In the mean time, Christ the true Sun afforded his rays, that is, the knowledge of his precepts, to this island, benumbed with extreme cold, having been at a great distance from the Sun: I do not mean the sun in the firmament, but the Eternal Sun in heaven." And Tertullian, a celebrated father of the church, in one of his controversial treatises, written in the year of our Re-

demption 209, declareth, "That those parts of Britain into which the Roman arms had never penetrated, were become subject unto Christ."

I am the more particular in referring to these writers of undoubted authority, as giving weight to the unanimous consent of Scottish authors, and indeed of all tradition whatsoever, that the Christian religion was established in our land, by royal authority, in the seventh year of the emperor Severus, by Paschasius, a Sicilian, who found the people wonderfully predisposed to the reception of the truth. This year Archbishop Usher hath determined to be the year 199 or 200, and not 203, as fixed in those traditionary verses cited by Fordon and Major, by which the memory of this blessed event was preserved.

Christi transactis tribus annis atque ducentis
Scotia Catholicam cæpet inire fidem.

In years from Christ two hundred and three,
Scotland a Christian kingdom came to be.

We are not, however, to believe that king Donald among the Scots, to whom the glory of this act is given, nor yet king Lucius in the South, who brought his British kingdom under Christ some forty years before, were moved thereto by an impulse of their own all at once received, but by the gradual propagation of the truth throughout their dominions, and the growing inclination of their people to receive it. Indeed nothing will account for the wonderful readiness with which the people received the new discipline, but the belief that they had been already well leavened with the new doctrine. In the Roman armies during these two centuries it is well

known that great multitudes of Christians served; and
every conquest which they made in Britain was secured
by a Roman colony, wherein Christians sought refuge
from the persecution which raged in all other quarters
of the empire. Now, before the close of the first century, the Roman arms had penetrated to the foot of the
Grampians; and in the second, all the country south of
the Friths of Forth and Clyde were secured by fortifications: beyond which lay the region at that time, or afterwards, occupied by the Scotch in the West, and the Picts
in the East; to whom alone, therefore, Tertullian can refer, when he declares in the year 209, that " those parts of
Britain into which the Roman arms had never penetrated,
were become subject unto Christ." The only region " into
which the Roman arms had not penetrated," even in the
first century, was that which lieth within the line of the
Grampians; and when he asserteth, that " this region
had become subject unto Christ," he must be understood
to mean, that therein superstition and heathenism had
yielded to the Gospel; not in a few solitary instances,
but had found a seat among the people. And the
language of Theodoret, quoted above, bears that the
Apostles themselves had preached in the regions of
Britain, beyond the bounds of " the Roman subjection."
This question is altogether disconnected with the great
historical questions concerning the origin of the Pictish
and Scottish nations, and the times of their several settlements within our realm. No one doubts that there was a
people intrepid of heart and powerful in arms, called by
the Roman authors Caledonians, who kept their fathers'
fields unconquered, and successfully contended with
the masters of the world for freedom and independency.

Amongst these people, whether the same with the Picts
and Scotch or not, we have shewn from various sources
that the Christian verity was made known before the
end of the first century, and established by royal
authority towards the end of the second. For which
let the Lord be devoutly acknowledged ; seeing it is a
glorious pre-eminence yielded to this island, of having
been the first region in the world under the government
of Christianity, which was not till more than one hundred years after established by Constantine upon the
throne of the Roman empire.

Three things mainly contributed to the early establishment of the Christian religion, both in the northern and
southern parts of this island. The first of these was
the destruction and almost eradication of the Druid
superstition, which from the most ancient times prevailed in Britain, with a strength unexampled in any
other part of the world. By their learning, and their
knowledge of arts and sciences, by their richness in patriarchal traditions, and their legal and political wisdom,
the Druids of Great Britain held almost absolute authority over this island ; and their fame extended to Germany
and Gaul, and it is believed even to Greece and the
East. This corrupt form of the patriarchal faith withstood the progress of the Christian religion, which is
the true form of that faith ; and there is no saying how
powerful a barrier it might have presented in the way
of the truth, had not God, in his wrath and mercy,
almost rooted it out by one single blow. This preparation
for the Christian faith, by a condign punishment upon
the idols and the idol priests, took place about forty
years after the resurrection of our Lord, and was accom-

plished by the instrumentality of the Roman governor and his legions, who drove the Druids before him into the island of Anglesea, their sanctuary and high place; and there, as Jehu did of old by the priests of Baal, he slew them without distinction of sex or age, hewed down their groves, and sacrificed the priests upon their own altars. In this stern act of vengeance the hand of the Lord is the more to be discerned, when we remember that the Romans made it an invariable rule to patronise all religions, and adopt into their Pantheon, or temple of all gods, every idol which had any name amongst the conquered nations. But the Druids being of an elder and deeper stock, and holding their religion from an age anterior to the worship of God in houses and by images, set at nought such patronage, and would not yield their empire of knowledge and superstition to the arms of Rome, and by their stern resistance brought upon themselves swift destruction.

This removed out of the way the chief opposition with which the Christian faith would have had to struggle; and though we find relics of the Druid family in Scotland for many centuries after, they existed without a head, and had no power to present any effectual opposition. The same grace did not God shew to any other land at so early a period; no, not for two centuries after this was Paganism suppressed in the other parts of the Roman empire by the hand of the emperor Theodosius; and to this cause I do mainly attribute the easy plantation and early establishment of the Christian faith among our fathers. Druidism and Judaism fell together, almost in one year; and perhaps when God saw it good to remove his church from her ancient seat

in Judea, he thus prepared for her a refuge amongst the
Britons, " divided from the rest of the world." Certain
it is, as we shall see in the sequel, that this island hath
ever since been, what still she is, the bulwark of the
Christian faith. " Not unto us, O Lord, not unto us,
but unto thy name be the glory.".

The second cause which principally conduced to the
early settlement of the Christian faith amongst us, was
the blessed exemption which we enjoyed from the seve-
rities of the first nine general persecutions. From the
time of Nero, before whom Paul twice appeared for the
testimony of Jesus, till the time of Dioclesian, a period
of nearly two centuries and a half, every other part of
the Roman empire was nine times by imperial edict
searched, as with candles, for Christians to destroy them;
but this the land of our fathers was left unmolested, to
propagate and enjoy the faith; and to open her arms as
a refuge of the faithful, who were permitted, nay commanded by the Lord, " when persecuted in one city to
flee unto another." And when at length, in the days of
Dioclesian, the sword of persecution visited the Roman
province of Britain, and made havoc of the churches
there, our unsubjugated Caledonia opened her arms,
and welcomed the holy men who fled to her for
their lives. For it is a noble distinction which Scotland
hath amongst the nations of the earth, that, come from
what quarter they would, honest and humble Christian
ministers have been ever received with open arms;
while haughty men, who would lord it over God's heritage, have ever been resisted and cast out. When
the tenth and severest persecution arose, our fathers
reaped the reward of their valiant and noble stand for

national independency, by receiving amongst them the most distinguished of the Christian confessors and Christian ministers of Britain; by whose piety and learning the cause of the church, planted about a century before, was greatly promoted amongst us. To this event our best historians refer the origin of the name Culdees, given to the primitive ministers of the Scottish Church; which, according to the best explanation of the word, doth signify either the servants of God, or the men who worshipped in lonely cells or chapels, as these faithful witnesses who fled from the sword of persecution were wont to do. Some, however, are inclined to think, that this name was not appropriated by our church till the time of Columba, nearly two centuries onward, who came over from Ireland with twelve co-presbyters, and established in Iona a monastic institution for learn-ing and religion; whence, as from a fruitful mother, Scotland was planted with many such holy families, preserving the same name and following the same rule, and, in spite of Papal oppression, continuing to sur-vive almost till the dawn of the Reformation: so that, however little acknowledged, it may with perfect safety be asserted, that Scotland since the second century hath not wanted a primitive apostolical church, and an or-thodox faith, over which the Papacy came like an eclipse that soon passed away.

The third reason to which we impute the rapid pro-gress and easy establishment of the Christian church in this island, is God's good preservation of the British churches from those numerous and frightful heresies, which during this period disfigured the beauty and ex-hausted the strength of Christians in other parts. And this is the more remarkable, as our fathers derived their knowledge of the Gospel from the disciples of St. John, and in all controversies leaned to the Greek Church, the fruitful parent of all those monstrous opinions. But haply, from having harder work on hand, and full occupation in defending their independence as a people, they were prevented from falling into those subtleties of thought which led the Eastern Church astray; and afterwards when the monastic institutions of the Culdees might have nourished the same spirit of refinement, they were directed into the more excellent way of charity, impelling them to go forth into all lands and preach the Gospel to every creature under heaven. Certain it is, however, that the Gnostic heresies, which corrupted the simplicity of the truth with the mixtures of the Eastern philosophy, falsely so called, concerning the origin of evil and the creation of the world, which denied the reality of Christ's body and the truth of his sufferings; the Ebionite heresies, which added to the Gospel the ceremonies of Moses and the traditions of the elders; the Manichean heresies, which represented the God of the Old Testament as different from the God of the New, and subverted the authority of all Scripture; and the Montanist heresy, or schism, which patronized an ignorant clergy, and introduced will worship and bodily exercises; all these forms of error, by which Satan perplexed the path and exhausted the strength of the faithful in other parts of Christendom, were wholly unknown in Britain, where the church was preserved in the unity of the faith, and permitted with unbroken strength to extend itself amongst the body of the people. Not until the fourth century did heresy shew its face

amongst us under the forms of Arianism, which denies
the Divinity of our Lord; and Pelagianism, which cor-
rupts the doctrine of salvation by free grace.   When I
reflect upon these three great advantages, the suppression of idolatry, the freedom from persecution, and the
preservation from heresy, which God bestowed upon
the primitive churches in this island of Great Britain,
my heart is filled with thankfulness and praise; and
I perceive the signs of a special purpose of grace
which God had towards us from the beginning, and
which he hath continued with us until now, notwithstanding our many provocations.   And I may add my
conviction, that this special purpose of God's grace was
to raise up a kingdom in the midst of the Roman empire; one amongst the ten into which it fell asunder;
and to make it for a testimony and a barrier against
that form of Papal superstition destined, under the name
of Christianity, to obtain the dominion over all the
rest; where, as upon a chosen eminence, he would
erect the beautiful structure of a true church, and exhibit
the power and the blessedness, whereof it is the parent,
unto every nation which will with wisdom and with
strength maintain its ordinances against the deadly and
destructive efforts of Antichrist.

The Christian verity having been thus established in
our Scotland, by those into whose hands God hath committed that highest prerogative, nothing occurreth of any
moment in the ancient traditions of our country until
the reign of Fincomarcus, towards the end of the third
century, in whose time the intestine wars between the
Scotch and Picts being composed, and his own mind
inclined to peace and good government, the church of

Christ in Scotland received no small strength and confirmation. For in his days the churches in South Britain
began to be visited with that direful persecution of Dioclesian which afflicted the whole Roman world, with a
violence unknown in any of the nine persecutions
before it. Wherefore that time hath been distinguished from every other by the name of " the age of
the martyrs." This trial of the Church was so sore, that,
according to the venerable Bede, "the faithful Christians hid themselves in woods and deserts, and hidden caves, and the churches were laid level with the
ground;" and "many of both sexes, in several places,
having endured sundry torments, and their limbs torn,
after an unheard-of manner, sent their souls by perfect
combat to the joys of the heavenly city." Amongst
whom, for the martyr's name ought ever to be recorded,
are mentioned Albanus, whose martyrdom gave name to
the town of St. Albans, and Aaron and Julius, citizens
of Chester. The sorrow of the church in the South was
made joy to the church in the North of Britain, where
peace at this time prevailed, and a king reigned of a
good disposition to the truth; who, according to our
learned Buchanan, "being free of foreign cares, esteemed nothing better than to carry forward the Christian
religion: for which an occasion arose, in that many
Christians among the Britons fled to the Scots from the
terror of Domitian's savage cruelty. Of these not a
few, distinguished for their learning and integrity of
life, took up their abode in Scotland, and led a solitary
life, with such a universal esteem for sanctity, that the
cells in which they had spent their lives were converted
into churches; and from this the custom remained

among the ancient Scots of calling churches cells (Kilpatrick, Kilsyth, &c.)   Monks of this kind were named Culdees; which appellation lasted until a more recent institute of monks, divided into several sects, expelled . them, who were as much inferior to the Culdees in learning and piety, as they were superior to them in riches, ceremonies, and other external rites, which fascinate the eye and infatuate the minds of men.   Fincomarcus having composed the state with the highest equity, and brought his subjects back to a gentler form of life, thereupon departed this life in the forty-seventh year of his reign." [A. D. 290—300.]   Whether this be the true origin of the Culdees, or whether that event is to be postponed for more than two centuries, till the coming over of Columba, hath, as was said, been made a question, upon which one of our latest and most learned antiquarians hath thus delivered his opinion: "That whether the name and order existed before that time, or not, there seems no good reason to doubt that the doctrines by which the religious of the Colomban order were distinguished had been held in North Britain long before;" and, for my own part, bearing in my mind the things which have been set forth above, I see no reason to doubt, but every reason to believe, the traditions of our earliest and best historians in this matter.

The establishment of the Christian religion in any country is a work of great labour, especially amongst such a vexed people as our fathers were: and though the work began under such good auspices in the end of the second century, and received much confirmation in the acts recorded above, it wanted much of embracing the great body of the nation, and, indeed, may be hardly said to have yet obtained more than a seat. In consequence of the great overthrow which the Scots endured from Maximus, the Roman Lieutenant, afterwards Emperor, the ministers of religion were scattered abroad to various places of exile, along with the Scottish nation, who were in like manner dispersed. For at this time the Picts, both of the South and of the North of Scotland, were mostly in a state of Paganism, from which they were converted, as we shall shew hereafter; the former by Ninian, and the latter by Columba. But soon rallying themselves, the suffering church and kingdom found their support in Grǽmus, or Grǽme, a man of great valour, whose name and exploits are made famous in the designation *Grǽme's Dyke,* by which the Roman wall between the two friths of Forth and Clyde continued to be known after his time amongst the Scottish people. That fortification the Romans, before taking their departure from Britain, had repaired, and left as a bulwark against the inroads of the Picts and Scots, whom they sought to shut up amongst their mountains, while they retained all the low countries for the provincial Britons, their subjects and allies. But our fathers, being a very warlike people, and possessing in Grǽme a man of great valour and conduct, broke through the rampart once and again, from which time forth it received the name of Grǽme's Dike. This man, so valiant in the field, and possessing the guardianship of the kingdom for his nephew, yet a minor, did, after reconquering that part of Scotland between the wall we have mentioned, and another, which ran from the head of the Solway frith to the mouth of the river Tyne, proceed to give a greater security and permanence

to the monks and teachers of the Christian religion, for
whom he appointed an annual income out of the fruits
of the ground:, which, saith the historian, "though
slender, as being in those times, the moderation and temperance of the men considered as ample." It pleaseth
me much to find our fathers in the Scottish church thus
well reported of: may the same slender livings continue, through the same moral atmosphere, to appear
ample! Such augmentations are cheap and blessed.
Thus the second step towards the establishment of a
church was taken: the first gave it authority and
patronage, by the king's submitting himself and his
family to baptism; the second gave it provision and
permanency, by appointing a first-fruits of the soil to
be devoted to its support. It is not generally known,
that to the same Græme, who was God's instrument to
trample upon the Roman fortifications, we owe this
second great act towards an ecclesiastical establishment
in our country.

From this time, being the beginning of the fifth century,
nothing is recorded in our ecclesiastical affairs till after
the accession of Eugenius; by whom, in the year 431, the
important step was taken of soliciting help from the
bishop of Rome against the heresy of Pelagius. But before
entering upon this it will be necessary to make honourable mention of an apostolical man who laboured much,
and with a great blessing amongst our countrymen, before the heresy of Pelagius arose. This is St. Ninian, a
native of Britain, of noble family, who having received a
good education, travelled to Rome, which still remained
the chief seat of learning in the West, as Alexandria
was in the East. He perfected himself there in all the
knowledge needful for the work on which his soul was

bent; and returning thence, he devoted himself to the
work of an apostle amongst the southern Scotch and
Picts, who dwelt between the Roman walls, having
been repossessed of that region by the valour of Græme,
as is set forth above. He founded the monastery, or seat
of piety and learning, called *Candida-Casa;* in the vulgar
language, Whitehouse; being the same, it is believed,
with Whithorn, in Galloway. This foundation, to which
the date of 413 is given, became one of the most famous
nurseries of religion and learning in these parts. From
which seat of piety and learning and industry the good
St. Ninian went forth amongst the people around, and
was eminently successful in converting them to the
faith. I know not whether this venerable churchman
hath received commemoration in the name of the parish
of St. Ninians, but certain it is his name brought an
odour of sanctity to his monastery for many ages after
his death. Concerning this apostolical man Bede thus
writes : " For the Southern Picts, who dwell on this side
of these (Grampian) mountains, had long before, as is
reported, forsaken the errors of idolatry, and embraced
the faith of truth, by the preaching of Nynias, a most
reverend man, and a most holy bishop of the
British nation, who had been regularly educated at
Rome in the faith and mysteries of truth." Whether
he came into contact with the Pelagian heresy or
not, is no where said; but most likely not, for the
Pelagian heresy was not condemned till the Council of Carthage in the year 415, whereas the date of St.
Ninian's labour is given as 412. Now it is not to be
believed that Pelagius returned into his native Scotland till he was driven from the heart of the field by
Jerome and Augustine, whom he early knew as inti-

mate friends, and afterwards as most determined antago-
nists. If we suppose him to have returned immediately
hereupon to Britain, and to have begun to propagate
his errors in Scotland, we have full fifteen years from
the date of Ninian's work to that of the mission of Palladius; during which, it is to be believed, that Pelagius
and Celestius made no small progress, aided as they
were by all the learning and accomplishment of the
Alexandrian school.

It is a remarkable feature in the history of the church,
that from Britain to Thrace, every one of the nations
which were used by God as his scourge against idolatrous Rome, took on about the same time some heretical form of the truth;—the Franks, the Vandals, the
Goths, and Visigoths, who overran Gaul, Spain, Italy,
and Africa, being infected with Arianism, the Scots
and Picts with Pelagianism. These heresies have their
origin in the carnal mind, which will insist upon satisfaction in knowledge before belief: whereas there can
be no true knowledge otherwise than through faith; as
it is written, " add to your faith knowledge." Among
the Roman nations it was quite otherwise: for with
them the faith was corrupted through the sense, which
always desireth an ostensible and visible form of every
truth. The symbolical and the ritual parts of religion
amongst them prevailed to overcloud the truth; whereas
amongst the northern nations the subtle speculations of
the intellect made it void. This bespeaks a very characteristic difference between the cast of mind and disposition of the Latin and the Gothic nations. After
Arianism had struggled about three hundred years for
the supremacy, it was put down by the heavy op-

c

pression of the Papacy: but wherever that weight has been removed by the Reformation, the old character of the Gothic nations appeareth, as is to be witnessed at this day in the foreign Protestant churches, which are overwhelmed with Arianism in its basest form; and in the British churches, which are overrun with Pelagianism, or, as they call it, Arminianism; and truly the tenets of the dominant parties, both in the churches of Scotland and England, at this day, is the Pelagian doctrine of merit. It is very curious to observe how a nation, as an individual, when converted to the Gospel, is not changed in its substantial character, but only overruled by the power of God, which being withdrawn, the old man appears in his proper features, as clear and distinct as ever. But it is now time that we give some account of Pelagius and his heresy.

Pelagius, a native Briton, if not a Scotchman (as I think) was born in the year 354, the same day and the same year with Augustine, his great opponent: and his disciple and friend Celestius was certainly a Scotchman. These heretics, before they left their own country, had made great progress in their studies: and being both of them very learned men, it proves that towards the middle of the third century, and before it, there must have been in Scotland both men and schools of Christian learning, according to the account given above by Buchanan. In the canons of the African code (can. 108—116) his opinions are anathematized as follows: First, He held that Adam was by nature mortal, so that he must have died whether he had sinned or not. (2.) He denied original sin, and that infants are baptized for the remission of sin. (3.) He denied that justifying grace

strengthens men against sin. (4.) He denied the necessity of grace in order to obedience. (5.) He said,
that it is in humility, not in reality, that *we ought . to
say, we have no sin.* (6.) He said, that saints say for
others, not for themselves, *Forgive us our trespasses.*
(7.) Or say it in humility, not in truth. These most
·heterodox,doctrines he and his disciples succeeded in
disseminating in Scotland, helped on by the happy ignorance and entire separation in which that church lived
towards Rome ; also by the great learning, severe self-
denial, and sound ecclesiastical views of their authors,
who boldly withstood the encroachments of bishops, and
their ambition to become prelates : and I think I discern
a third reason, in the subtle character of the Scottish intellect, which even then delighted to lose itself in abstract questions concerning the freedom of the will and
the decrees of God. To me it is apparent that these errors
could only originate and grow amongst a people of a
metaphysical turn of mind, and of sequestered habits of
life : when they began to be published in the church of
the South Britons by Agricola and Julianus, the British
clergy would not receive them ; but yet could not reply
to them, being -more inclined to visible symbols of
truth, and less to abstract conceptions. It is curious to
·perceive the strong and striking characteristics of the
Scotch and English people of the Scotch and English
churches thus early revealing themselves. Before passing on to consider the effectual remedies which were
applied to this disease in Scotland, and the great results
to learning and piety which arose out of it, I cannot
omit one remark with respect to heresy in general :
that, though the origin of it be doubtless in the unbe-

lieving heart and depraved mind of man, it is not permitted to enter into the church without a very evil occasion and for a very good end. The occasion is gross ignorance, into which, when the church falleth, heresies or errors of knowledge are the inevitable consequence and needful cure. Heresy is an accommodation of truth to that ignorance, and therefore doth at first catch like an infection; the ignorance being at once its occasion and its sustenance, as the filth of foul houses and the exhalation of putrid marshes are the occasion and continuance of fever and pestilence. The end of permitting the heresy to arise is to clear away the pestilent ignorance in which it was bred, and to bring out the truth still more beautiful and complete: and as an Arius brought forth an Athanasius in the church, and a Pelagius brought forth an Augustine, so will a heresiarch always bring forth a mighty champion of the faith. In the works of Augustine are contained confessedly by far the most perfect demonstration of those doctrines of grace which Luther, taught and sustained in no small degree by Augustine, preached abroad; and for the revival of which we need, I think, in our times, both the pen of an Augustine and the trumpet-voice of a Luther.

To withstand the progress of the Pelagian and Celestian heresy, the instrument whom God employed was Palladius, who had already commended himself to the work by the pains which he took to persuade pope Celestine to send Germanus and Lupus, two bishops of the Gallican church, into the southern parts of Britain, in order to stay the progress of Pelagianism there. He was then a deacon; and a short while afterwards received

from the same Celestine a commission to proceed to
the Scots who believe in Christ. Some would have it
that this commission was to the Scotch people in Ireland,
and not to the Scots who in conjunction with the Picts
possessed the northern parts of Britain. But there is
little reason to doubt, both from the language of Prosper
of Aquitaine, a contemporary, and of Bede who follows
him, that it was to the Scots of Britain, our fathers, that
Palladius was sent; and not to the Scots of Ireland,
who were afterwards brought to the true faith by our
countryman Patricius, commonly styled St. Patrick.
The words of Prosper I shall quote, not for the sake of
the controversy but for the end of information :—" Pope
Celestine was not less diligent in delivering Britain
from the same infectious doctrines, when he banished
from their country some enemies of the faith, appointed
a bishop in Scotland, and not only endeavoured to preserve in the Roman island the exercise of the Catholic
religion, but also converted a barbarous country to
Christianity." This Celestine was an orthodox, but an
ambitious, pope : orthodox in that he resisted both the
Pelagian heresy,which invalidates grace and redemption,
and the Nestorian heresy, which attaineth the same evil
end by asserting two persons to be in Christ, instead
of two natures in one person;—ambitious in that he
contended with the African bishops, concerning the right
of appealing from them to the bishop of Rome, a point
which containeth in it the assumption of entire supremacy.
In the exercise of this zeal for the orthodox faith and the
Roman supremacy, I doubt not that he sent Palladius
into Scotland ; which till then had never acknowledged,
and for six centuries thereafter would never acknow-

ledge any superiority whatever, much less supremacy, to be in the bishop of Rome. Eugenius, our king, being then in the tenth year of his reign, over whom Græme had been tutor, did, with a good disposition to the well-being of his subjects and the prosperity of the Gospel, grant without price to Palladius, and the great company of clergy which was with him, a place to dwell where-ever they chose to ask. When, in our old writers, it is said that Palladius came with a great accompaniment of clergy, it is to be understood of elders and deacons and other inferior persons; who, in the language of those times, were called clergy; nothing being so common in the canons of the church as the expression, "bishop, presbyters, and deacons, and other clergy." In one of the manuscripts of the Scottish chronicle of Fordon, it is added that he made choice of Fordun in the Mearns; which also answers well to the traditions and relics of him still surviving there.

There can be little doubt, from the many footsteps of the same event in our Scottish records, that whether Palladius's mission might have included the Irish Scots or not, he certainly laboured amongst the Caledonian Scots, or rather Picts, who dwelt chiefly in that eastern side of the island. With what success his mission was attended during his own life-time we have nothing but loose accounts, such as that given by Prosper above; but that it did not prevail to the extirpation of the Pelagian heresy, is too manifest from the letter which pope John III. wrote to the Scots in the year 639, two centuries after the mission of Palladius, wherein he thus expresseth himself:—"And we have also understood that the poison of the Pelagian heresy again springs up

among you: we therefore exhort you that you put from
your thoughts all such venemous superstitious wickedness.   For you cannot be ignorant how that execrable
heresy has been condemned; for it has not only been
abolished for two hundred years past, but it is also daily
by us buried in perpetual anathema : and we exhort
you, that you do not rake up the ashes of those whose
weapons you know are burnt.   For who will not detest
their insolence and impious proposition, who say, That
man can live without sin of his own free will, and not
through God's grace?. And in the first place it is the
folly of blasphemy to say, That man is without sin;
which no man can be, but only the Mediator of God
and men, the man Christ Jesus, who was conceived
and born without sin ; for all other men, being born in
original sin, are known to bear the testimony of Adam's
prevarication, even whilst they are without actual sin,
according to the saying of the prophet, For behold I was
shapen in iniquity; and in sin did my mother conceive
me."—This passage of the letter of pope John, which
expresseth well both the heresy of Pelagianism and its
refutation, proveth that, however the labours of Palladius
at that time might have prevailed to lop the branches, the
root of it still remained in the soil of the Scottish Church ;
where, as I have said, it is at this day the form which
the hatred of the truth continues to assume.   But certainly as a church we are much beholden to pope Celestine for this timeous help; and though it brought along
with it some of the seeds of Romanism, we are thankful that they did not take root amongst us ; or rather, I
should say, God by other eminent servants, and especially by Columba, counteracted the evil of Prelatical
and Papal supremacy, which Palladius brought along

with him, and of which it is said by Buchanan he introduced the beginnings.

It is a subject of great gratitude to those who know and reverence the place of kings, as the chief magistrates and lieutenants of Christ, to perceive that those heresies which were permitted to occupy the throne both in the East and West and the Gothic kingdoms, never received any such sanction in Scotland; where not only did Eugenius graciously receive and royally entertain and settle Palladius and his great company, but likewise his successor Dungardus, who inherited the wisdom of his father, and of whose services in the cause of the church Buchanan thus writes: "His mind being delivered from this fear, gave itself wholly to the care of God's worship. For the churches were still troubled with the relics of the Pelagian heresy; for the refutation of which, in the reign of Eugenius, Celestine, the Roman pontiff, had sent over Palladius, by whom very many, being grounded in learning and pious living, grew to be famous; especially Patricius, Servanus, Ninianus, and Kentegernus. This same Palladius is believed to have been the first to create bishops in Scotland: for up to this time the churches were governed by monks without any bishops; with less ceremony and pomp indeed, but with greater simplicity and sacredness. The Scots, intent upon the care of purifying their ecclesiastical matters, and cultivating their mind, escaped," &c. It will be sufficient to explain for the present, that by the bishops, here truly represented as a novelty in Scotland, are meant prelates who then began to assume authority over many altars and parishes; an evil which to this day is to be lamented in many churches, which had no existence in the primitive church; but is expressly prohibited in the 24th canon of the code of the primitive church, commonly called the Apostolical Canons: "If any priest [presbyter or elder] despising his bishop, gather a separate congregation and erect another altar, being not able to convict his bishop of any thing contrary to godliness and righteousness, let him be deposed as one that affects dominion, for he is an usurper; as also the clergymen [as explained above] that are his accessaries; and let the laymen be suspended from communion. Let these [censures] be passed after a first, second, and third admonition from the bishop." Now the order which Palladius introduced amongst us, was an order of men who should have authority over many altars and congregations. For as to a bishop in the New-Testament sense, or "an elder who ruleth in the word and doctrine, and is therefore worthy of double honour;" there were such in every church in Scotland as there are now. But of prelates there were none, and are none, and ought never and no where to be any. Thus was the Pelagian heresy brought under for the present; and though it had a certain root two hundred years after, as it will ever have either overtly or covertly in every church, it certainly never again shewed any head or strength, or disposition to propagate itself in the kingdom of Scotland, until the rise and progress of the moderate party in the church during the last century, of whose preaching it may safely be said that the chief ingredient was Pelagianism. There is this difference in our times, that the leaven worketh all unseen; it hath joined hypocrisy to heresy; it subsisteth in concert with an orthodox confession of faith: but my conviction is, that it prevails at the present day in the church to a far greater extent than it ever did before.

We now come to make mention of one whose name cannot be held in too high esteem. We mean Columba, a man of royal descent; who, with twelve co-presbyters, his kindred and friends, passed over from Ireland in their wicker boats covered with hides, about the year 563, and settled in Iona, an island contiguous to Mull, which was bestowed upon him by Conal, king of the Western or Dalriad Scots. He was a man of great sanctity of manners, and of high authority even in the courts of kings, insomuch that they referred their quarrels to his arbitration. Aidan, who afterwards became king of the Western Scots, was not satisfied with his title until he had received unction from Columba; and before he engaged in battle, he was accustomed to seek the prayers of the elders of Iona; and, as might be expected, he grew to be the greatest conqueror of his time, and wrought out great privileges for his people. Columba was also a man of a large and charitable heart; and in the great council of Drumcea in Ulster, he was the apologist of the Irish bards, who, by their flatteries, had drawn down on them the wrath of their king; and he there also maintained the liberties of his country. Columba is said to have founded an hundred monasteries, and some extend the number even to three hundred, including the churches; he administered unction to kings; and in the great council above referred to, he appeared as the representative of the clergy of North Britain; and there are at least twenty churches still existing, or upon record, which are called by his name. His life was written by

two of his successors, Cumin and Adomnan; and
in these latter times by the Rev. Dr. Smith. Our
object in this sketch is to be brief, though comprehensive; and therefore we shall not trouble ourselves to
speak of this eminent saint, to whom, perhaps, the
church of Christ owes more than to any single man who
has lived since the days of the Apostles ; and to whom
Scotland certainly owes a debt which she can never repay;
and England also, whereof the north and central parts
were converted by those who followed in his footsteps :
yea, and foreign parts of the world also.

We should form an idea the most remote from the
truth, if we were to suppose that the monasteries of the
Culdees, which he established, had any resemblance
whatever to those monkish institutions which in after
times prevailed over Christendom. In nothing do they
agree but in this, that in both they lived together according to a rule, but, unlike the other monastic institutions
which even in the fifth century had become proverbial for
their licentiousness, the Culdee monasteries continued,
till within three centuries of the Reformation, distinguished for their piety, simplicity, purity, and zeal for religion. The reason of this difference is to be found in many
things; and chiefly in this, that from the beginning, and
for several generations, they steadily resisted all commerce with Rome, and proved themselves, even so late
as the thirteenth century, steady opponents to the pre-
latic invasions of that apostate church. Aidan, who
converted the Northumbrians and the Angles to the
Christian faith, would never conform to the Roman customs, and yet was held in reverence by his
opponents. Colman, one of the disciples of Columba,

resigned the bishopric of Lindisfarn, in Northumberland, rather than submit to the papal traditions and
rites. The famous Alcuin, the preceptor and religious
adviser of Charlemagne, in his letter "to the most
learned men and fathers in the province of the Scots,"
bears testimony that none of the laity confessed to the
priests; shewing that auricular confession had no place
amongst them : yet beareth he testimony to the wisdom
and piety and holy living of the monks, and to the
religious conversation of the laity, and their most chaste
lives. St. Bernard, in his life of Malachi, who went to
Armagh in the twelfth century, speaks of the Christian
people there as most barbarous and savage, for their rejection of auricular confession, authoritative absolution,
the sacrament of confirmation, and other papal inventions.
Now the Irish, especially in the North, were almost
entirely taught by the Culdees. They baptized in any
water they came to, without respect to consecrated
chrism. One of their bishops, Sedulius, whether of
Scotland or Ireland matters little, but certainly of one
or the other, seeing he subscribes himself a bishop of
Britain, of the nation of the Scots, in a commentary on
the Epistle to the Romans, when treating of these words,
"Do this in remembrance of me," hath no allusion
whatever to the doctrine of transubstantiation, but
speaks in a manner which any Protestant might subscribe to. They dedicated their churches to the Holy
Trinity, and not to the blessed virgin or any saint: and
without entering into further particulars, we conclude
by observing, that to the minutest matter, as the rite of
the tonsure, which yet in those days was esteemed very
important by the Romanists, they resisted until the

eighth century. This same spirit continued amongst them, in a greater or lesser degree, until the extinction of the order; and to this their preference of primitive customs over papal innovations, I refer, in a great measure, the blessings of holiness amongst themselves, and of prosperity to the church of Christ, whereof this order was the instrument. Among other things in which they resisted the innovations of the Church of Rome, and differed from all monastic institutions whatever, was their rejection of celibacy and their honour of God's ordinance of marriage. They lived together with their wives and children in their monastic establishment; nor was it until a late period in the history of the order, that their wives and children lived in houses apart. Nay, in such esteem was this sacred relation, that not unfrequently son succeeded to father in their holy ministries. Unlike the Papal institutions, when they died their property was divided amongst their wives and children, and nearest relatives, and went not to aggrandize the order. Moreover there was no superstition attached to the rule itself, as if there was religious merit in the observation thereof. They merely conformed to it as a thing most convenient for the ends of brotherhood, and piety, and learning, and religious duties. These religious societies consisted partly of -clergy and partly of laity. There were twelve elders, or presbyters, or priests, and over them an abbot or superior, who likewise was no more than an elder, presbyter, or priest: and as one died, they elected another in his room. These men devoted themselves exclusively to the service of God and of religion, in the va-

rious ministries of the church. They followed after
learning with great diligence, and employed themselves
much in transcribing the Holy Scriptures, in fasting,
and in prayer. They went forth from the monasteries,
and preached the Gospel to the people in the neighbouring country. They administered unto them the
sacraments and consolations of religion. They composed their quarrels; they blessed their families; they
received the gifts of the rich and dispensed them amongst
the poor. They rebuked wickedness; they withstood
violence; they healed breaches; they composed wars:
in one word, the life of Columba, the life of Aidan,
and, in general, the lives of all the Culdees, which are
on record, are above all praise. They are the nearest
to the lives of the Lord and his apostles which I have
either read or heard of in any language or in any country: and what is remarkable, I know not an instance recorded of impurity, treachery, arrogance, or self-seeking, amongst these followers of the Lamb. While
thus the clerical part of the household went about the
services of God in the proper way, of study, meditation, prayer, preaching, and transcribing the sacred
volume, the lay members of the fraternity employed
themselves in cultivating the land, and raising food for
the community and the poor; in practising the arts of
life, and bringing them to perfection; and in propagating useful inventions amongst the people; so that,
while upon the one hand these Culdee establishments
were the centres of evangelical truth, from which the
preaching of it went forth, they were also the centres of
civilization, from which the well-being of the present

life went likewise forth. They ministered that godliness in its full measure, which hath the promise both of the life which now is, and of the life which is to come. In what other light, therefore, may we regard these institutions, than as houses which wisdom built for her own habitation, in times when the world was rude and unaccustomed to the rights of man, and the restraints of law. Here religion retired, not to dwell alone and become stagnant and corrupt, but to protect and reinforce herself with studies and devotions, that she might go forth with renewed faith, and tame the fierce passions of mankind.

Our fathers of the Scottish nation were a mighty and a valiant people, who dwelt in the face of all their enemies, nor were afraid to encounter the might of them all. God hath put within the people of Scotland an indomitable spirit, which will not be enforced by the power of man. Our fathers may be said to have lived for centuries in the tented field; yea, and to have slept by night with their arms in their hands; and had they not been of such a temper, long ere this the name of Scotland would have been lost amongst the nations. Romans, Saxons, Danes, and Normans, and, above all, our sister England, unsurpassed in arms, would have annihilated the Scottish church and state, had it not been for that patience and perseverance, in asserting their rights and liberties, which, beyond all nations in the world, the Scottish people have manifested; and for their endurance they have been rewarded with no second place amongst the nations of the earth.

These trophies of our nation are not to be attributed to her mountains, and marshes, and other natural defences, but to the spirit of valour, and of endurance, and of single-handed adventure, with which God hath endued the people for great ends of his providence; and for this, among the rest, the end of preserving the primitive forms of his church against all the innovations of Papal Rome. Now amongst such a people where the comparatively modern division of the land into parishes, and the settlement of parish churches, with their several pastors under their several presbyteries, was utterly impracticable; what method was there left but this, which the Culdees adopted, of planting the land far and near with these sanctuaries of religion, learning, and civilization; wherein might be reared up a learned and holy order of men, to fill the offices of the church and of the state; also to administer law and equity amongst the people; whither the poor might resort in time of need; where the charities of life might dwell; whence the prayers and intercessions needful for a wicked land, might ever ascend to God; and from which the preachers of glad tidings might go forth over the world? Ah me! I could almost wish myself transported back to Iona; and living, amongst the presbyters of Columba, their life of piety and love.

At the time when this institution appeared amongst us, for no less an end, I believe, than the preservation of the pure faith of Christ, our land, having recovered from its wrestling with the power of Rome, had begun to act offensively against the southern parts of Britain, now deserted by the Romans, and visited with poverty and pusillanimity of spirit, through the corruption and licentiousness which had crept into all classes, and especially through the ignorance and want of learning which prevailed in the church. To meet these the stern reprisals of our fathers, the British people, instead of looking unto God, joined league with the idolatrous nations of Germany; and introduced into their country not only a new oppression but a fresh superstition; and the remnants of the British church were forced to take refuge in the mountains of Wales. Then began a series of bloody wars between the Saxons and the Scotch, waged with various success; through means of which fierce conflict God propagated, by the Culdees, the Christian faith amongst the idolaters. Oswald, a prince of the Angles, having during his exile received baptism and Christian education amongst the Culdees, when he was restored to his kingdom sent to the island of Iona for a bishop (*antistes*, overseer), by whose teaching and ministry "the nation of the Angles which he governed might learn both the benefits of the faith of our Lord, and receive his sacraments." The presbyters or elders sent Colmar from amongst their number, devoting him to this object by the laying on of their hands; "who having, through the severity of his nature, ill succeeded, returned into his country; and in the assembly of the elders he made relation, how that in teaching he could do the people no good to the which he was sent, forasmuch as they were folks that might not be reclaimed, of hard capacity and fierce nature. Then the elders, as they say, began to treat at length what were best to be done." Whereupon Aidan having spoken his fears that his brother had proceeded with over much haste and severity, it is written by the same venerable Bede, "that the eyes and ears of all who sat together in council being turned upon himself, they did diligently discuss

d

the thing which he had said; and decree that he himself was worthy of the episcopate, and was the man
who ought to be sent to teach the unbelieving and unlearned people, as being a man proved to be before all
things imbued with the grace of discretion, which is the
mother of virtues; and so they ordained him, and sent
him to preach the Gospel." And by this same Aidan,
a missionary worthy to stand by the side of an Apostle,
was the nation of the Angles [the English] converted to
the Christian faith. King Oswald himself deeming it
nothing beneath his dignity, nor beside his royal calling,
to act as his interpreter, which he was able to do, having
been reared among the Scots.

From this time, the same venerable author relates,
that many of the Scots began daily to come into the
provinces of England, and with great devotion to preach
the Gospel, and such of them as had received the degree of priesthood administered the sacraments. I need
not point out, as I proceed, how exactly the Culdee
discipline accords with the discipline of the Scottish
church unto this day; according to which, any one
may preach who hath submitted his gifts to the inspection of the eldership; but those only may administer
the sacraments who are thereto ordained by the laying
on of the hands of the presbytery. Bede is not ashamed
to say, " The English, great and small, were by their
Scottish masters instructed in the rules and observances
of regular discipline."

This is only one instance amongst many of the diligence and success with which the Culdees laboured in
the propagation of the Gospel in foreign parts. It is mentioned in one of the histories of Columba, that Cormuc,

one of the presbyters of Iona, being minded to go to some islands in the northern main, where he might plant the truth as it is in Jesus, was brought by the providence of God to the Orkney Islands, and there by his faithfulness converted the people.   Two things connected with this mission beautifully illustrate the character of the Culdee priests.   After the missionary had proceeded on his perilous way in his lonely wicker-boat, there arose a great tempest, directly in the face of his course ; whereupon Columba said unto his monks, "Come, let us hasten unto the church and pray for our brother, that the Lord would preserve him and speed him on his way ;" and praying in faith they had soon the answer of their prayer granted to them.   Columba, about the same time, happening to be at the court of Brudius, king of the Picts, met there a prince from the Islands of Orkney, who, being much taken with the sanctity and wisdom of the aged man, besought how in any way he might do him a grace; whereupon Columba said, " When thou returnest to Orkney, if thou shouldest hear of our brother now on his way thither, give him thy countenance and help."   This same prince afterwards saved the Culdee missionary's life; and was the means of helping forward the work of the Lord in those parts.   The number of Culdee settlements along the Western Islands, shew how diligent they were to plant the waste parts of the earth with the tree of life.   Their numerous establishments throughout the mainland of Scotland, shews how diligent they were to give to the church already in existence the advantage of learning and permanence, which the monastic institution, when thus constructed, did certainly confer.

I count it good, in this place, to make relation in a
few words of the services which my native country and
my mother church have been honoured to render, from
the earliest times of their own conversion, to the cause
of the propagation of the Gospel in foreign parts; and
this I do with the more willingness, because in these
days they seem to be forgotten in the events of the
Reformation, and the noise and bustle of the money
missions which characterise our times. Nor will I be
nice in deciding, whether the persons whom I am about
to name, were of the Scots of Ireland or Caledonia,
seeing their religious institutions were nearly or entirely
the same. What I aim at is, to shew forth the true
spirit of apostolic zeal to propagate the Gospel with
which the fathers of the Scottish church, who resisted
both papacy and prelacy, were informed. Before the
age of Columba, not only had Pelagius and Celestius,
but many others, as St. Cœtalidus and St. Fridoline,
travelled into foreign parts, and settled there with great
odour and sanctity, which lives to this day in the monasteries dedicated to the latter somewhere on the Rhine.
I speak not of the labours of the royal Constantine of
Cornwall, and of Kiernan, because they laboured
chiefly upon the Clyde, and in Kintyre, and other regions of Scotland itself. We have already mentioned
Sedulius; and we may add to him St. Triobelline, who
cultivated learning and established schools and monasteries for religion in Germany and France, at a time
when these nations were yet unconverted pagans. Columbanus, nearly contemporary with Columba, and
sometimes confounded with him, went forth with twelve
companions and founded the abbey of Luxeville in

Burgundy; whence, after twenty years, being exiled by
the persecution of Queen Bonnnechilde, he went forth and
preached the word to the Boii, the Franks, and other
nations of Germany; and after labouring amongst the
inhabitants of Swisserland, he at last settled in Lom-
bardy, and there he founded the abbey of Bolio, where
he died in the year 615. From his writings concerning
the keeping of Easter, against the Romanists, he seems
to have been a man of no mean science for those times,
as well as of apostolic zeal in preaching the Gospel,
and likewise of skill in the orthodox faith, which he defended against Arius in a work now lost. Amongst
the companions of Columbanus was St. Giles, who was
instrumental in converting many thousands in Swisserland to the Christian faith. Yet so strict was he to the
forms of his church, that he refused the bishopric, or
prelacy, of Constance. Contemporary with him was
Jonas, who made great proficiency in theological learning, and wrote the lives of many of the saints of those
days, and amongst others of Columbanus, in the number
of whose companions also they reckon St. Gall, who
published the Gospel amongst the Helvetii and the
Suevi. That same spirit of the Culdees which spread
the Gospel over Scotland and Ireland, and the northern
parts of England, extended itself into foreign parts
with the same purity and zeal, and was mainly instrumental in converting the heathen nations. Some also
amongst them, though few, as St. Chilian, fell away
to the Roman church; and some, both at home and
abroad, addicted themselves to solitary devotion, though
the great body of these learned and apostolical men
gave themselves, like Columba, and Columbanus, to

plant religious houses, wherein learning and piety might have their refuge, and dispense their healing beams over the wilderness around. I have not made much mention of St. Kentigern, or Mungo, and his disciples, as the ascetic Balthere, nor of St. Patrick, because their labours were chiefly in our native land. St. Patrick was assisted in his conversion of Ireland by many natives of Caledonia, amongst whom are mentioned St. Mael Gildus Albanus, the historian, and St. Benigne, one of St. Patrick's disciples. Though the events of these times be obscured and disfigured by the manner in which they have been reported to us, still there can be no doubt that God, during these ages, so dark in other parts of Christendom, was serving himself with the labours of the uncorrupted church established amongst our fathers.

I might be tempted in this place likewise to make an enumeration of the services which were rendered to learning by these the fathers of the Scottish church, and successors of the apostles in the conversion of the heathen nations, who had such a reputation during the dark ages as to obtain for their country the name of " learned Scotland ;" but this belongs not so much to my subject. One thing, however, is most worthy of notice, that the last effort on a large scale against the progress of Papal idolatry and darkness, in the time of Charlemagne, was made chiefly through the instrumentality of learned and pious Scotchmen entertained in the court of that prince. Though Alcuin was an Englishman, he belonged to those regions of Northumbria and Mercia which had been converted by the ministry of the Culdees, and received their primitive discipline ; and Albin, who has sometimes been mistaken for him, was a Scotchman born, who wrote a treatise against image-worship at this time, favoured by the second council of Nice. So also was Clement, who wrote on the same subject, and withstood Boniface, a great promoter of the Papal superstitions. By these, and other men, mostly of this island, a school of learning and of theology was established under that munificent monarch, which for several ages withstood, both by learning and by reasoning, and likewise by decrees, as in the council of Frankfort, the Papistical spirit, and asserted the rights of private judgment against the authority of fathers and councils, with which the church now began to be overwhelmed. In the train of these men arose others; such as John Scotus Erigena, also of Culdee origin, and Samson, and John of Melrose, and Sedulius, and others, who maintained the conflict against the Papal see. How high was the reputation of our country in these times is well asserted by Muratori, in these words: "To Britain, Scotland, and Ireland, is due great praise for surpassing the other western nations in literary acquirements;" and with what zeal they went forth to bless other nations with their knowledge of philosophy, as well as of religion is declared by Hericus, in the dedication to Charlemagne of one of his works: "Why speak I of Scotland? almost that whole nation, setting at nought the perils of the sea, resort to our country with a numerous train of philosophers," &c. Indeed the services, which they did to foreign parts, continue to be acknowledged to this day, in the foundations for Scotchmen, which exist in many of the chief towns and university seats of Germany and France.

, I mention these things, because they prove, beyond a question, that the Scottish Church, with its simple and primitive forms, did more to preserve the light of knowledge and the life of true religion over the world, during these dark ages, than all Christendom besides. Our fathers were possessed with that true missionary spirit which is the surest token of a true church of Christ; and however much I admire the Reformation, I am forced to confess, that we look there in vain for any such generous efforts. In that glorious work our nation put forth its ancient magnanimity, and defied the efforts of Papacy and Prelacy to impose their inventions upon a primitive church. Again I am forced to confess, that neither the apostolical spirit of propagating the Gospel, nor the Culdee spirit of cultivating learning, hath yet arisen to any strength amongst us since the Reformation. I grieve to see the multitude of our preachers who, having little or no occupation at home, remain unmoved by the spirit of our fathers to carry the Gospel into heathen parts. The reasons of this will better appear in the sequel of our discourse: but I cannot leave this glorious epoch of our ecclesiastical history without calling upon the youth of my native land, and mother church, to be ashamed of the lethargy, and seek after the spirit of the ancient time.

PART II.

: The Church of Scotland wrestling against Antichrist.

THERE is no greater mystery.in the providence of God,
.than the permission in his church of that spirit of Anti-
.christ, which, beginning in the days of the·Apostles,
went on .until it. made for itself an. habitation and a
name, in, the. city of Rome, whence it went forth with
an·iron sceptre, to counteract and destroy the work
which our Lord and his disciples had wrought over the
earth: wherein God doth hold up to view, the.wicked-
ness of Satan and of man, in darker colours than ever
had been seen before. . In the, oppositions which were
made to the .preaching, of .the Gospel, and the persecutions of the primitive church, by an unbelieving·world,
was manifested the work and power of Satan in·the
natural heart of man, which, though made by Christ,
would not acknowledge him its maker; and though
enlightened by that true Light which lighteth every man
that cometh into the, world, preferred the darkness
to the light, and·when, the light·shined the darkness
comprehended it not: but in the mystery of iniquity,
wrought up into the Papal system, the. light which was
in the church was converted into. darkness; the life
which,was in the church was by violent hands, of the
church herself put to death; the candle of the Lord
was hidden under a bushel by those to whom he had
entrusted it, and whom he had honoured to be its
upholders, for the illumination of the world. The
pagan opposition to the truth was the great proof given

of the darkness and love of falsehood, which the father
of lies hath engendered in the human heart; the Papal
suppression of the truth was the manifestation of that
positive hatred of God, and of godliness, and preference
of the devil and wickedness, which is wrought by Satan
in the hearts of men ; and both together complete the
evidence and establish the proof of man's utter debase-
ment under the dominion of Satan, his love of his
bondage, and his inability to be helped out of it by
any external advantages, by any thing short of a new
heart and a right spirit put within him. Let every
mouth be stopped, let every tongue be silent, and let all
the world become guilty before God, while beholding not
only the kingdoms of the world, but likewise the ordinances of the church, yea, and the very doctrines of the
truth themselves, in the hands of men joining against
God and his Anointed, saying, " Let us break asunder
their bands, and cast their cords from us."

While thus, in the growth of the Papal superstition,
the power of wickedness to transmute light into darkness, good into evil, was shewing itself, the Spirit of
God was at the same time shewing his superior power,
by enabling the poor things of this world, and the things
that are despised, and the things that are not, to resist
the coming on of darkness, and to shine as lights in the
midst of the world : for God is great, and there is none
able to withstand him. The Father hath given unto
Christ a seed, and none shall pluck them out of his
hand. This is the very way whereby God proveth his
being, and his power, that in the midst of manifest
resistance of all things, when they plunge, and rear, and
foam against him, he can, whenever he pleaseth, and he

doth ever please, to still the psssionate storm, and make his creatures obey whatever his pleasure is.   We, who are his, cannot make any separation betwixt ourselves and the common flesh and blood of mankind; in whose Pagan opposition to light, and Papal destruction of light, we see that spirit which we are naturally of; and in our hatred of darkness and love of light, and transmutation of darkness into light, we come to know that it is not we, but God, who is more mighty than we, that hath translated us out of darkness into the kingdom of his dear Son: and thus all wickedness in the world enables all saints to give all glory unto God.   Therefore is it most necessary, in order to shew that the devil had not taken the world all unto himself, that God should keep up a body of faithful witnesses, to whom he should give power to witness for Christ and the truth, against the devil and the mother of lies, during all the period of her appointed regency in the realm of darkness. To point out, in a brief and cursory way, the resistance and protestation which was maintained in the realm of Scotland by the servants of the Lamb, until they got the victory in the Reformation, is the second object which we propose to ourselves in this Introductory Essay.

Palladius, as hath been said above, was the first man who came to our fathers from the see of Rome, and naturally introduced into our country the notions both of Prelacy and of Papacy, which, at that time, were both in being in the Latin church; the one having existed for a good while, the other just coming into existence. The constitution of the primitive church was equality of bishops, each appointed to minister word and ordinances to one, and only one, flock.   When they met in council, it was necessary to appoint some one who should preside; and ofttimes this their president would be continued, for his life, and sometimes it would be claimed as the privilege of one, perhaps the mother church of the province; but that there was no right in one minister of the word to rule over another, is a point of the last importance to maintain, for in it stands, and with it falls, the headship of Christ. Prelacy, however, stands in the denial of this; and when I speak of Prelacy, I mean that system of ecclesiastical policy which subordinateth one minister of the word unto another, one bishop of the church unto another. A superintendant authority may be permitted, though dangerous, in such cases as prevent the ministers from meeting in presbytery; but a prelatical authority, where one hath lordship over another, cannot for a moment be admitted. It would seem, from his appointing Servan to the Orkneys and Tervan to the Northern Picts, that Palladius brought with him, and sought to promote, the false system of diocesan prelacy. But it took not with the nation; for in the next century, by the conjoint labours of Congal in the kingdom, and Columba in the church, the ministers of religion were gathered together, into cloisters or colleges, according to the rule laid down above; in which our scholars and antiquaries have made it to appear, beyond a doubt, that there was no such thing as superiority of one above another, except that which choice conferred for the sake of order and discipline. From the time of Palladius there was no communication with Rome until the time of Augustine the monk, who came over to England from Gregory the Great, in the year 600, to claim and take possession of the

island in his name, a usurpation which was resisted by
the British church with one consent, and with circumstances of great indignation. . His successor Laurentius,
claiming to be archbishop of Britain in his room, followed up his ambition by a letter to the Scottish church
in Ireland, which, as we have said, was one in government and often in name with the Church in Scotland, in
which he was joined by two of his ambitious coadjutors,
Melitus and Justus. "To our most dear lords, our
brother bishops and abbots over all Scotland, Laurentius, Melitus, and Justus, bishops, servants of the
servants of God. When the apostolical see, as its custom is over all the world, did direct us to preach to the
pagan nations in these Western parts, and we happened to come into this island which is named Britain,
believing that they walked according to the custom of
the universal church, we, in our ignorance, held both
the Britons and the Scots in the greatest veneration
for their sanctity. But, upon knowing the Britons, we
had thought the Scots to be better than they, until, by
Dagamus, a bishop, who is come hither, and Columbanus, an abbot among the Gauls, we have learned that
they differ nothing from the Britons in their walk and
conversation; for Dagamus the bishop, upon coming to
us, not only would not break bread with us, but not
even partake of it in the same inn where we lived." This
letter speaks volumes with respect to the antipathy
which there was between the Scottish presbyters or
bishops and these bishops of the antichristian school.
I can well understand the indignation which moved the
Scottish Culdee presbyter when he entered the presence
of the successors of Augustine, who came into Britain

with all the pomp and arrogance of a Papal legate, and
carried himself towards the British church with all the
cruelty and pride of the Pope himself: and yet this
man, and his master Gregory, (proh pudor!) hath in
these times been held up by a Protestant and Evangelical divine as the fathers of religion amongst us. They
were the fathers of prelacy and papacy, and other lies,
the enemies of true apostolical bishops, and of the Gospel
of truth: they were the greatest curses that this island ever
saw. Indeed such was the opinion of the Britons with
respect to this newly-imported religion, that, according
to Bede, it was their custom in his day to hold it in no
account, and to have no more communion with them
than with pagans. Shortly after this came a letter from
Pope John, referred to in the former part, concerning
the keeping of Easter and the Pelagian heresy. It is
addressed in like manner to certain bishops and presbyters; some of whom were certainly of Ireland, and
one, at least, is known to have been of Scotland, and
abbot of Iona. But there is no record of any answer to
these epistles. That, however, they were utterly ineffectual in their object of bringing the Culdees round
to the papal discipline, was soon after evidenced in the
synod of Streoneshalch, now Whitby, in Yorkshire,
which being convened to settle the question concerning
Easter, Wilfrid, a Northumbrian abbot, appeared for
Rome, against Colman, who defended the customs of
the Culdees, as derived immediately from John the
Apostle. And when it was determined against Colman,
he, and many other priests of the Scottish nation, rather
than be imposed upon in ecclesiastical matters, forsook
the English territory, and retired again into the land

from which they had come forth; for it seems to be a
national feature in the Scottish character to resist oppression, whether in church or state.   It cannot be won-
dered at, that there should have been such dislike to every
thing which comes from Rome, when we read of what kind
was the life and conversation which these Scottish presbyters introduced into England.   Bede, though strongly set
against their ignorance and obstinacy, as he deemed it,
dismisseth Colman and his monks from the realm of
England with this noble testimony, in which every
mind, enlightened in the state of the Roman church in
the seventh century will discover the root of that ab-
horrence which they ever shewed to the uncanonical,
that is, unpapal bishops of the Scots.   "The place he
governed shews how parsimonious he and his prede-
cessors were; for there very few houses besides the
church were found at their departure, that is, only so
many as without which, civil conversation could not
subsist.   They had no money, but cattle; for if they
received any money from rich persons they immediately
gave it to the poor, there being no need to gather money or provide houses for the entertainment of the great
men of the world; they never resorting to the church,
but only to pray and hear the word of God.   The king
himself, when opportunity offered, came only with five
or six servants, and having performed his devotions in
the church, departed.   But if they happened to take a
repast there, being satisfied with only the plain and daily
food of the brethren, they required no more : for the whole
care of those teachers then was to serve God, not the
world; to feed the soul and not the belly.   For this
reason the religious habit was at that time in great

veneration; so that wheresoever any clergyman or
monk happened to come, he was joyfully received by
all persons as God's servant; and if they chanced to
meet him upon the way, they ran to him, and, bow-
ing, were glad either to be signed with his hand or
blessed with his mouth. They also gave great attention
to their words of exhortation; and on Sundays they
flocked eagerly to the church, or the monasteries, not to
feed their bodies, but to hear the word of God; and if
any priest happened to come into a village, the inhabitants, flocking together, were diligent to ask the
word of life of him; for the priests and clergymen
went not into the villages on any other account than to
preach, baptize, visit the sick, and, in few words, to
take care of souls; and they were so free from all
worldly avarice, that none received lands and possessions for building of monasteries, unless they were
compelled to it by the worldly powers; the which custom was in all points for some time after observed in the
churches of the Northumbrians."

The next attempt which was made to reduce this
surviving relict of the primitive church to the will of
Rome, was made about forty years after, by that Adomnan who wrote the life of Columba, and was himself
Abbot of Iona. Having proceeded to the court of
Alfred, king of the Angles, in order to conciliate peace,
he was won over to the Papal opinions, and sought,
when he returned, to win over his brethren; but failing
there, he proceeded to Ireland on the same errand, and,
as it is said, with more success; from whence returning,
he sought again, but without success, to carry his point
with the Scotch, who persisted thus stedfastly in their

opposition to Rome. For this they had the honour of receiving the censure and condemnation of the synod of Vernon, in France, held in the year 755, who speak of them as " bishops who wandered about, having no parish;" that is, like the Apostles, seeking in all regions of the world heathen to convert: " neither do we know what kind of ordination they had;" that is, they had it from themselves in the bosom of their own apostolical church, and would hold it neither of the Roman pontiff nor of any other usurper. The other was the council of Châlons, held in the year 813, in the acts of which it is thus written: "There are, in certain places, Scots who pronounce themselves to be bishops, and neglecting many," that is, the Romanists, who despised or under-valued their ordination, and called the bishop of Rome master and father, "ordain elders and deacons without licence of lords or superiors." Could a more exact description have been given of an evangelist after the school of Timothy or Titus, who were appointed by Paul to ordain elders and deacons in every city? So these men, having been set apart by their presbyteries to preach and plant the Gospel, felt like the servants of the Lord, that they were authorised to found churches, and to ordain elders and deacons wherever he gave faith to the people to whom they preached the everlasting Gospel. I rejoice in these men; and I feel that their spirit lives in their children still. It is not the spirit of misrule; but it is the spirit of an ordained minister of Christ, whose mouth being opened to preach the word, and his hand privileged to minister the sacraments, hath in him a sacred power invested, whenever he comes into heathen parts, to plant churches, and not ask liberty—

e

yea he may not ask liberty—of any man on earth. I mean not that he should thus carry himself in Christian lands, already under ecclesiastical government, for that were to patronise schism ; but that he may and ought so to do in all lands, where the Gospel is not preached and the church is not established. These same Culdees,when, in the council above referred to, they had their Christian liberty taken from them by king Oswy and his son Alcfrid, sought not to set up another church. within his realm, but went forth into other parts. It is as needful for an ordained minister of the word to know and maintain his rights, as it is for an anointed king.—The next attempt of the bishop of Rome to impose upon our fathers was made by Boniface, archbishop of Mentz, whom we willingly enough resign to those who maintain that he was of English birth. He came into Scotland, after having brought many nations to submit to the see of Rome, amongst whom the Bavarians, Thuringians, Hessians, and others are mentioned, thinking to reduce our fathers to the same denial of Christ, and adoption of the pope, as head of the church. But even in his attempts abroad he was encountered by two of our nation, Clement and Samson, who, being in those parts, rose up against him, and in their sermons publicly denounced him on these charges :—First, " That he studied to win men to the subjection of the pope, and not to the obedience of Christ; 2dly, That he laboured to establish a sovereign authority in the pope's person, as if he only were the successor of the Apostles, whereas all bishops are their successors as well as he; 3dly, That he went about the abolishing the priests' marriage, and exalted the single life beyond measure ; 4thly, That he caused masses to be said for the dead, erected images in churches, and introduced divers rites unknown to the ancient church :" for which most complete protestation Clement was excommunicated and condemned for an heretic, in a council holden at Rome; and with him Samson and several others, who sought to be heard and to plead their cause, but were not permitted : and for poor Clement, he was given over to the secular arm, and devoted to the flames. In Scotland itself Boniface met with an able opponent in John of Melrose, who likewise impugned the Papal impositions upon the truth. Yet we lament to say, that the Papal leaven began now to work in our land ; and this same Boniface met with no small success, especially in the Northern and North-Eastern quarters of the kingdom : so that many of our countrymen, seduced by his example, as is recorded by Balæus, went forth and laboured amongst the nations in the same antichristian service. These things bring us down to the time of Charlemagne, and the opening of the ninth century, when, as we have already said, so many of our countrymen went forth and assisted that munificent prince in the stand he made against the rapid progress of Papal errors, which, indirectly, he himself had so much hand in establishing by the munificent grants which he made to the see of Rome.

The Scottish Church began soon to be pressed from a quarter where she might have expected better things, even from that realm of England which she had been chiefly instrumental in delivering from idolatry: but while the Culdee presbyter travelled from the North, bearing with him the prayers and ordination of his brethren, the Papal legate proceeded from the South, bearing with him the panoply of darkness; and England was divided between the truth and the lie, until at length the latter prevailed over the Saxon people: yet was Alfred the first king who consented to receive unction from Rome. We have seen the controversy of these two ways; the way of godliness, and the way of iniquity; in the matters of the keeping of Easter and the tonsure, small indeed, but most important, as denying the right of Rome to interfere in the Church of Scotland; important, according to that maxim of the Lord, He that is faithful in the least is faithful in the greatest, and he that is unfaithful in the least is unfaithful in the greatest. But now, in the council of Celilythe or Ceal-hythe, held in England in the year 816, our church received at the hand of England a most unnatural and ungrateful wound. The substance of the 5th canon of this synod is, That no Scotchman should be permitted to exercise any clerical ministry, as baptism, celebration of the mass or the eucharist, "because they had no order of metropolitans, and gave not honour to others." This shews that in those days the Scots had none amongst them above the rank of a presbyter, priest, or bishop, and that they gave no reverence to any superior orders. The thing most worthy of observation in this canon of the council of Ceal-hythe is, That the Scottish Church not only did not adopt, but contemned and protested against, the orders which sprung from the ambition of Rome.

About this time occurs a most important event in the history of our church; the parliament held at Scone, by Constantine the son of Kenneth, about the year 862, wherein various laws were enacted concerning church-

men; without acknowledgment and without presence
either of pope or prelate: It was ordained, " that
churchmen should attend Divine service diligently, and
abstain from all civil affairs ; that they should live content
with the patrimony of their churches; that they should
preach the word of God unto their people, and live as they
teach ; that they should be free from all charges of wars ;
that they should not feed horse nor hounds for pleasure ;
that they should have no weapons nor judge in civil
actions : and if they do, they should pay for the first
fault a sum of money, and for the second they should
be degraded." In this we see the light struggling with
the darkness; the memory and presence of a better
state of the church struggling with the growth of corruption and error. We see the soil preparing for the seed
of the enemy ; we see Christian Scotland, that had been,
and still is, struggling with Papal Scotland, that is coming into being. Yet though we be more than two centuries and a half in advance from Pope Gregory's time,
when ecclesiastics attained their freedom from courts
of justice, we have not the least hint of such a thing
recognized in Scotland, we have not even the shadow of
a protestation against it. But it was near for to come
In the very next reign of Greg, or Gregory the Great as
he is called, the Church of Scotland is said, in the language of the Romanists, to have received liberty. Greg
gave liberty to the persons of ecclesiastics, and the right
which heretofore had lain with the Culdees passed over
to the bishopric of St. Andrews, which was first established in these times, and gradually grew to the supreme lordship, or primacy, over God's heritage in our
realm. From this time forth the Papacy had the upper

dissolve the relationship between king and people, and to excommunicate the emperor, not in that Christian sense in which Theodosius was placed by Ambrose amongst the penitents,—a power which the church may never forego in respect to any worldly dignity, but in the antichristian sense of dissolving the authority of the magistrate, which is ordained of God, and making the allegiance of the subjects to be in the keeping of the man of sin and his synagogue of Satan. From these enormities he was not withheld, by the witnesses whom God now raised up, in the person of Berengarius, and a great company of famous men of all ranks and orders, who followed him in denouncing this most daring of the sons of pride, whose long-handed ambition would have seized the supremacy of England also, but that he found in William the Conqueror a man both willing and able to defend his rights. " Loyalty," said he, " I would not give ; nor will I, because neither have I promised it, nor do I find that my ancestors have done it unto thy ancestors." But now poor Scotland was destined to a trial of another and a more insidious kind, in the persons of her sovereigns, who, from the time of Malcolm Canmore and his Queen Margaret, the sister of Edgar Atheling, down to the time of the good king Robert the Bruce, lent themselves with an extraordinary zeal to bring in swarms of Romish monks, who overlaid the life of the kingdom, and introduced that darkness which, in the opinion of a most competent judge, the biographer of Knox and Melville, was deeper and grosser in Scotland than in any other of the papal kingdoms. Though Malcolm, being bred chiefly in England, and Margaret in Hungary, introduced into the kingdom many priests from these subject churches, they found the temper of the nation so firmly set against Rome, that though they erected new diocesan bishoprics, and founded one abbey of papal monks, they did carry themselves in all these acts with great reverence of the Culdees, to whom also they made several munificent grants, as had been done by Macbeth and other kings before them. ' This Margaret, who, if I err not, was canonized for her services to the Church of Rome, is much celebrated, in the monkish legends, for the controversies which she was wont to hold, both in person and by her attendant monks and Romish priests, against the clergy of the national church. The Romish writers report, that the Scottish Church received a reformation according to the rites of Rome by her procurement. Her son Edgar went forward in the same evil course, founding various monasteries and making many grants to the bishop of Durham; and his successor Alexander went further, in translating the prior of Durham to be bishop of St. Andrews, who was consecrated, as hath been said, by the archbishop of York with great pomp, to proselytize the Scottish church, wherein he had but poor success, dying of disappointment; and the like defeat had John, bishop of Glasgow, in the like undertaking. The king's great difficulty was to get his church brought under Rome, without passing under the yoke of the Church of England. For, according to the canons, the bishop of St. Andrews must be consecrated by an archbishop, of which order poor Scotland possessed none, and must needs be beholden to York or Canterbury. But this the stubborn spirit of the Scottish kings would not submit to : wherein we see no small advantage arising from the hereditary warfare between the two kingdoms. At length, however, in the reign of David, his brother, commonly called the saint, this point was yielded, and the bishop of St. Andrews was consecrated by the archbishop of York, as had been done before. This led to the most impudent claim which perhaps was ever made, that the Church of Scotland should become thereby subject to the Church of England. This was in the reign of Henry II., who, in the Constitutions of Clarendon, having asserted the independency of the Church of England, must needs disgrace the nobleness of his own deed, and enact the part of the pope by the Church of Scotland, whereto he was encouraged by the acknowledgment and fealty done by Malcolm and his brother, for the lands of Northumberland; whereas, in former times, the heir of the crown did only perform that ceremony. The narrative of this transaction, as given by our historian Petrie, is as beautiful as the deliverance itself was wonderful. Scotland, in her most trying calamities, hath been always delivered by the hands of singular men. If it be the dignity of other kingdoms to produce societies and social institutions, it is the dignity of Scotland to produce men, and now at this crisis God raised up, in a youth, one who by his words of wisdom saved the independence of his church. I shall give the narrative in the words of the historian above referred to.—"The same Henry did claim the lands of Northumberland and ——— from the Scots. Malcolm the Maiden and his brother William at two several times went to London, and did homage to the king for their lands; whereas, in former times, the heir of the crown only performed that ceremony. But then Henry would have more, that all the bishops of Scotland should be under the yoke of

the archbishop of York as their metropolitan.   At the
first meeting at Norham, the Scots put it off, but with
slender delays.   The next year Hugo, cardinal de St.
Angelo (sent into England), was for Henry in this purpose, and did cite the bishops of Scotland to compear
before him in Northampton.   They went thither, and
the cardinal had a speech of humility and obedience,
all to persuade the Scotch bishops to submit themselves
unto the primate of York, who was a prelate of great
respect, and whose credit in the court of Rome might
serve them to good use.   A young clerk [by name
Gilbert Murray] stood up and spake in name of the
others.   His speech is written diversely : I shall shew it
as I have copied it out of an old register of Dunkeld
(by the favour of bishop Alexander Lindsay).

" It is true, English nation, thou mightest have been
noble and more noble than some other nations, if thou
hadst not craftily turned the power of thy nobility and
the strength of thy fearful might into the presumption
of tyranny, and thy knowledge of liberal science into
the shifting glosses of sophistry : but thou disposest not
thy purposes as if thou wert led with reason, but being
puffed up with thy strong armies, and trusting in thy
great wealth, thou attemptest, in thy wretched ambition
and lust of domineering, to bring under thy jurisdiction
the neighbour provinces and nations; more noble I will
not say in multitude or power, but in lineage and antiquity; unto whom, if thou well consider ancient records, thou shouldest rather have been humbly obedient, or at least, laying aside thy rancour, have
reigned together in perpetual love.   And now, with
all wickedness of pride that thou shewest, without any
reason or law, but in thy ambitious power, thou

seekest to oppress thy mother the Church of Scotland,
which from the beginning hath been catholic and
free, and which brought thee, when thou wast straying
in the wilderness of heathenism, into the safeguard of
the true faith, and way unto life, even unto Jesus Christ
the Author of eternal rest. She did wash thy kings and
princes and people in the laver of holy baptism; she
taught thee the commandments of God, and instructed
thee in moral duties; she did accept many of thy nobles and others of meaner rank, when they were de-
sirous to learn to read, and gladly gave them daily
entertainment without price, books also to read, and
instruction freely; she did also appoint, ordain, and con-
secrate thy bishops and priests, by the space of thirty
years and above; she maintained the primacy and pon-
tifical dignity within thee on the North side of Thames,
as Beda witnesseth. And now, I pray, what recom-
pence renderest thou unto her that hath bestowed so
many benefits on thee? Is it bondage? or such as
Judea rendered unto Christ, evil for good? It seemeth
no other thing. Thou unkind vine, how art thou
turned into bitterness? We looked for grapes, and thou
bringest forth wild grapes; for judgment, and behold
iniquity and crying. If thou couldest do as thou
wouldest, thou wouldest draw thy mother, the Church
of Scotland, whom thou shouldest honour with all reverence, into the basest and most wretched bondage.
Fie, for shame, what is more base when thou wilt do
no good to continue in doing wrong: even the serpents
will not do harm to their own, albeit they cast forth to
the hurt of others: the vice of ingratitude hath not so
much moderation, an ungrateful man doth wrack and
massacre himself, and he despiseth and minceth the

benefits for which he should be thankful, but multi-
plieth and enlargeth injuries. It was a true saying of
Seneca (I see), The more some do owe, they hate the
more; a small debt maketh a grievous enemy. What
sayest thou, David? It is true they rendered me evil for
good, and hatred for my love. It is a wretched thing
(saith Gregory) to serve a lord who cannot be appeased
with whatsoever obeysance. Therefore, thou Church of
England, doest as becomes thee not : thou thinkest to
carry what thou cravest, and to take what is not granted.
Seek what is just, if thou wilt have pleasure in what
thou seekest. And to the end I do not weary others
with my words, albeit I have no charge to speak for the
liberty of the Church of Scotland; and albeit all the
clergy of Scotland would think otherwise, yet I dissent from subjecting her; and I do appeal unto the
apostolical lord, unto whom immediately she is subject; and if it were needful for me to die in the cause,
here I am ready to lay down my neck unto the sword :
nor do I think it expedient to advise any more with my
lords the prelates; nor, if they will do otherwise, do I
consent unto them, for it is more honest to deny
quickly what is demanded unjustly, than to drive off
time by delays, seeing he is the less deceived who is
refused betimes."

When Gilbert had so made an end, some English,
both prelates and nobles, commended the young clerk
that he had spoken so boldly for his nation, without
flattering, and not abashed at the gravity of such authority; but others, because he spoke contrary unto their
mind said, a Scot is naturally violent, and *in naso Scoti
piper*. But Roger, archbishop of York, who princi-

pally had moved this business to bring the Church of
Scotland into his see, uttered a groan, and then with a
merry countenance laid his hand on Gilbert's head saying, *Ex tua non phareta exiit illa sagitta;* as if he had said,
When ye stand in a good cause do not forethink what
ye shall say, for in that hour it shall be given unto you.
This Gilbert was much respected at home after that;
and Pope Celestin put an end unto this debate, for he
sent his bull unto King William, granting that neither
in ecclesiastical nor civil affairs the nation should answer unto any foreign judge whatsoever, except only
unto the pope, or his legate specially constituted. So
far in the register of Dunkeld."

The learned baronet above referred to when speaking
of Berengarius, and of the Albigenses, hath these words
which I quote, as containing the judgment of a most
competent, if not the most competent man, with respect
to the time at which the Church of Scotland first acknowledged the authority of the Latin church.—

" I come now to give an account of the state of religion
in Scotland, in the year 1138, from Richard, prior of
Hexham, treating of Alberic, Bishop of Ostie, legate by
Pope Innocent the Second, to the Scots, as well as to
the English, after a description of his person, and the
occasion of his mission; and of the pope's character,
and of the schism by the anti-pope Petrus Leo, and
that he had come the length of Hexham, and relieved
William Cummine, King David's chancellor, out of
prison, he afterwards advanced to ' Carlisle, quarto die
ante festum Sancti Michaelis ad Carlel pervenit, ibique
regem Scotiæ cum episcopis, abbatibus, prioribus, ba-
ronibus suæ terra reperit.' Of whom our author adds,

the following character: ' Illi vero diu a Cisalpina, imo fere ab universa ecclesia discordantes, exosæ memoriæ Petro Leoni et apostasiæ ejus, nimium favisse videbantur. Tunc vero Divina gratia inspirati, mandata Innocentii Pape et legatum ejus, omnes unanimiter cum magna veneratione susceperunt, &c.' Here is a plain acknowledgment that the Scottish nation, both clergy and laity, had been a long time in schism and discord with the Cisalpine, and almost with the universal church, that is (in the sense of the author, a Romanist, and who lived at that time) with the Romish church, and many churches over the world adhering to her. He does not say simply the universal church, but with the restriction of almost; for besides the Scottish church, there were great multitudes in Italy itself, France, Germany, and Flanders, who differed from the Romish church, not in rites and smaller matters, but in the doctrines concerning the sacrament of the Lord's Supper, and other points of faith, and renounced their communion, and erected churches separate from Rome." Dalrymple's Collections, pp. 258, 259.

The Latin words, quoted in the above extract, are taken from a description given of the Scottish Church, by Richard Prior of Hexham, when treating of his book De Bello Standardi, concerning this mission : " But they [the heads of the Scottish church and nation] differing of a long while from the Cisalpine, yea from almost the universal church, seem to have favoured overmuch Peter of Lyons, of execrable memory, and his apostasy; but at this time, inspired by Divine grace, they almost unanimously with great veneration received the mandates of Pope Innocent and his legate." This.

is a distinct testimony, that, up to that time, the Scottish church were identified in doctrine with the Waldenses, or Lyonites, as they were sometimes called, from Peter Waldo of Lyons. In this age the honour of our church and country was supported in foreign parts by Richard de Sancto Victore, who wrote much and well concerning various points of the orthodox faith, though he is said to have been the first who taught that the virgin Mary was born without original sin,—a notion which is appearing again in Scotland, amongst those who hold that Christ was of her substance, and yet that it was not a sinful substance.

In the reign of Alexander II., an interdict was laid upon the kingdom for having levied war against England, which King John had put under the protection of the pope. This the legate would not take off again without large contributions of money; on which account the clergy of Scotland having complained against him to Pope Honorius, obtained judgment in their favour, and power withal to hold a provincial synod without the presence of a metropolitan. Understanding, or affecting to understand, this privilege as of perpetual authority, they drew up a code of ordinances for all such synodal meetings, and instituted an office-bearer by name, 'Custos Statutorum,' keeper of the statutes; and they continned to assemble without application to the Holy See. The next attempt of the pope, against the liberties of our church and kingdom, met with a reply from King Alexander the Second, which shews, that, however much attempted in the former reign, a legate from the pope had never yet exercised authority in Scotland. It was at the conference held at York 1237, between Henry

and Alexander, when Otto the Pope's legate desired
to go to Scotland, as he said, to redress the affairs of
the church, to whom the Scottish king made reply,
—" I remember not that ever a legate was in my
land, neither have I need of one, thanks be to God;
neither was any in my father's time, nor in any of
my ancestors; neither will I suffer any so long as I
may." Nevertheless he suffered money to go forth of
the kingdom for the use of the pope. The clergy,
in the days of Alexander III., positively refused to
meet the cardinal legate at York, and would not
observe the canons there enacted, but enacted others of
their own, in a council holden at Perth, whereby the
liberties of the church were established, and a good understanding prevailed betweeen the civil and ecclesiastical state. In the same century the pope gave, or rather
sold, letters summoning a number of Scotsmen to appear
in England before his legate, which they despised to do
alleging the privilege of Scotsmen to answer to no
power without the kingdom; and so his mandate fell to
the ground.

And now we come to the most glorious era in
the history of our land, when the character of our
church and nation was put to the sternest proof which
was ever endured by any people under heaven, except perhaps the Jews in the time of Maccabeus; when
God raised up, in the persons of William Wallace
and Robert the Bruce, two mighty men of war, who
vindicated the rights of our nation against the might
of England, led by the mightiest of her kings. When
I look at the unwearied valiancy of Scotland, a mere
handful of men compared with the might of France

which bowed before the conquering Edwards and Henrys,
I can account for it in no way, save by our comparative
freedom from the superstition· and wickedness of the
papal religion. Patriotism was yet unbroken by appeals to Rome. Loyalty was not yet enervated by
the supremacy of a priest, the bands of natural life were
not broken by the impostures of the Papacy; the fear of
God, and not of the pope, was in the land; and therefore, I believe, the people were so mighty and could not
be broken. It is recorded in the annals of the wars of
Bruce, that when the good lord James Douglas·sent
one day a·person to reconnoitre a solitary house, he reported that he heard the inmates use the devil's name in
their conversation; then, said James of Douglas, they
must be English soldiers, for none of·our people would
so speak. And so it proved to be, when having beset the
house he took them prisoners, and amongst them Ran-
dolph his future companion in arms, and next to the king
and himself the greatest saviour of his country. This shews
under what a bridle the people were wont in those days
to keep their tongue, which an Apostle hath pronounced
one of the best proofs of a perfect man. · I cannot look
upon the great national controversy of this age without
seeing in it the hand of God withstanding not only the
usurpation of England, but likewise the usurpation of
the pope; who, when he was appealed to in the question, forbad Edward from proceeding, "because," said
he, "the sovereignty of Scotland belonged unto the
church." This opened the eyes of the people to the
ambition of the Roman see, which was still further disclosed, when after the battle of Bannockburn the pope
sent a legate to·restrain the Scots from troubling Eng-

land till he should have decided on King Edward's claim to the crown of Scotland. " But in this," said the good King Robert, "his holiness must excuse me, for I will not be so unwise as to let the advantage I have slip out of my hands ;" whereupon the kingdom was laid under an interdict, which, at the entreaty of the nobles, was soon after removed. There are several other acts of our kings resisting the usurpations of the pope which it may be as well to mention in a few words, and so finish the subject of the Culdees, and the resistance which they were making during these reigns. In the third parliament of James the First, an act was made that all subjects should be ruled by the king's laws only; and in the eighth parliament, that if any did fly or appeal from the king's judgment, he should be accounted a rebel, and punished accordingly. In the reign of James the Third holding of livings *in commendam*, that is, without a resident and officiating minister, was forbidden within the realm; and it was under pain of rebellion that any one should purchase or accept such *commendams* otherwise than for the space of six months : and other acts in the same reign and the following one, were made still further to withstand Papal encroachments ; and thus things continued with little alteration until the time when the whole Papal system was rejected at the Reformation.

We should be far from the truth if we were to suppose, as some have done, that, because the Culdees withstood the Papacy in the matter of Easter, and of the tonsure, they therefore deemed the essence of religion to stand in such observances, or that they had no other grounds of difference with Rome : the truth is, that

they differed in, every thing, that constitutes the Christian church, distinct from the synagogue of Satan. In government they knew no order but presbyter and deacon ;
and when from the number of the elders one was to be
appointed to any set office, it was done by the consent
of those with whom he was associated, as we have seen
in respect to those bishops who converted the English
to the Christian faith. In respect of doctrine they rejected confession to the priest, and absolution of the
priest ; they baptized in any water they came to by
immersion, without the consecrated chrism ; they had
no sacrament, nor, ordinance of, confirmation ; their
churches were dedicated to the Holy Trinity, and not to
any saint ; they denied the intercession of the living for
the dead ; they rejected works of supererogation, denied
all merit of their own, and hoped for salvation only from
the mercy of God, through faith in Jesus Christ. They
celebrated their office after their own manner ; and
when the monastic orders of Rome were introduced
into Scotland, it was " for extending and exalting the
worship and honour of God, and for serving him after
a canonical manner." They abhorred the ordinance of
the Papal church which forbad priests to marry ; and
in one word, whether we look positively, to that which
is testified of them, or negatively, to that which is
denied to them by the Papal writers, directly to the
resistance of the Culdees resident in our own country, or
indirectly to the resistance which their sons in foreign
parts made to the Papal inventions, we cannot doubt
for a moment that in the sum and substance of what
constitutes religion and a church, they were directly
opposed to the inventions and doctrines of Rome.

With respect to the extent of this holy ministry in Scotland we are able, from the learned work of Dr. Jamieson, to
lay down their principal seats. At Abernethy, the ancient
capital of the Picts, was a foundation of the greatest antiquity, reaching back, as some suppose, into the fifth
century; and it continued to exist till the latter end of
the thirteenth century, when it fell into the hands of the
canons regular. It was also a great school of learning,
for in this respect the Culdees alway followed the example of Iona. It was not a bishopric, as some have
said ; but within the diocese of Dunblane, after diocesan episcopacy came into Scotland, an innovation made
at the conclusion of the ninth century. At Lochleven,
beside Kinross, there was a monastery of Culdees, dating
its origin so far back as the year 700, which received various gifts from our Kings, Macbeth, Malcolm the Third,
Edgar, and Etheldred, and from three of the bishops of St.
Andrews. It was founded by St. Serf, or Servanus, contemporary with Adomnan, Abbot of Iona. At Dunkeld,
there was "founded an illustrious monastery by Constantine, king of the Picts, from his devotion for St. Columba,
at that time patron of the whole kingdom, where he placed
those religious called Kuldees, having wives according
to the custom of the oriental church, from whom they
kept themselves while they ministered in courses."
There is reason to believe " that after Iona was destroyed by the Danes, anno 801, or after its power over
the Pictish churches ceased, the Abbot of Dunkeld,
a Culdee, was for a time regarded as supreme of the
Pictish churches :"—supreme, that is, in the sense in
which the Abbot of Iona was supreme, being, as it
were, the parent stock from which this order arose ;

but having no shadow of episcopal jurisdiction or prelatical dignity; for Dunkeld did not become a bishopric
till the time of Alexander, in the twelfth century. The
foundation of St. Andrew's, or Kilremont, as it was called,
though it is ambitious of an earlier origin, was made by
Hungus, in the year 825. "Kilde, in the year 943, became a bishopric; at the close of the same century, the
bishop being elected by the Culdees, received an order
of canons in the time of David the First, by whom
the Culdees were dispossessed, though not without a strenuous resistance, at the end of the thirteenth
or the beginning of the fourteenth century. In the time
of Kenneth (this is he who gave the great city of Brechin to the Lord), a Culdee monastery was established
there in the year 970; to which was added a bishop in
the days of king David, who yet, as was commonly the
case, respected both the Culdees and their prior. The
foundation at Dunblane takes its origin about the year
1000, in the time of Kenneth III., and after 124 years
grew to be a bishopric, in the time of David I. The
Culdees of Moneymusk, in Aberdeenshire, though not
of so early an origin, are entitled to honourable mention,
for the steadiness with which they resisted the invasions
of the bishops of St. Andrews in the twelfth and thirteenth centuries, and the honourable and independent
privileges which they secured for themselves, which yet
did not prevent them, like their brethren of St. Andrews, Loch Leven, Dunkeld, and Brechin, from being
driven away by the invasions of the canons regular, the
standing army of Rome. But I make no doubt that this
was ordered in mercy to the suffering Church of Scotland, to the end that these confessors against the Papacy

might be forced home upon the people, and preserve in the recesses of the country, the record of a better age, and plant in the memory and traditions of Scotland that love of primitive simplicity which, at the Reformation, burst forth in its strength, like Samson out of his sleep, and shook off the bonds of darkness with which it had been bound. Besides these, there was an establishment at Portmoak founded in the ninth century; at Dunfermline, from the time of Malcolm Canmore till the time of David, who introduced monks from Canterbury: at Scone, which was reformed after the Papal mode in the time of the first Alexander; probably also at Kircaldy (Kirkculdee, cella Culdeorum), at Melrose, founded by Aidan, who converted the Northumbrians, and brought with him twelve youths, after the manner of Columba. This house was destroyed in the ninth century, and again rebuilt in the time of David I. Besides these, which are of chief account, there were founded monasteries by Columba, in Crusa, and Oronsay, two of the western isles. And others are mentioned, as Achaluing in Ethica, Himba or Hinbu, and Elen-naohm; also Kill-Diun, or Dimha, at Lochava, or Lochorr; also at Govan, on the Clyde, Abercorn, so often mentioned by Bede. The Culdees certainly planted the Gospel in the Orkneys also, and, there is reason to believe, even in Ireland. The chapels dedicated to the memory of Columba are so numerous and wide-spread, as to leave no doubt of the extent to which he and his followers propagated the Christian faith.

. For six centuries, commonly called the dark ages, they preserved in Scotland the light of Divine truth, the love of sacred learning, the reverence of apostolic tradition, the obedience of the Holy Scriptures; and they sent forth over all 'Europe lights to enlighten the nations; men of might to contend against the man of sin ; which made the Scottish name to be identified during those times with piety and learning : 'and when they could no longer preserve their king and country from the depredations of the lovers of darkness, they retired into their cells, the fastnesses of their piety and religion, and thence maintained a noble resistance for the relics of their order. Though much corrupted and greatly fallen from their primitive purity and valour, they did still preserve a steady warfare against the Roman name. Nor do they cease to be visible on the stage of history until about the time that Grosteste, bishop of Lincoln, defied the pope, and Wickliffe denounced the monks as the servants of the devil. But no eye of history can penetrate into the homes and habitations and hearts of a people ; and therefore no one can say, how long, after the beginning of the fourteenth century, when we lose sight of them in the existing records of our country, they may have subsisted amongst the people, like the Druids and the bards of preceding ages ; and preserved throughout the land a certain leaven of better things, the memory of departed liberty, the hope and the desire of liberty again. To me, reflecting upon the long-lived traditions of my native land, evidenced by the poems of Ossian and the minstrelsey of the Border, and those tales which have appeared in our own day, and of which ten times more than have yet appeared, do circulate among the people of Scotland ;— to me, I say, reflecting upon the traditionary lore of my native land, and the reverence for antiquity which characterizes the people of the Scottish name, it is a thing beyond doubt, that the wrestlings of the Culdees against the Papacy did disseminate through Scotland that hatred of Roman superstition, and preserve that love of religious liberty, and preference of a primitive church, without pomp or ceremonies, which have distinguished and blessed us amongst the nations of Christendom.

Before proceeding to search out the dawnings of the Reformation, which almost meet with the last twilight of the primitive Culdee Church; and to inquire particularly into the character of that event, as a mighty work of God, and the corruptions which the wickedness of man hath brought upon it, until it be now almost, if not altogether destroyed; we may be permitted to pause, and make a few reflections upon the long ages of which we have been rendering some account.

And, first, The hearts of all Scottish people should be filled with gratitude, that God did so early take a favour for our land, and plant amongst us the incorruptible seed of his word, and preserve, from the second, if not the very first, century of the Christian era, a succession of faithful witnesses for " the truth as it is in Jesus :" and not only so, but made the Gospel to sound forth from us into many foreign parts, and especially into our sister-land, the realm of England, with which we are now so happily united in national community. The preceding narrative, brief and meagre as it is, hath brought to my own soul a strong confidence that the Lord will not easily suffer his truth to be trodden down and trampled under foot in the land of our fathers, which he hath so long and so constantly loved: and though I were to see the combination against it many times more strong and stern than it is, my heart would not fail me, so long as the mouths of those who know the Lord are opened to proclaim his truth among the people. But if they will stand in fear and dread of wicked and worthless shepherds, who feed themselves, and not the flock; or, if they will fondly think to propagate the truth otherwise than by preaching, they will but vex their hearts in vain, and leave the enemy to prevail. "Let Scotland flourish by the preaching of the word."

Secondly. It ought to be matter of great thanksgiving unto our God, that he preserved amongst us for long centuries, such distinct doctrines and ordinances of the primitive church, divested of the Papal doctrines of devils and inventions of Satan. And it is a great consolation to be able to take lessons of instruction in ecclesiastical government and discipline from that institution which, for more than ten centuries, not only preserved the light in our native Scotland, but shed it abroad over many nations. Now, of the Culdee or primitive Church of Scotland the government was of the simplest kind; consisting of so many Presbyters, or Elders, who chose from amongst themselves one to preside over their councils as their head: standing exactly in the same relation to the rest as the Minister does to the Eldership of the Session of a Scottish Church. To these elders under their head, all rule and government pertained. They might send out any whom they pleased from their number into any quarter to preach the Gospel; who, being set apart to his duty by the laying on of hands, had power conveyed to him of ordaining elders and deacons in every city, who might choose from amongst themselves one to be over them; and so become a sacred college,

.to propagate the truth and watch over the church in those parts. These ordinances were not peculiar to the Culdee churches, but were in fact the universal constitution of the primitive church, wherein the elders did commonly from amongst themselves make choice of one to be their bishop in room of him that was departed. And with this superior and the elders lay the power of sending forth missionaries and evangelists into all parts where Providence pointed their way. The idea of many separate churches, each complete in itself, being necessary to this work of ordaining elders and deacons, and sending forth preachers of the Gospel, is one which hath grown up amongst us since the Reformation; but was not from the beginning, nor during those long centuries, during which the preachers sent forth from Scotland established the Christian faith in all parts of the world. And, since it hath come into practice, the Church of Scotland hath ceased from being missionary at all. Of all the Reformed churches she hath done the least for propagating the Gospel: of all the primitive churches she did the most. The Presbytery of the Apostolical and primitive church was not a collection of delegates from many churches, but the minister and presbyters of a church representing the rule and government thereof, and, with its concurrence, having full power of trying the doctrine, detecting heresies by the promulgating of the orthodox faith, exercising discipline, inquiring into the gifts of the members of the church, and sending them forth into all parts of the world, with full powers to preach the Gospel and to plant churches. Upon this right I believe the present practice of the Church of Scotland to be as great an invasion as the prelacy of the

Church of England; whereby the number of those competent to licence in the one country is reduced to some seventy or eighty; in the other, to some twenty or thirty.

Add to this the most unwarrantable imposition, that before any one can be sent out to preach the Gospel, he must give himself, whatever be his age and gifts and learning, to study seven or eight years in a university. Vile substitution of natural accomplishments of learning and eloquence, instead of the gifts and callings of the Holy Ghost! And, as if God would mark this oppressive imposition with his withering curse, what are those school-furnished preachers found to be? Are they filled with zeal to feed the flock? No; but to feed themselves out of a good living. Are they stirred up to go into foreign parts to preach the Gospel to perishing sinners? No; but it is as a banishment for them to cross the Tweed. Of what service are they? To fill churches as they become vacant, and, for the most part, to vegetate therein; or, being stirred up with a spirit, it is the spirit of casting out the truth. Oh, heavy-laden Scotland! what a burden of lethargic ministers and preachers— for the most part perverters of the Gospel, and, I think, a great many of them apostates from the faith—thou hast lying like an incubus upon thy breast! In which most calamitous state of the church I feel that this labour, small as it is, may be blessed of God, to shew her the primitive simplicity and faith by which she won such celebrity as a preacher of righteousness. It may be the means of awakening some of the ministers and preachers and elders within her pale to reflect upon the present awful state of formality and error into which she

is fallen, and to bestir themselves for her deliverance.
And, as they are cast out one by one for their faithfulness, it may, under God, be the means of suggesting to
them the steps proper to be taken, in order to revive the
work of the Lord, both at home and in foreign parts.
The ministers must assert their freedom; the elders,
their dignity; and, acting together in brotherhoods over
the country, they must wait upon God, and cry unto
him mightily, till he stir up amongst them a spirit of
going forth to preach the Gospel in the desolate Church
of Scotland, and in the more desolate churches and
nations over the face of the earth; and, having taken
the proof of those men, they must send them forth, like
Aidan to the Angles, or Cormac to the Orkneys, in
order to preach the Gospel, to ordain elders, and plant
churches, of such as receive faith to the saving of their
souls, that they may be filled of the Spirit with all gifts,
and wait for the coming of the Lord.

And now I proceed to the period of the Reformation;
that mighty work of God, which may now almost be
written of as a thing that hath been and no more is.
But this cannot be brought within the compass of
an Introductory Essay; and must be left for another
opportunity.

PREFACE TO THESE DOCUMENTS:

CONTAINING

AN ACCOUNT OF THEIR ORIGINATION,

AND

REMARKS ON THEIR CONTENTS.

PREFACE TO THESE DOCUMENTS.

THE Church of Scotland was no sooner born by the Reformation into a new life, than she had, like her Divine Master, to seek shelter in foreign parts; as also had the Church of England; where, under the protection of Geneva and the free towns of Germany, they grew up in love, like twin sisters, knowing and loving one another better in their adversity than afterwards they did in their prosperity. In consequence, and in token of which, our Reformers adopted, as the first symbol of their faith, that enlargement or commentary of the Apostle's Creed, which had been adopted by the English Church at Geneva as the confession of their faith. Of the documents now reprinted this is the first in date, though, as not being the offspring of the Church of Scotland, we have placed it in the Appendix, where it standeth the first in order.

REMARK FIRST.—This Confession is strong and explicit upon the orthodox doctrine now controverted in our church; namely, that Christ's

g

death was " a sacrifice to purge the sins of all
the world;" and, which is still more important,
that the same proceedeth out " of God's free
mercy, without compulsion.". This is most important as giving to the atonement its true
moral character, for the expression of a disposition of mercy, ever existing in the bosom of
God, to every creature under heaven. There is
a class of theologians, who treat of the work of
Christ, as if it were the providing a huge stock
of merit, not only sufficient for this world but
for a thousand worlds; which is to make it
virtually the same with St. Peter's great trea-
sury of merits, provided for sin-indulgence.
The atonement is the expression of a disposition in the mind of a Person towards other persons, which they may ever, and at all times,
calculate upon to that amount,—the expression of God's love to all men, even to the chief
sinners of mankind.

REMARK SECOND.—This Confession is likewise good as to the doctrine of the resurrection, to which it doth " attribute our resurrection;" and maketh "the victory of our faith
to stand" thereon, so that, without the faith of
the resurrection, we cannot feel the benefit of
the death of Christ.

REMARK THIRD.—It is sufficient also as to
the important point of Christ's identity with us
in all things, except sin, " became man, in all
things like unto us, sin excepted;" " born of
the virgin Mary according to the flesh;" " and
forasmuch as he, being only God, could not

feel death; neither, being only man, could overcome death; he joined both together, and suffered his humanity to be punished with most cruel death, feeling in himself the anger and most severe judgment of God, even as if he had been in the extreme torment of hell, and therefore cried with a loud voice, My God, my God, why hast thou forsaken me?"

· REMARK FOURTH.—The Confession is also sufficient in what respects the church both as to its "consenting in faith hope and charity;" and also to its "using the gifts of God, whether they be temporal or spiritual, to the profit and furtherance of the same." What gifts are here to be understood no one will question, when he taketh into consideration these references at the foot of the page: Acts ii. 41, &c., iv. 32, &c.; Rom. xii. 4, &c.; 1 Cor. xii.; Eph. iv. 7, 11, 12; which are the very passages of Scripture that contain the account of what they are pleased, in these our days, to term "extraordinary," and to deny to be for continuance in the church. The Church of Scotland, in adopting this Confession, approves their continuance; and I delight here to shew also what was the mind of the Church of England on this subject, as stated in the Homily concerning the Holy Ghost (Part i.): "The Holy Ghost doth ALWAYS DECLARE HIMSELF by his fruitful and gracious gifts—namely, by the word of wisdom, by the word of knowledge, which is the understanding of the Scriptures by faith, in doing of miracles, by healing them that are diseased, by prophecy, which is the declaration of God's mysteries, by discerning of spirits; diversities of tongues, interpretation of tongues, - and so forth. All which gifts, as they proceed from one Spirit, and are severally given to man according to the measurable distribution of the Holy Ghost; even so do they bring men, and not without good cause, into a wonderful ad-. miration of God's power."

REMARK FIFTH. — This Confession is defective, and I think somewhat evasive, in the matter of the descent into hell, explaining away that necessary part of the faith, into the dolours which our Lord's soul endured on the cross : whereas, in the Apostle's Creed, as in the Holy Scriptures, it is stated as a fact, giving to us assurance, under that part of death which consisteth in the soul going to hades, to wait till judgment; whether Christ's soul also went, yet remained not captive, but led the captivity captive, and emancipated the souls of all believers from that imprisonment, as he shall emancipate their bodies from the grave in the day of the resurrection. There are some other points wherein this Confession is defective from, though not contradictory of, the truth ; as the first resurrection, and the reign of Christ on earth, whereof we shall have to speak under the next head. But, upon the whole, it is an excellent document, drawn up with great plainness and simplicity ; with as much brevity as is consistent with clearness, and with as much openness of charity as is consistent with soundness in the faith.

THE SCOTTISH CONFESSION.

The next document is the pillar of the Reformation Church of Scotland, which hath derived little help from the Westminster Confession of Faith: whereas these twenty-five articles, ratified in the Parliament of Scotland in the year 1560, not only at that time united the states of the kingdom in one firm band against the Papacy, but also rallied the people at sundry times of trouble and distress for a whole century thereafter; and it may be said even until the Revolution, when the church came into that haven of rest, which has proved far more pernicious to her than all the storms she ever passed through. For, though the Westminster Confession was adopted as a platform of communion with the English Presbyterians in the year 1647, it exerted little or no influence upon our church, was hardly felt as an operative principle either of good or evil, until the Revolution of 1688; so that the Scottish Confession was the banner of the church, in all her wrestlings and conflicts, the Westminster Confession but as the camp-colours which she hath used during her days of peace; the one for battle, the other for fair appearance and good order. This document consisteth of twenty-five articles, and is written in a most honest straight-forward manly style, without compliment or flattery, without affectation of logical precision, or learned accuracy, as if it came fresh from the heart of laborious workmen, all the day long busy with the preaching of the truth, and sitting down at night to embody the heads of what they continually taught. There is a freshness of life about it, which no frequency of reading wears off. Upon this also I would make one or two remarks.

REMARK FIRST.—This Confession is most precious on this account; that it hath guarded as well as could be against the abuse of Confessions, by being advanced into a certain lordship over the consciences of the members and ministers of the church, yea and of the word of God itself. So little did the writers of it think, that they were binding the Church of Scotland to the very words and sentences and even matters of this their deed of faith, that they declare themselves to be bound by it, only so long as they should see it to be according to God's word, and no longer. And so little did they think with our present authorities, who claim to be their representatives, that after it had been agreed on by the church, and ratified by parliament, it cannot be changed, and if any one differ from it he must go out of the church, that they solemnly promise and protest their willingness to submit it, at all times, to the arbitriment of God's word, and to modify it thereto ; themselves to become the willing instruments of amending it. And why ? Because they trembled at God's word. And why is it not so now ? Because the church doth no longer tremble at God's word, but trembleth for her own security, ease, and comfort. The passages are many to this effect.

Take this, of which I know not whether to admire more the elegance or the honesty : " Protesting, that if any man will note in this our
Confession any article, or sentence, repugning
to God's holy word, that it would please him of
his gentleness, and for Christian charity's sake,
admonish us of the same in writing ; and we
upon our honour and fidelity do promise unto
him satisfaction from the mouth of God (that
is, from the holy Scriptures), or else reformation of that which he shall prove to be amiss."
When an able and a pious and a learned preacher
took up this office, and asked satisfaction from
the Scriptures upon one or two points from the
last General Assembly, he was treated as an
insolent fellow, and deprived of his licence
without one word of explanation or even of
examination.

> Tempora mutantur, et nos mutamur in illis.

"The times are changed, the men still more."
See also the whole of Article xx. " Of General
Councils, of their power, authority, and cause
of their convention."

REMARK SECOND.—This the native and proper Confession of our church, is very strong
upon the nature of faith, as being no doubtsome, wavering, unresolved persuasion, but a
firm and strong assurance of our own personal
interest in Christ ; and so this they make to be
not only of the essence, but the very essence of
regeneration, and the one work of the Holy
Ghost, " which regeneration is wrought by the

power of the Holy Ghost, working in the hearts
of the elect of God an assured faith in the promise of God, revealed to us in his word; by
which faith we apprehend Christ Jesus with the
graces and benefits promised in him." Art. iii.
—And speaking of faith as it were in an inci-
dental manner, they never hesitate to inter-
change it with assurance; for example (Art. xii.):
" This our faith, and assurance of the same,
proceeds not from flesh and blood, that is to
say, from no natural powers within us, but is
the inspiration of the Holy Ghost."

REMARK THIRD.—This Confession of ours
is very strong and stable upon the subject of
the Incarnation of the Son of God, and the
nature of the flesh in which he was incarnate.
First, As to its mortality and corruptibility in
itself, and its receiving immortality and incor-
ruption from the Godhead : " As the eternal
Godhead hath given to the flesh of Christ Jesus
(which of its own nature was mortal and corruptible) life and immortality; so doth Christ
Jesus, his flesh and blood eaten and drunken
by us, give unto us the same prerogatives." (Art.
xxi.) And the proofs adduced of this, are the
passages of the four Gospels, where he is declared to have yielded up the Ghost. The ar-
gument being, his flesh was mortal and corruptible because he did die.—Secondly, As to
his being of the substance of his mother, and
not any other, as of Adam : " Who took the
nature of mankind, of the substance of a woman,
to wit, of a virgin, and that by operation of

the Holy Ghost, and so was born the just seed of David." (Art. vi.) Again : "It behoved, that the Son of God should descend unto us, and take to himself a body of our body, flesh of our flesh, and bone of our bones." (Art. viii.) —Thirdly, With respect to " imbecility," or weakness of his flesh : " But because the only God-head could not suffer death, neither yet could the only Man-head overcome the same, he joined both together in one person, that the imbecility of the one should suffer, and be subject to death, (which we had deserved,) and the infinite and invincible power of the other, to wit, of the Godhead, should triumph, and purchase to us life, liberty, and perpetual victory."—Finally, With respect to its being substantially and completely this nature of ours : " We confess and acknowledge Immanuel very God and very man, two perfect natures, united and joined in one person : by which our Confession, we condemn the damnable and pestilent heresies of Arius, Marcion, Eutyches, and Nestorius, and such others, as either did deny the eternity of his Godhead, or the verity of his human nature, or confounded them, or yet divided them."—And thus are we clearly taught, that Christ took our whole nature ; and that his human nature was not essentially, but only through union with God and unction of the eternal Spirit, incorruptible, mighty, and holy.

REMARK FOURTH.—This, the Confession of the Protestant Church of Scotland, is mighty upon the Sacraments, that strongest hold of faith, which superstition is ever endeavouring to possess, and infidelity to undermine. For example: " And thus we utterly condemn the vanity of these that affirm sacraments to be nothing else but naked and bare signs; no, we assuredly believe, that by Baptism we are engrafted in Christ Jesus, to be made partakers of his justice, whereby our sins are covered and remitted: and also, that in the Supper, rightly used, Christ Jesus is so joined with us, that he becometh very nourishment and food to our souls: not that we imagine any transubstantiation of bread into Christ's natural body, and of wine into his natural blood, as the Papists have perniciously taught, and damnably believed; but this union and conjunction, which we have with the body and blood of Christ Jesus, in the right use of the sacraments, wrought by operation of the Holy Ghost, who by true faith carrieth us above all things that are visible, carnal, and earthly, and maketh us to feed upon the body and blood of Christ Jesus, which was once broken and shed for us, which now is in heaven, and appeareth in the presence of his Father for us : and yet, notwithstanding the far distance of place which is between his body now glorified in heaven, and us now mortal on this earth; yet we most assuredly believe, that the bread which we break is the communion of Christ's body, and the cup which we bless is the communion of his blood. So that we confess, and undoubtedly believe, that the faithful, in the right use of the Lord's table, do so eat the body, and drink the blood of the Lord Jesus, that he remaineth in them, and they in him; yea, they are so made flesh of his flesh, and bone of his bones, that as the eternal Godhead hath given to the flesh of Christ Jesus (which of its own nature was mortal and corruptible) life and immortality; so doth Christ Jesus his flesh and blood, eaten and drunken by us, give unto us the same prerogatives."—Again: " And therefore, whosoever slandereth us, that we affirm and believe sacraments to be naked and bare signs, do injury unto us, and speak against the manifest truth. But this liberally and frankly we confess, that we make a distinction between Christ Jesus in his eternal substance, and between the elements in the sacramental signs; so that we will neither worship the signs, in place of that which is signified by them; neither yet do we despise and interpret them as unprofitable and vain, but do use them with all reverence, examining ourselves diligently before that we so do; because we are assured by the mouth of the Apostle, that such as ' eat of that bread, and drink of that cup unworthily, are guilty of the body and blood of Christ Jesus.' "—It was this article which delivered me from the infidelity of evangelicalism, which denies any gift of God either in the work of Christ, or in the sacraments, or any where, until we experience it to be within ourselves; making God a mere promiser, until we become receivers; making his bounty and beneficence nought but words, till we make it reality by accepting thereof; in one word, making religion only subjective in the believer, and not elective in God,—objective in Christ, in order that it may be subjective in the believer; a religion of moods, and not of purposes and facts; having its reality in the creature, its proposal of reality only in God. The true doctrine of the Sacraments will always strike this infidelity upon the head. It revolutionized my mind; and that not till after I had been the object of attraction to a nation; shewing me how vain are natural gifts to discern spiritual realities. I can never express the obligations which I and hundreds, both of ministers and members of the church of Christ, whom it hath pleased God through me to benefit, owe to the straightforward, uncompromising, thorough-going boldness of that twenty-first Article of our Confession, which both parties in the church, moderate and evangelical, as heartily repudiate as ever they did repudiate that holy man of God, John Campbell, from the ministry, for maintaining the substance of the same truth; namely, the veritable gift which Christ is to the reprobate as much as to the elect. *Hinc illæ lachrimæ.* My mother! oh my mother!

REMARK FIFTH.—The Confession is good against the modern notion of a spiritual coming of Christ (as they term it); that is, a work done in the spirit, but not in person, for the end of bringing all things under him upon the earth, Antichrist and all, some thousand years before the judgment. Doctors in our church have laboured hard in those days to place the days of refreshing before the coming of Christ in person to judge the earth, and they have spoken of his going away from the earth again with his people as a point of unquestionable orthodoxy. Here what our Reformers declare thereon: " Received all power in heaven and earth, where he sitteth at the right hand of the Father, inaugurate in his kingdom, Advocate and only Mediator for us; which glory, honour, and prerogative, he alone, amongst the brethren, shall possess till that all his enemies be made his footstool, as that we undoubtedly believe that they shall be in the final judgment, to the execution whereof, we certainly believe, that the same our Lord Jesus shall as visibly return as that he was seen to ascend; AND THEN we firmly believe that the time of refreshing and restitution of all things shall come, insomuch that these that from the beginning have suffered violence, injury, and wrong, for righteousness' sake, shall inherit that blessed immortality promised from the beginning; but contrariwise, the stubborn, inobedient, cruel oppressors, filthy persons, idolaters, and all such sorts of unfaithful, shall be cast into the dungeon of utter darkness, where the worm shall not die, neither yet shall their fire be extinguished." This is sound doctrine; I, who am a Millenarian, ask no other confession of my creed; understanding the day of judgment as the same expression is used in the Scriptures of the time when the day of grace endeth.

REMARK SIXTH.—The idea of a church (not *the* church) given in this precious symbol of our faith, and the faith of our fathers, is true and well worthy of particular notice, in these days, when it is believed that there are but two churches in all this island, The Church of Scotland, and the Church of England; which, in truth, are the only two things so named, that are, properly speaking, not *churches,* but religious nationalties; or national communions of churches: a church hath the same relation to *the national church,* which *a person* hath to *the community.* " Wheresoever then these former notes (sound doctrine preached, sacraments rightly administered, and discipline uprightly ministered,) are seen, and of any time continue (be the number never so few, about two or three), there, without all doubt, is the true church of Christ, who, according to his promise, is in the midst of them: not that universal of which we have before spoken, but particular, such as were in Corinthus, Galatia, Ephesus, and other places, wherein the ministry was planted by Paul, and were of himself named the churches of God: and such churches, we the inhabitants of the realm of Scotland, professors of Christ Jesus, profess ourselves to have in our cities, towns, and places reformed, for the doctrine taught in our churches, contained in the written word of God; to wit, in the books of the Old and New Testaments: in these books we mean, which of the ancients have been reputed canonical, in the which we affirm, that all things necessary to be believed for the salvation of mankind are sufficiently expressed." The integrity of a church within itself, its power to act in all ways for Christ, its Head, its completeness in all respects, hath nothing to do with Presbytery, Synod, or General Assembly, or establishment by the state, or the like circumstances; which arise out of other obligations, but are in nowise necessary to give a church the same noble standing as the church of Corinthus had, or of Ephesus, with all its gifts of the Holy Ghost, and office-bearers within itself, and power of sending forth men into every region to preach the Gospel. In one word, the church of which I am a minister, while doctrine, sacraments, and discipline are rightly administered in it, is, in the eye of our Reformers, as true and complete a church, as if it were the limb of a Presbytery, Synod, or General Assembly. This is an awfully important conclusion, and I thank the Reformers for being so explicit upon it. I learned it not from them, but from the patient study of the seven epistles in the Apocalypse. But I rejoice to know that it is the doctrine approved by the Church of Scotland.

I now dismiss this document, with the highest encomium which I am capable of bestowing upon a work of fallible man. It hath been profitable to my soul, and to my flock. For several years I was in the habit of reading it twice in the year to my people; and once upon a time when two men whom I wished to make elders had their difficulties in respect to the

Westminster Confession, I found them most cordial in giving their assent to this. So that I may say my own church is constituted upon it. I love it for another reason, that it is purely a Confession of Faith, containing neither matters of church government nor discipline. And if, as I foresee, the faithful of all churches should be cast out of their communions, they could, without forfeiting any of their peculiarities of government and of worship, find in this standard a rallying point. Its doctrine is sound, its expression is clear, its spirit is large and liberal, its dignity is personal and not dogmatical, and it is all redolent with the unction of holiness and truth. With a very few enlargements of what is implied, but not fully opened, with no changes or alterations, I could give it forth as the full confession of my faith, and I earnestly recommend to the ejected brethren, to think seriously of this which I now suggest.

THE FIRST BOOK OF DISCIPLINE.

This was drawn up by the same ministers who drew up the Confession, immediately upon the dissolution of the Parliament 1560, wherein the Confession had been ratified and confirmed by the assembled estates of the kingdom. " The parliament dissolved, consultation was had, how the church might be established in a good and godly policy, which by the Papists was altogether defaced. Commission and charge was given to Mr. John Winrem sub-prior of St.

Andrews, Mr. John Spotiswood, John Willock, Mr. John Douglas rector of St. Andrews, Mr. John Row, and John Knox, to draw in a volume the policy and discipline of the church, as well as they had done the doctrine, which they did, and presented it to the nobility, who did peruse it many days. Some approved it, and willed the same to have been set forth by a law; others, perceiving their carnal liberty and worldly commodity somewhat to be impaired thereby, grudged, insomuch that the name of the Book of Discipline became odious unto them. Every thing that repugned to their corrupt imaginations was termed, in their mockage, devout imaginations. The cause we have before declared; some were licentious, some had greedily gripped the possessions of the church, and others thought that they would not lack their part of Christ's coat, yea, and that before that ever he was crucified, as by the preachers they were oft rebuked.......Yet the same Book of Discipline was subscribed by a great part of the nobility; to wit, the duke, the earl of Arran, the earls Argyle, Glencairn, Marshal, Monteith, Morton, Rothes, lord James after earl of Murray, lord Yeaster, Boyd, Ochiltrie, master of Maxwel, lord Lindsay elder, and the master after lord barrons, Drumlanrig, Lothingwar, Garleiss, Bargany, Mr. Alexander Gordon bishop of Galloway, (this bishop of Galloway, as he renounced Popery, so did he prelacy; witness his subscription of the Book of Discipline, as the rest of the prelates did, who did join to the Reformation) Alexander

h

Campbell dean of Murray, with a great number
more, subscribed and approved the said Book
of Discipline in the tolbooth of Edinburgh, the
27th day of January, the year of our Lord God
1561, by their approbation, in these words :—
' We who have subscribed these presents, having advised with the articles herein specified,
and as is above-mentioned from the beginning
of this book, think the same good, and conform to God's word in all points, conform to
the notes and additions thereto, asked, and
promised to set the same forward at the uttermost of our powers; providing that the bishops,
abbots, priors, and other prelates and beneficed
men, which else have adjoined themselves to
us, bruik the revenues of their benefices during
their lifetimes; they sustaining and upholding
the ministry and ministers, as is herein specified, for preaching of the word, and ministring
of the sacraments.' "

As the First Book of Discipline is large, I
thought it better to print the short sum of it,
which was drawn up some few years afterwards
by direction of the church, and faithfully expresseth the substance of the other. The original document was submitted to Parliament,
with the following faithful and dutiful com-
mendation :—" To the great council of Scotland
now admitted to the government, by the providence of God, and by the common consent
of the estates thereof. Your honour's humble
servants and ministers of Christ Jesus within
the same, wish grace, mercy, and peace from
God the Father of our Lord Jesus Christ, with

the perpetual increase of the Holy Spirit. From
your honours we received a charge dated at
Edinburgh the 29th of April, in the year of our
Lord 1560, requiring and commanding us in the
name of the eternal God, as we will answer in
his presence, to commit to writing, and in a
book deliver to your wisdoms our judgments
touching the reformation of religion which
heretofore in this realm, (as in others,) hath
been utterly corrupted : upon the receipt whereof, (so many of us as were in this town,) did
conveen, and in unity of mind do offer unto
your wisdoms these subsequents, for common
order and uniformity to be observed in this realm
concerning doctrine, administration of sacraments, election of ministers, provision for their
sustentation, ecclesiastical discipline, and policy of the church ; most humbly requiring
your honours, that as you look for participation
with Christ Jesus, that neither ye admit any
thing which God's plain word shall not approve,
neither yet that ye shall reject such ordinances
as equity, justice, and God's word do specify.
For as we will not bind your wisdoms to our
judgments further than we are able to prove
by God's plain Scriptures : so must we most
humbly crave of you, even as ye will answer
in God's presence (before whom both ye and
we must appear to render accounts of all our
facts), that ye repudiate nothing for pleasure
and affection of men, which ye be not able to
improve by God's written and revealed word."
Upon this document also we shall make a few

remarks, making our quotations from the larger work.

REMARK FIRST.—The First Book of Discipline is a most comprehensive scheme for the well-ordering of all the churches, and for bringing about a unity of faith and practice in the nation; it belongs to the church considered as national, and is the basis upon which the churches which had grown up in Scotland might confederate into one. With a high hand it sets at nought and abolishes the doctrine of transmission of ordination through a regular succession of bishops, and even excommunicates the Roman-Catholic clergy from the number of those who have a lawful calling to the ministry. And if the Church of Scotland be a true church of God, it is so in despite of hereditary ordination, to which it gave no heed, and even went so far as to set aside the imposition of hands also. This, however, was soon restored by the Second Book of Discipline set forth some twenty years thereafter. Yet were our Reformers very considerate in their provisions for appointing ministers; none more so, perhaps none so much so as they. And first, they reverence the call of the Holy Ghost, and require the gifts for each office to be sought for and found before any one should desire the office or be inducted thereinto : secondly, they require the call of the people after he hath made proof of his gifts before them : and, thirdly, the examination and approbation of the ministers and elders of the church : and finally his admission by the preaching and prayer and exhortation of some godly minister before the people, without any signature of confession or formula, without the laying on of hands or any ceremony of whatever kind. If the church did not present a person so gifted to the neighbouring ministers for examination, which was the proper order, the ministers might present one unto the church; and require of the church to accept him if no good reason were found against him. This is the original constitution of the Scottish Church. There is no mention whatever of attendance at schools or universities for any term of years; and yet there is a strict proviso that the ministers should be learned as well as godly. And in point of fact, the ministers of this period did as far surpass in learning, as they did in godliness, those who now study in the universities for eight years at the very least. When I look at the blessed liberty and godly order which Christ's church had amongst us at the Reformation, and compare it with the bondage of forms, and the obstruction of times and circumstances, which now prevails, I am grieved at my heart, and cry out in the bitterness of my soul for some deliverance. The gifts of the Spirit for the office are not looked for by the Presbyters, but certificates of professors, and petty attainments in literature and science, a smattering of every thing, and of theology, that is, Calvinistic divinity, among the rest; and floods of such unspiritual ungifted persons are poured upon the churches. And from these they must make their choice, or be without ministers altogether. This is clean contrary to the platform of our Reformers, who gave the church the privilege not merely of calling from amongst those whom the ministers approved, but expected the church to choose out from among themselves fit persons for the examination and approbation of the ministers and elders. This was the apostolical method, and the method of the early church, and ought to be the method of every church, and without it faithful ministers will never be obtained. The Holy Spirit's supremacy to divide the gifts according to his will, and his judgment, or discrimination expressed by the members of the church, are prior to the approbation of the ministers and elders, with whom is deposited the power to invest and institute the person to that office, whatever it is, for which the Holy Ghost hath furnished, whereto the church hath called him. I think the Reformers were wrong in doing away with the act of laying on of the hands of the eldership, which is the sign of giving him the sanction of their authority; but it is a secondary thing compared with those great rights which they carefully preserved, and it was soon restored again. There is not, I believe, a more bold rejection of the Papistical impositions, nor yet a more reverent preservation of the apostolical ordinances, than is exhibited in this part of our church discipline; which is now not a dead letter merely, but a perverted ordinance. And what is the fruit of its perversion? Hundreds of preachers who have no heart to the work nor success in it; hungry

hangers on, waiting for a bit of bread, instead
of bold and fearless propagators of the Gospel.
I am one who feel the bondage of this system,
and wait on Divine Providence for a call, and
the work of the Spirit for a warrant, to restore
to the church its ancient liberty. And I believe
that I shall not wait long. When it shall please
the Holy Ghost to furnish men with gifts to
fit them for apostles, prophets, evangelists,
pastors and teachers, powers, helps, govern-
ments, discerners of spirits, speakers with
tongues, and interpreters of tongues, I am prepared for my part, and will seek to shew to
my brethren their duty to concur with me, in
setting such apart, and sending them forth in
their several charges. Meanwhile, we must
keep what we have, be faithful over it, and
wait for better things.

· REMARK SECOND.—The other office-bearers
were Superintendants, but only for the present
necessity, until the churches should be supplied
with faithful and able ministers; after which
the church seems to have contemplated no su-
perintendance save that of the Provincial Synods
and the General Assembly. Readers were men
set to read the Scriptures, with a view to their
growing up into the gift of explaining them,
and exhorting the brethren; after which they
might take upon them to administer the sacraments. For our Reformers did well consider
that the chief thing necessary for the holy
office of ministering the sacraments, was the
gift of explaining and applying the same.
The gift of preaching they considered as the
title to minister the sacraments; the laying on

of hands as the appointment to power over that
and the other ordinance in a particular place.
And because the Papist priests did not minister
any word of explanation and exhortation, their
ordinances were held not to be rightly administered. And in this I heartily concur. This
office of reader ought to be revived, in order that
the Spirit might have liberty to draw out the
gifts of his servants, and shew himself in the
church, which at present he is entirely prevented
from doing. Not a man may open his lips in
a church of a thousand persons, save one only.
What a shame, what a divergence from the
primitive church, and from the platform of our
Reformed Church. Elders and Deacons are required to be in every church, and many of each
sort are contemplated; and lest the office should
be burdensome, election is required annually.
This was changed in the Second Book of Discipline, whereby the office was made perpetual;
as doubtless it was intended to be, unless some
fault requiring deposition should arise. The
office of the deacon is now all but entirely
disused in the Church of Scotland, through the
shameful neglect of all discipline; and the office
of an elder is little else than a name, or a lay-
office. And yet we boast of our primitive simplicity, and have almost extinguished these two
superior orders of the clergy. Better have
an ordinance in any form, however altered,
than have it altogether neglected or abolished.
My wonder is, that the Church of Scotland,
having swerved so far from her original foundation, and from the only true foundation of the
word of God, should stand at all. It was said

truly in the late debates, that by Acts of Parliament they stood, and that they might not,
without forfeiture, make any alteration from
the constitution by Act of Parliament established. And yet this is the church which yielded
up so many martyrs for Christ's royal office in
his house!

.. REMARK THIRD.—There was an ordinance
entitled, "The Prophesying or Interpreting of
Scripture;" or, as it is called, "The Exercise,"
founded upon this passage, "Let the prophets
speak, two or three, and let the others judge;
but if any thing be revealed to another that
sitteth by, let the former keep silence. For ye
may one by one all prophecy, that all may
learn, and all may receive consolation. And
the spirits of the prophets are subject to
the prophets." This exercise was to be
weekly, to the end "that the kirk have judgment and knowledge of the graces, gifts, and
utterances of every man within their body;
the simple, and such as have somewhat profited,
shall be encouraged daily to study and to
prove in knowledge; and the whole kirk shall
be edified: for this exercise must be patent to
such as list to hear and learn, and every man
shall have liberty to utter and declare his mind
and knowledge to the comfort and consolation
of the kirk." I ask, where is this ordinance
now? It is sunk into disuetude. How earnestly bent the church was upon this exercise,
with additions, is declared in the following extract: "And, moreover, men in whom is supposed to be any gift which might edify the
church, if they were well employed, must be

charged by the minister and elders to join
themselves with the session, and company of
interpreters, to the end that the kirk may
judge whether they be able to serve to God's
glory, and to the profit of the kirk in the vocation of ministers or not: and if any be found
disobedient, and not willing to communicate
the gifts and special graces of God with their
brethren, after sufficient admonition, discipline
must proceed against them, provided that the
civil magistrate concur with the judgment and
election of the kirk. For no man may be permitted as best pleaseth him to live within the
kirk of God, but every man must be constrained
by fraternal admonition and correction to bestow his labours, when of the kirk he is required, to the edification of others. What day
in the week is most convenient for that exercise, what books of Scripture shall be most
profitable to read, we refer to the judgment of
every particular kirk; we mean, to the wisdom
of the minister and elders."—An ordinance of
the like kind obtained in the Church of England,
which, when Archbishop Parker was required
by Queen Elizabeth to suppress, he preferred
rather to lay down the primacy. I have no
hesitation in saying, that, for want of this
ordinance, the Holy Ghost hath been more
grieved and quenched than by almost any thing
besides; and our church-meetings, from being
for edification of the brethren by the Holy
Ghost shewing himself in the variously gifted
persons, have become merely places for preaching the Gospel, and not for edifying the church.
No one feels more than I do the importance of

public preaching, with which I would not interfere; but, surely something is wanting besides this for the edification of the church
within itself.   There are some vestiges of this
ancient order in Rosshire, under the name of
"The day of the men," before the administration of the Sacrament.   To revive it, as our
churches are now constituted, would cause
great confusion, and perhaps do more harm
than good; but the same end might be served
by elders gathering the people of their several
districts together and presiding over such a
holy exercise in their own houses, after the
manner of fellowship-meetings.   Something of
this liberty must be permitted, or else the gifts
of the Spirit will never be fully manifested.
God help us to set this thing in order.

REMARK FOURTH.—There was a book of
common order, according to which John Knox
conducted his church in Edinburgh, and which
was commonly adopted by others.   This contained a set of prayers and offices for the common occasions of the church, and our Reformers
were of opinion that there should be daily
service in the church, either for sermon or
common prayers, with some exercise of reading
of Scriptures.   It was required, moreover, that
one day in every week there should be public
worship with a sermon, during which there was
to be cessation from business and labour, as
well by servant as by master.   The Lord's
Supper was to be administered at the least
four times in the year.   Public examination
was to be had annually of the knowledge of

every person in the church; and a regular
treatise of fasting for the church was prepared
by the General Assembly; and many other
things which I cannot particularize, all of them
betokening the life of the church, as our present
condition betokens her nighness unto death.
What, though to countervail these blessed ordinances, there be in the First Book of Discipline
some erroneous doctrine on the subject of the
duty of the civil magistrate towards profaners
of the holy Sacraments, and of the name of
God, as if such were not worthy to live; it is
only one proof amongst many that there still
did cleave unto the Reformers some of the
evil savour which their spirits had been baptized into by the accursed Papistry, as they
term it. Upon the whole, therefore, take it
for all in all, I admire the First Book of Discipline, as a very mighty work of the Spirit of
holiness and charity and good order. And I
devoutly wish we had in our churches one half
of the liberty and privilege which we are there
required to use. I am much pressed in spirit
upon this subject, and beseech the brethren to
seek the Lord and set things in order.

THE SECOND BOOK OF DISCIPLINE.

No one, who is not acquainted with the history of the Church of Scotland, can conceive
the unwearied travail which his ancestors underwent between the years 1564 and the year
1581 in preparing the Second Book of Discipline, not with the view of superseding, but of
perfecting the other; and though they pre-

vailed not to obtain the ratification and legal enforcement thereof by the civil magistrate, it ought to be looked upon as by far the most deliberate, and excogitated document, and almost the unanimous voice of our Reformers upon the subject of Discipline. With the more diligence, therefore, let us consider wherein it adds to the correctness and completeness of the former.

REMARK FIRST.—While it is declared (chap. ii.) that three out of the five ministers of the word, namely, Apostles, Evangelists, and Prophets, were extraordinary and temporary, it is not declared that they are done away with; but, contrariwise, that God " extraordinarily for a time may stir some of them up again." This comforts my mind, which can find in Scripture no hint of any withdrawal of the gifts and callings of God, but, on the other hand, a continual testimony that they are without repentance. And I do continually pray, both publicly and privately, that the Lord would restore such gifted persons to his church for the perfecting of his saints, for the work of the ministry, for the edifying of the body of Christ. I think if ever a man had the gift of apostleship sealed upon him, it was Knox himself, whose labours and whose success are almost unprecedented in the annals of the Christian church. And before him, in our land, the same may be said of Columba the Apostle of the Picts, and of Aidan, the Apostle of the Northumbrians and Angles. And in the latter days I may say the same of Schwartz and Brainerd. I do not mean to place them, or any other men, by the side of the twelve Apostles, who had from Christ the power of bringing the gift of the Holy Ghost into the church by ·the laying on of hands. That faculty has ceased; gifts are now in the church, and not in any order of men. But, because this vice-regal function hath ceased, we may not, without warrant of Scripture, say that the apostolic office hath ceased; and as to the prophetic office, I believe it to be in the church at this day, exercised and practised by those persons who have received the gift of tongues. To the doctrine, that they have been withdrawn by any act of God, I can never subscribe: to the fact that they have not been apparent, I confess with shame and confusion of face; to the hope that they are all reviving and will soon be all manifested, I cleave with strong assurance. And for this I call upon all Christians to pray. Even common parlance hath denominated Bernard Gilpin the Apostle of the North, and St. Patrick the Apostle of Ireland: and I hope to see the day when not ecclesiastical .courts, of which we hear nothing in Scripture save for emergencies; but persons apostolical, evangelical, prophetical, pastoral, and doctrinal, shall ·rule over the word of God. As things are at .present, I would as soon commit any question concerning doctrine to the town-council of a burgh as to the Presbytery of the bounds, or even to the General Assembly itself.

REMARK SECOND.—The rule over the word is committed to the Pastor, and Doctor or

Teacher: of which orders there should be one in every church; the former to take the cure of souls, the latter to travail in the word; the one to administer consolation, edification, exhortation, word, and sacrament; the other to wait on teaching, and doctrine, and catechising. The elders have no part nor lot in this matter, to whom belongeth government or discipline; to the deacon, gathering and distribution of the goods ecclesiastical. This division of offices is I think sound, and it were well for every church that it were faithfully observed. The office of doctor or teacher hath failed, and where it still remains in the collegiate churches, it is not according to the ordinance, but merely as a second minister. I have lived to see it revived, and to preside over the revival of it, in the person of one, whom the General Assembly cast out without permitting him a trial by the Holy Scriptures; and whom, therefore, I consider as a sufferer for righteousness' sake. May the Lord speedily revive this office in all the churches.

REMARK THIRD.—These four offices of Pastor, Doctor, Elder, and Deacon, without which the Reformers consider no church rightly constituted, are all put upon the same footing in respect of admission; three things being necessary: First, the calling of God and inward testimony of a good conscience: secondly, election by the judgment of the eldership, and consent of the congregation; none to be intruded contrary to the will of the congregation, or without the voice of the eldership: thirdly, ordination by fasting, earnest prayer, and imposition of hands of the eldership. All this I deem to be well ruled; but I dissent from a limitation put upon the call of God in these words: "There are two sorts of calling; one extraordinary, by God immediately, as was that of the Prophets and Apostles, which, in kirks established and already well reformed, hath no place." Until I see authority for this in the word of God, I must regard it as a hasty conclusion drawn from a low and faithless estate of the church, and which, if permitted to remain, will perpetuate that estate. I believe that the call of God is neither more nor less than the gift of the Holy Ghost for that particular office; which, being received by any one, he exerciseth before the church, and the church, discriminating the nature and experiencing the edification thereof, doth ask him to be by the proper authority of the eldership instated in that office; which, being accomplished, every thing is done to preserve the invisible Head, the visible government, and the whole church, in their several rights and immunities. The invisible Head acts in the spirit of the person by the Holy Ghost, working in him a certain power of teaching, miracles, tongues, wisdom, knowledge, or otherwise: the whole church recognizeth this, and are thankful, and they wait upon their rulers with their wishes, who, giving heed thereto, and being well satisfied therewith, do straightway institute him in his office. This, I feel assured, is the completeness of the rule. It is very remarkable that *the word of wisdom* and *the word of know-*

ledge, which are manifestations of the Holy
Ghost (1 Cor. xii.), should be assigned as the
gifts which severally qualify for the offices of
the *Pastor* and the *Doctor.* Our Reformers
were right in the substance; they were led
astray merely by the use of that distinction,
extraordinary and ordinary, for which I cannot
find a shadow of authority in the Scripture.

REMARK FOURTH.—As in the church of Jerusalem, Antioch, or Ephesus, those elders who
ruled in the word, and those who ruled in the
discipline, might and did meet together for the
well-ordering of all things within the church,
and for sending out men, as Paul and Barnabas,
to see how the other churches fared, and to water
them, yea, and to plant churches where none
already were; so our fathers, looking reverently
to apostolic authority, did ordain likewise; and
the assembly so convening they called the
Presbytery or Eldership : for there is no mention in the Second Book of Discipline of a
kirk-session as distinct from a presbytery.
But, on the contrary, the assemblies of the
church are declared to be " of four sorts; for
either they are of particular kirks and congregations, one or mo (more), or of a province,
or of a whole nation, or of all and divers nations professing one Jesus Christ." The first
of these is as complete in one congregation as
in more ; the former being the rule, the latter
the exception; as is set forth in these words :
"When we speak of the elders of the particular
congregations, we mean not that every particular parish-kirk can, or may, have their own

i

particular elderships, especially in landward; but we think three, four, more or fewer particular kirks, may have one eldership, common to them all, to judge their ecclesiastical causes." Accordingly, in the towns all the ministers and elders did convene together as it is at this day: and this is the true idea of the Presbytery or Eldership; being in truth derived from the order of the seven Apocalyptic churches, and of the primitive Culdee colleges, as is distinctly set forth in these words: "This we gather out of the practice of the primitive kirk, where elders, or colleges of seniors, were constitute in cities and famous places." Now to have copied the model, there should have been not a moderator elected at every meeting, but a permanent *angel* (to use the Scripture expression), or a *bishop* (to use the expression of the primitive church), or an *antistes* (abbot, superior, to use the style by which the Culdees expressed the same truth). I maintain, therefore, that a church with its minister, one or more; its doctor, one or more; its elders and its deacons, is complete within itself for all purposes whatsoever, either of self-preservation or of propagation: and that the Presbytery, mentioned in Scripture, and in our Books of Discipline, consisted of the eldership of such a church, and I do feel in this respect perfect liberty, acting as the head of the eldership of a church, to do all the acts to which a bishop in the Church of England or a Presbytery in the Church of Scotland feel themselves to be competent. Moreover, I feel assured that it is the duty of every church so to act. And this is the ordinary jurisdiction; provincial synods, and national assemblies, and œcumenical councils being extraordinary, to meet emergencies. But when the emergency ariseth, as it did at the last General Assembly of the Church of Scotland, that orthodox men are deposed for heresy, it is the bounden duty of a man to appeal to a General Council of Christendom, and, until the appeal be redressed, to keep his footing and do his work only the more valiantly because multitudes have risen up against the truth. These are things which it deeply concerneth the church to know and to hold in times like the present, when discipline, in the hands of blind and presumptuous men, threatens dissolution to the truth and to the church itself.

CRAIG'S CATECHISM.

The next official and authoritative document of the Church of Scotland which we have republished, is entitled, "A Form of Examination before the Communion," drawn up by Mr. John Craig, and commonly called Craig's Catechism. It was drawn up by order of the General Assembly, read in their hearing, in the meeting 1592; and by them publicly approved, and ordered to be used in all the churches. My reverence for the authority of the church, as well as my own high satisfaction in this little Catechism, first moved me to use it in my own church for examination of communicants; and finding it so very advantage-

i 2

ous, I resolved to republish it at my own
charges; and doing this, I thought it would
not be unseasonable to publish along with it
the other ancient documents of our church,
which now are hardly known, save to a few
men of antiquarian research;—insomuch that
lately, in a meeting of synod, all appeal to
them was ridiculed, as if one should talk of
the vitrified forts of Scotland.

Anterior to this time, our church, in that
loving spirit of fraternity, of which we have
noted another instance, did receive the Catechism of the Genevan Church, commonly
called Calvin's Catechism, and also the Palati-
nate Catechism. There was also the little Catechism for young persons before communion, and
the Latin Catechism used in schools. Nor were
these ever annulled, but continue to this day
symbols of that faith upon which our church
was founded. I had thoughts of reprinting
these four Catechisms, but preferred the Larger
Catechism of the Westminster Divines, in testimony of my reverence for the labours of that
Assembly, and because it is so very ample and
sufficient upon all points of doctrine and practice. With respect to Craig's Catechism, I
have nothing to say, except that it is a most
precious depository of vital truth, and, with
one alteration, the best catechism I know. The
grounds of this judgment, I will now express.

REMARK FIRST.—It hath an advantage over
the Shorter Catechism, in being so entirely divested of a systematic form, and being expressed almost entirely in Scripture terms.

Each question and answer generally contain
one simple truth, with one text of Scripture
to confirm it. And it is so much shorter than
the Assembly's Catechism, that I almost wish it
might supplant it both in families and schools.
Besides the whole subject of our union with
Christ, and our deriving nourishment from
him in the way of life, sorely overlooked in
the Shorter Catechism, is in this excellently set
forth. The Shorter Catechism is systematic;
Craig's Catechism is Scriptural and simple.
The Shorter Catechism is intellectual; Craig's
Catechism is vital.

REMARK SECOND.—The subjects of our bondage through Adam, and our redemption by
Christ, are treated of as altogether independent
upon our participation with Christ, as mysteries
of the faith outward to us, done in God for all,
and by us to be believed on, anterior to, and
in order to, our coming into the participation
thereof. Then that participation through union
with Christ by faith, is beautifully opened; and
faith is defined to be " a sure persuasion that
he is the only Saviour of the world, but ours
in special who believe in him." Here is the
common redemption, the particular appropria-
tion, and assurance combined together in the
definition of faith. Would one believe that the
men who cast out the Rev. John Campbell, are
the successors of those men who sanctioned
this Catechism ?

REMARK THIRD.—There is somewhat of in-
distinctness in the vth section, of which the
first question, " What good things may we

do now, being regenerated?" is well answered,. " We may serve our God freely and uprightly."' But the following question; " May we do it perfectly according to the law?" is, if I understand it right, erroneously answered, "No, truly; for our regeneration is not perfect:" and I say so, because it is expressly written, " That the righteousness of the law might be fulfilled in us, who walk not after the flesh, but after the Spirit " (Rom. viii. 3). This inaccuracy leads to one or two more, all arising out of one or other of these two notions, that it is sinful to have temptations in the flesh, or that regeneration is not good against those temptations, utterly to triumph over them. Now, the truth is, that to have the law of the flesh is indeed one part of our original sin, from which we are delivered by Christ's perfect conformity to the law; as we are delivered from the power of death by his resurrection. But the presence of this law of the flesh is no impediment to the holiness of the regenerate man, regeneration being a power of God, able to triumph over it, and to be holy against all its temptations. I would not be the means of publishing what may have the remotest chance of conveying error; and therefore I would alter Questions 37, 38, 39, 40, 41 in this way:—

Q. 37. May we serve God freely and uprightly, and perfectly, according to the law?—A. Yea, truly; because the righteousness of the law is fulfilled in us, who walk not after the flesh, but after the Spirit (Rom. viii. 3).

Q. 38. What followeth upon that?—A. A

continual crucifixion of the flesh, with its corruptions and lusts, and living unto God by the power of the Holy Ghost (Rom. vii).

Q. 39. Is the presence of the law of the flesh in our members to be accounted sin?—A. No surely, while we serve it not, but do ever gainsay and overcome it (1 Pet. iv. 1).

Q. 40. Whence hast thou assurance of this continual victory over the flesh?—A. From the spiritual generation, holy life, and spotless death of Christ, notwithstanding he was bone of my bone, and flesh of my flesh.

Q. 41. What are we then who believe in Christ?—A. Just in him, and ever deriving from him the will, and the way, and the power to be holy, as he is holy (1 John iii. 6, 7).

Q. 42. How is this?—A. Through a constant faith in Christ, and crucifixion and burial of the natural man.

The Reformers were so intent, upon the one hand, to establish Christ's righteousness, as the only fountain head of righteousness, and, on the other, the liberty to come at once and be saved by faith in the same, without the works of the law, that they did not give themselves so strenuously as they should have done to define and maintain holiness in the believer as the continual requirement of God, which Christ enabled him to fulfil. They looked at Christ's righteousness for the chief of sinners, as a thing to bring us at once into acceptance with God, and to set us up in a clear conscience; they did not consider it also as a continual sustenance in the same state of acceptance, through

the preservation of the conscience clean. They
spake of the virtue of Christ's blood to cleanse
the conscience at all times, but not of the
power of Christ's resurrection to uphold us in
perfect obedience and purest holiness at all
times. It was an omission, not an error;
though, as in the case before us, it betrayed
them into forms of doctrine highly pernicious
to holiness, and which have now wrought out
the heresy, that to say Christ had the law of
the flesh is to say he had sin. I wish, instead
of the word *imputed,* were continually substi-
tuted *inherent, but derived.* Though the Catechism comes short in this statement of the
Creed, it is always right, in the spirit of its
faith; and upon the subject of the Sacraments,
it is altogether admirable.

THE NATIONAL COVENANT.

The first document in the Appendix is the
Confession of the English Church, referred to
at the beginning of this Preface. Concerning
the second document, entitled, " The National
Covenant, or the Confession of Faith," we have
to observe, that it consisteth of two parts, separated at page 137 by a short black line; of
which two, the former is of date 1580, and the
other of date 1638. These are, properly speaking,
not ecclesiastical, but national, emanating not
from the church but from the state. The Confession itself is one of the most nervous protestations
against the Papacy that was ever penned; in which,
amongst other things, " his desperate and uncertain repentance, his general and doubtsome faith,"

are condemned along with his other abominations. Now this is exactly what has been recently approved by the General Assembly, who have condemned the true doctrine as the height of presumption, and the root of Antinomianism. The latter part contains a succession of acts and statutes, confirming the above Confession, the Coronation Oath, and other muniments of the kingdom, for which the people of all ranks and estates declare themselves willing to live and die. Whether it was right for the nation to do this in the face and without the consent of their king, and in the strength of it to defend themselves against their king, is a question which began to be agitated both in England and in Scotland, and in all other lands at the time of the Reformation. And I have no hesitation in saying, that both Knox and Buchanan took up erroneous doctrine on this subject, in maintaining that the king of a Christian people might be lawfully resisted by his Christian people, when violating the laws and constitutions of the kingdom, and trampling under foot the oaths and covenants whereby he had bound himself. The principle of *Lex rex*, The law the king, is essentially an erroneous one, inasmuch as it makes the supremacy to stand in a book, and not in a person, and diverteth the ordinance from the ordinance-administrator, and from the ordinance-head. It is by persons, not by truths, that God is glorified; and persons, not truths, doth he ordain for the government of his creatures; and the truth

was never perfected until it appeared in the
person of the Son of God, who said of himself,
I am the truth.   Buchanan's treatise, " De Jure
regni apud Scotos," and Knox's " First Blast
of the Trumpet against the monstrous Regi-
ment of Women," contain essentially false doctrine upon the subject of obedience to the powers
that be, which hath wrought like a leaven in
the church and realm of Scotland, and may
yet exhibit that country as the most formidable
seat of radicalism and rebellion in the world.
The jealous government of Elizabeth, the sage
counsels of her statesmen, and the deep in-
sight and reverence of the English Reformers,
resisted the same spirit insinuating itself into
England, and drew up one of their Articles in
distinct and explicit reprobation of it.   Driven
back by their measures, it sunk down into the
deep and secret parts of the nation, and wrought
there until it found a head among the the Independents, and produced the fury and havoc of
the Commonwealth, and remains securely seated
amongst that body until this day, waiting occasion to manifest itself: nor will it wait long;
its day of manifestation and perdition is just
at hand.   Ah me ! it was a sad thing that the
Reformers took the civil arm so much into their
service.   Had they been content to teach their
duties to kings as well as to all other men, and
left them to the noble liberty of the servants
of Christ Jesus, to give and to grant what char-
ters and immunities they pleased to the church
and the people, and taught the people to hold

these as boons during the good pleasure of their
rulers, and to resign them when Providence
required it, looking for a heavenly inheritance;
then the Reformation, instead of being the cradle
of insurrection and civil war, of free-thinking
and liberalism, as it hath proved, would have
been the cradle of witness and martyrdom for
the faith and hope of the Lord's coming.

While I make these allowances and abate-
ments from the excellent work of Reformation
in general, I must say for the Reformers in
Scotland, and their successors, the Covenanters,
that they were most disinterested, noble-mind-
ed, humble and patient sufferers for the cross
of Christ, though in this point they wanted
light. They thought that when the Sixth James
had sealed to the excellence of the Church
of Scotland, before assuming the English
crown, and when the Second Charles had done
the same by the Covenant, they might be lawfully resisted, if afterwards they should resile
from, and act contrary to, their obligations.
Which is to make the definition and dignity of
the royal office to be not of Divine ordination,
but of human agreement; and to bring in the
doctrine of the social compact, and the rights
of the people, whose natural fruit is revolution
and destruction of all social relations whatever.
It is as if a Mohammedan wife having become
Christian, should work upon her husband to
become Christian also; and so enjoy the privileges of a Christian wife; and afterwards,
because her husband fell back into Moham-

·medanism, should resist him, and refuse obé-
·dience to his commandments : or, as if children should obey the father while he was tender
and kind, but throw off their dutifulness when
he became rough and stern and wicked : or, as
if servants should serve only the gentle master,
but refuse obedience to the froward :. whereas
the Scripture doctrine is to obey all ordinances
of man for the Lord's sake. The relation of
king and subject, of husband and wife, of parent
and child, of master and servant, are older
than Christianity, which came to comfort and
mollify and redeem them from all evil, not to
destroy and subvert them. When they are
righteously exercised, let us be obedient and
give thanks ; when they are wrongously exercised, let us be obedient and rejoice that we
are counted worthy to suffer with Christ; who,
when he was reviled, reviled not again, when
he suffered, he threatened not, but committed himself to Him that judgeth righteously.—It was noble in the ejected ministers to
betake themselves to the mountains, and to
wander about in sheep skins and goat skins,
and to have their habitation in dens of the earth,
" of whom the world was not worthy;". but it
was wrong in them to take arms, or to permit
the people to take arms against the most ra-
venous and wicked of the spoilers of the land.
They should have taken joyfully the spoiling
of their goods, knowing they have in heaven a
better and a more enduring substance. It is
not a question of casuistry, it is a question of

plain and direct Christian morality. I hold
without a doubt, that in this matter of resistance
our fathers were wrong.

But should they have obeyed the king, and
observed his ordinances in respect to things
ecclesiastical; as, for example, in having these
beggarly curates who were thrust in upon the
church, instead of their right godly pastors?
No, not for a moment. The king of Great
Britain had as little right to interfere in the
Church of Scotland, as king Uzziah had to
interfere in the temple service. It was beyond
his ordinance. He could not dissever a pastor
from his people, whom God had joined together
in one. And I would have died a hundred
deaths rather than have allowed any power on
earth to dissolve that sacred relationship. What
then? The pastors must preach to their people;
and the king's hirelings must have their hire.
But if the king will not suffer the people to
hear their pastors? Then the people must obey
God rather than the king. No king, no husband, no father, no master, hath liberty or
power to make one of God's creatures do wrong;
that is what no servant of God can require; and
inasmuch as any ostensible office-bearer of God
doth so require, he is a real and efficient servant of the devil, who is the author and insti-
gator of all wrong.—But is not this resistance?
Yea; resistance unto blood. But resistance
for what sake? For conscience sake. Not for
the sake of rights political, nor properly ter-
restrial, but for the kingdom of heaven's sake:
not resistance with weapons of the flesh, but

with spiritual weapons, which are the girdle of truth, the breast-plate of righteousness, the helmet of salvation, the shield of faith, and the sword of the Spirit, which is the word of God, and the continual strength of prayer. Now, because the chief labour and persecution and death of the Covenanters was of this kind, patient suffering for righteousness sake, God did so abundantly countenance the work, and by such wonderful providences did bring it out triumphantly : so that I can glory in it as a great work of God, though I disapprove the ostensible creed which they gave out upon this subject of resistance, believing it to be the beginnings of that insubordination and revolution which now filleth Christendom. It was a root of bitterness which hath grown up and troubled the flock, whereby many, almost all, have been destroyed. The principle is, We must give up all the world contains for Christ willingly, yea joyfully ; but Christ we must not give up for all the world contains;—a truth which I am the more patient to inculcate, because there is hardly a man, save those who are looking for His coming, who believe it, and who is not ready at any time to act against it.

THE DIRECTORY FOR FAMILY WORSHIP.

While, with that single exception of a false opinion, rather than a false faith, I do heartily approve and greatly commend, yea and glory in, the wrestlings of the Church of Scotland during almost a whole century of grievous opposition and persecution from the powers that

be, I am still more delighted and rejoiced by
the unwearied care with which she gave herself
to cultivate amongst the people the seeds of
vital religion, and to order the whole kingdom
after a godly sort. One of these breathing times
of rest she enjoyed between the great assembly
of 1638, and the restoration of Charles II. in
1660 ; and notwithstanding that the Presbyterians of Scotland were agitated by so many
wars, first with the Royalists, and then with
the Independents, the church did address herself with so much faith and patience to the
work of evangelizing and edifying the people,
that it was like a second Reformation to the
land, and raised up a generation capable of
enduring the furnace of persecution which was
seven times heated during the thirty years following. One of the instruments by which the
spiritual husbandry was carried on, is exhibited
to us in the next of the documents, which we
have thought it good to republish. It is entitled, " The Directory for Family Worship," and
was agreed upon by the General Assembly in
the year 1647, and enjoined upon the observation of all the people. I earnestly commend
it to all families, especially to the families of
my own flock, with one or two remarks proper
to our condition in the heart of a great city.

REMARK FIRST.—The caution given (section
III.) against any one, however otherwise qualified, taking upon him the interpretation of
the Scriptures, unless he be duly called thereto
by God and the church, is very wholesome and
safe; provided it be not carried to the extent of

preventing the head of the family, or the con-
ductor of the worship from his proper function
as the instructor and counsellor of the family,
which the former hath in right of his baptismal
engagements, the latter hath delegated to him
as the leader of the worship, and the reader of
the word. For, while interpretation is inter-
dicted to all but those who are appointed to
rule in the word and doctrine, it is declared to
be a commendable thing, that all confer, and
make a good use of what has been read. The
church opens the mouth of the heads of families to every thing but trespassing upon the
office of the minister of the word, permitting
exhortation against sin, warning of judgment,
application of the promises for comfort, and
enforcement of the duties; and, in general,
pressing home of the things which have been
read. Moreover, it is very clear from section
VIII. that while the church requireth all her
people to be subject unto those who rule in the
word, and not to meddle with their office, it
doth expect that all heads of families should
give reverent heed to what is delivered in the
congregation, and break down the same to their
families afterwards. And if to their families,
they be required to hold forth the interpretations, doctrines, counsels, and instructions
which have been held forth to them in the
church, then surely to other families and com-
panies of ignorant people who may dwell beside them, far from the means of grace, and
the knowledge of the true God. In a country
like Scotland, which was all supplied with

ministers of the word, this case needeth not to
be provided for; but in a great city like London,
over the families of which there are no efficient
pastors, insomuch that not one family in a
hundred can be considered as so conditioned,
it surely is permitted to any godly person to go
forth from the congregation among the ignorant
and perishing people, and do whatever he can
to convey to them the instruction which he hath
himself received through the ministration of
the word.   I have seen too much the evil of
unproved men taking upon them to interpret
the word with authority, to desire that any of
the congregation should break loose from the
wholesome restraint here laid down; while I
devoutly desire, nay, and enjoin it as a duty
upon every one who has time and opportunity,
without neglecting his own duties, to go forth
and communicate the substance of that instruction which he hath heard and learned, and felt
to be profitable to his own soul.   The spirit of
the caution is, 'Do not take upon you to originate, but be at all pains to convey and communicate the interpretations which you have received through the ordinance of preaching. Be
not many masters or preachers in the word,
but be all communicators of the gift and grace
which you have freely received. Freely ye have
received, freely give.'

REMARK SECOND.—Persons of quality (section IV.) are encouraged to entertain in their
families persons approved by the Presbytery for
performing family exercises, and taking a spiritual charge of the household.   I do greatly

k

desire and continually pray that such families in our great cities, as can afford it, would entertain in their houses young men who have separated themselves to the preaching of the Gospel, that they may go in and out amongst the ignorant all the day long, and endeavour to bring the Gospel to the ears of the people, who are living as remote from it as if they had their habitation in the heart of the Arabian desert. And I give it as my opinion, that if God by his grace should stir up in the congregation young men, who were willing to forsake all for preaching the Gospel, and to submit their gifts to the inspection of the minister who rules in the word, with the consent of the eldership; that such an one might be lawfully set apart to the office, and might be profitably entertained by the heads of families in the flock to evangelize this heathenish city; and, if he desired it, might, yea, and ought to be sent into the villages round about, and into other nations, to the very ends of the earth. And I feel assured that the work of God will never be rightly done, while it is under the power of the unwieldy mechanism which is now brought to bear upon it. The General Assembly's Mission, as they call it, is the proof of what I say. I feel assured that this state of bondage cannot last; and that if God's people pray diligently, deliverance will soon come.

REMARK THIRD.—In section XII. of this Directory are contained instructions and injunctions concerning the work of mutual edification among the members of the body of Christ, out of which grew the fellowship-meetings and prayer-meetings, once so frequent throughout Scotland, and so profitable to the rearing up of men for the offices of the church. In them the Spirit began to shew himself, and the report was borne to the minister, who straightway took order that such a gifted person should be rightly trained up for the work of the ministry. Here also were the gifts for the eldership manifested, and for the other offices in the church. All this work of edifying the flock is now cast upon the minister, who, if he be faithful, hath too heavy a burden, and, if faithless, then the whole edification of the parish is shipwrecked during his incumbency. It is apparent from the whole scope of the direction, that, by this vitality of the whole body, the church expected that the body should be nourished, and that the pastor's part lay in superintending and overseeing the whole scene of religious activity. I thank God that I begin to see the same work of mutual edification beginning to revive in my flock; and I pray that it may grow up into that perfection which is set forth in the Epistle to the Ephesians : " From whom" (Christ, the Head) " the whole body fitly joined together and compacted by that which every joint supplieth, according to the effectual working in the measure of every part, maketh increase of the body into the edifying of itself in love."

OVERTURES OF GENERAL ASSEMBLY, A.D. 1705. Concerning this document, of which I have never been able to find another copy than that from which this is reprinted, I can find no further information than what is contained in a printed Act of Assembly 1704, and an Act of the Assembly 1705, not printed, but noticed in the list of unprinted Acts. The twenty-fifth Act of Assembly 1704, is entitled "An Act, anent preparing a Form of Process, and the Overtures concerning Church Discipline;" whereby a committee is appointed to prepare the same, and transmit them to the Presbyteries for their approval against the next Assembly, which is " to order what is to be done therewith, as they shall think meet." Among the list of unprinted Acts of the Assembly 1705, session 3, is this notice : " Recommendation anent buying the Overtures for Discipline, which are reprinted according to the twenty-fifth Act of the late Assembly." Not having access to the Assembly Records, I am not able to say whether the Presbyteries had approved these overtures, so as to give them the force of positive laws, but do suppose so from the tenor of the recommendation. However this may be, I have thought it good to reprint them for several reasons.

This document, bearing date 1705, exhibits the mind of the church on the subject of discipline at the beginning of her last period, the period of her freedom from persecution, which began at the Revolution. There is a great declension from the period between the famous Assembly at Glasgow 1638, and the Restoration in 1660, and still a greater declension from the brightest period of our Reformed church from 1560 to 1610. The Acts of Assembly from the Revolution, which begins this last period, I have read with great care, and cannot but lament how the gold is become dim, and the fine gold changed from the time of the first and second books of discipline.   There is a hard legal spirit, a character of business transactions, a hiding of principles, whether doctrinal or ecclesiastical, and in general an unlearned character, which bespeak the church fast falling from the catholic spirit of the universal church into the minute details of a body incorporated by Acts of Parliament.   One cannot but admire the diligence to plant Scotland with churches, and to take order for the good government of the whole kingdom. The Assembly is fulfilling its duty to the king and the country faithfully, so far as details and regulations go ; but its duty to the great Head of the church, to preach the Gospel to every creature under heaven, it is overlooking very much. That spirit of legal formality, of lifeless order, is growing, which is now consummated, like a huge system of agricultural labour, without any sowing of seed, or propitiating of the dews of Heaven. Plenty of management, but neither seed to sow, nor rain to moisten the earth. And, accordingly, so early as the Assembly 1720, we find the spirit of formality beginning to act against the spirit of doctrine in the matter of the Marrow controversy ; which hath gone on with a progressive course until this year, when it hath prevailed to trample all doctrine triumphantly under foot, both the doctrine of the Father's love to all men, of Christ's incarnation in the flesh of all men, of the Holy Ghost's working assurance in them who believe;

—yea and hath made the Confession of Faith, and not the Scriptures, the book of ultimate appeal; and hath condemned a book without exhibiting propositions of error, and placed its author under stigma of heresy without once citing him, or permitting him a hearing. Of which the like was not done by the Councils either of Constance or of Trent. There wanteth further but one other decree; to bring these acts to bear upon those who are seeking to enter the ministry, and upon those who are seeking sealing ordinances, in order to lock the church as fast in apostasy as Rome hath been since the decrees of Trent were embodied in the Creed of Pope Pius IV. And even this was attempted last Assembly, first by the overture of one evangelical doctor, and then by the motion of another. Oh! how little these poor forsaken men know what they do.

Nevertheless I have deemed it good to exhibit the form of the mind of the church at the beginning of the last century, that men may take it up and compare it with the present state of the poor Church of Scotland, " blind, miserable, and naked;" abounding in ignorance and pride, in formality and error, destitute, or almost so, of unction, orthodoxy, and charity.

REMARK FIRST.—The first six sections respect the Kirk-session which is composed of the minister, the doctor, the elders, the deacons, and the clerk, or scribe or recorder of each church; permitting thereto the ordering of every thing concerning the word and the sacraments and the discipline, in which the vitality of a church consisteth. It answereth to

the angel and the elders of the apostolical
times, the bishop and the clergy of the primitive church, the bishop and the elders of the
Culdee churches. And though the Presbytery,
hath now acquired a distinct and separate existence, which it had not according to the First
and Second Books of Discipline, it is only a
court of delegates from the several Kirk-sessions within its bounds, having no conformity
with any primitive institution, and being intended only for the supervision of the several
churches in order to preserve unity; not to
usurp any of their prerogatives, or to super-
sede aught of their jurisdiction. This is a most
important remark, because it hath come to be
not only opinion but also doctrine, that the
Presbytery, and not the Kirk-session, is the
thing written of in Scripture under the name
πρησ€υτερον, and in our symbolical books under
the name Eldership.' So also I find in the
Church of England that the bishops have con-
trived to get into their sole hands the power
and dignity which belong to the parish clergy.
This I steadily resist as an imposition. The
Kirk-session wanteth nothing to give it full
power to do every act which pertaineth to a
church; it is a complete responsible depository
of the authority of the great Head of the church.
And so far as I can understand it, the presbytery
is instead of the superintendant; and the superintendant is a sort of relic of the Apostle or
Evangelist. The Synod is the old provincial
council of bishops and presbyters. The General
Assembly is the national one. But what this
presbytery is, more than the eldership of any

church I cannot see, unless it be for doing by means of a court what was originally done by the Apostle or Evangelist; as they say in civil affairs, the putting of that personal right into commission until its proper owners shall appear. I hope the Holy Ghost will soon seal some men to the Apostolical and Evangelical office, and that the court of delegated commissioners will then resign their trust.

REMARK SECOND.—Let not the former remark be understood as intending any thing against the Presbytery, but as advancing the Eldership of each church, the Kirk-session, into its proper dignity. For, as hath been set forth above, while I believe that every church or communion of the faithful, under its eldership and its angel, is fully competent to, and altogether responsible for, the fulness of the Holy Ghost to do and to suffer, to preserve and to propagate the faith, I do likewise believe that to unite these churches under their several pastors and doctors into one, there is an ordinance of God sacred and essential to the completeness of the church, as the one body of Christ; namely, the ordinance of Apostles and Evangelists, who were as it were the bands and joints which linked and bound the many churches or memberships of Christ's body into one. For while every church hath an organic life within itself, to make increase of the body in love, all the churches do form one body, for the manifestation of the unity of the Spirit of Jesus Christ: and in holding this point the Presbyterians and Episcopalians have the advantage of the Independents; while these again have somewhat the advantage of us in maintaining, at least practically, better than we do, the completeness of each church within itself; this intercommunion of church with church throughout the whole world was preserved by an ordinance of the Spirit, which like all his ordinances standeth in gifted persons, not in ecclesiastical courts. "When he ascended up on high, he gave *some* (not *to some*) apostles, some evangelists, some prophets, some pastors and teachers, for the perfecting of the saints, for the work of the ministry, for the edifying of the body of Christ." Now the persons who bound the churches into one, were the Apostles and Evangelists. How these two were distinguished from each other I stay not to examine particularly; but my notion is, that the Apostle planted churches, the Evangelist watered the churches which had been already planted. Neither of these was the episcopal office, and to mix them up with the bishop, or the overseer, or the angel of a church, is to confuse things entirely distinct. This has been done in some measure in the Church of England; and in the Church of Scotland it was done also in the superintendant. These institutions are good, are better than the presbytery, inasmuch as they preserve the *personal* character of these bands and joints of the churches; but not so good, inasmuch as they confuse the vocation, and the gift, and office of the pastor with the higher calling of the Apostle or Evangelist, which the presbytery doth not. But the way of a presbytery is worse than the way of a bishop or superin-

tendant, inasmuch as it hath drawn away from
each church its independent and indefeasible
completeness, and made the same to stand in a
confederacy of some half dozen or even score of
churches, meeting once a month by delegation;
which is a nonentity in the Scriptures, and a
solecism in ecclesiastical polity, and not authorized by our Reformers, and hath crept into
use by the spirit of formality. As hath been
said above, I look upon the presbytery as a
body of commissioners holding the office of the
apostleship or evangelist *in commendam* until fit
persons for taking it in charge be raised up by
the Holy Spirit;—a time which I believe to be
near at hand.

Nevertheless I am exceedingly pleased with
the instructions given to presbyteries in these
Overtures on Discipline, as exhibiting a very
beautiful and complete view of the constitution
and occupation of these bodies, which makes
me blush with shame upon every remembrance
of what I have witnessed in the present goings-
on of presbyteries. The matter is digested into
two chapters; which are the viith and viiith;
whereof the former entreateth of the "method
of proceeding," the latter of the "parochial
visitations." They ought to meet every third
week, but in the first and second periods of the
church when the idea of presbytery was the
eldership of each church, or the collected eldership of one or two contiguous congregations or
churches, and not a delegation from the several
elderships, they were required to meet every
week. They were to be opened by one of the

brethren *exercising* or *making* upon a text after
the manner of the doctor, and *adding* after the
manner of the pastor; to qualify us for which
excellent ordinance we are required when students
of divinity to write such an exercise with
additions. This being finished; the presbytery
proceeded to *censure* or give their judgment
upon the exercise; and thereafter they held a
public disputation upon some common head of
doctrine every first presbytery of the month.
They then were to proceed to the work of examining
the gifts of those who sought office
in the church, and of ordaining them to their
several charges; and after this they sat as a
court of appeal, to hear any causes of discipline,
and to heal any breaches, which the several
churches had not been able to settle within
themselves.—In all this I perceive a very godly
ordinance, as unlike that which now passeth
under the name as well can be; and likewise
I discern a relic of the old apostolic power
which Paul exercised of gathering the elders of
the church together and giving them a charge,
which is also kept up in the episcopal visitations of the Church of England: likewise of the
angel's power over the several congregations or
churches in any city, like Ephesus for example:
but I can find no authority for dispensing with
a constant head, and adopting in stead thereof
a changing moderator. There is something
surely uncanonical in this ordinance; which I
have no doubt hath come from the presbytery
regarding itself in the light of a synodical
court. It is a strange mixture of synodical,

personal, and congregational rights, which I cannot justify though I can thus shew the fountains of the several jurisdictions.—The laying on of hands for authority, is an assumption of that which belongs to the angel and eldership of each church, the visitation of the churches is a right derived from the apostólical office, and perhaps the exercising upon a passage of Scripture from the evangelist, and certainly the sitting as a court of review with an elective moderator, is derived from the provincial synod.—The viiith section, entitled "Of Parochial Visitations by the Presbytery," opens more light into the state of the church at these times, compared with its present state, than whole volumes could do. I do recommend it to the perusal of all persons in the Church of Scotland, as fitted by God's blessing to do away with that vain confidence and self-sufficiency which hath swallowed up all humiliation and confession of sin, and brought every man from being a mourner for the corruptions of our Zion, to be a champion, and too often a bully, for every thing, the very worst, which is there found smelling rank to heaven and crying for vengeance.—The ixth, "Of Visitation of Families," the xth, " Of Sanctification of the Lord's-Day, and observing Fast and Thanksgiving-Days," are all full of the odour of sanctity; and contain most wise precautions against the growth of wickedness in the church. Whence then the present distress? From the shepherds, from the unfaithfulness of the administrators to these excellent ordinances, who have gradually let

them drop out of use, and out of mind, until
they have become a dead letter, or are revived,
as in the case of the visitation of the parish of
Row, in order to convert the salutary rod of
discipline into a sceptre of iron for dashing out
the brains of faithful ministers. The universities, and above all the University of Edinburgh,
where the ministers of the church are reared,
the abuse of patronage; the self-seeking of the
heads of corporations, and the public func-
tionaries, or, as they might be called, factiona-
ries of Scotland; the secularity of the church
courts, the growth of a legal spirit, the miserable
state of preaching for three quarters of a century, have made the well-watered and fruitful
garden of Scotland to become a spiritual waste,
her presbyteries to become business and con-
vivial meetings, or scenes of low and vulgar
strife; her kirk-sessions to become almost non-
entities; the order of deacons to be abolished;
the office of priest or elder to be prostituted to
the vilest interests; and all things, in one word,
from the preaching of the Gospel downward, to
become a sore and grievous evil in the sight of
God; which, if not repented of, will bring
down his wrath and indignation upon that
whole land like a whirlwind. Of all this evil
I impute the chief and almost only blame to
the shepherds, who, having such admirable
canons of discipline, all and every one of which
they bound themselves to observe, have fallen
into the grossest ignorance with respect to
them, and are at this day found living in the
utter neglect, yea, and contempt of them all;

which things I speak plainly, because the poor
people are blinded,—and sorrowfully, because I
would move compassion in the heart of the
people, that they may cry unto God for their
mother, and find help for her in his tender
mercy, which endureth for ever.

THE WESTMINSTER ASSEMBLY'S LARGER CATE-
CHISM.

In this historical enumeration of the authorised documents of the Church of Scotland, I
have refrained from noticing the Confession
of Faith and Catechisms of the Westminster
divines, which were examined and approved by
the General Assembly of the Church of Scotland in the year 1648. And this I have done
because the Church of Scotland had to do with
them not directly but indirectly. It is true we
had some half-dozen Commissioners in that
Assembly of Divines; but the great body were
Puritan ministers of the Church of England,
assembled not by warrant of the king, but of
the long parliament, when, by common consent,
the constitution of this kingdom was under
abeyance; a being essentially an issue of re-
publican and revolutionary principles. I never
liked that assembly, and would much rather
our church had never adopted its books. As
it is, however, we must bow to the awards of
Providence, and make the best use of them.
While I prefer beyond all measure the labours
of our Reformers, which took so many years
to complete them, and grieve exceedingly that
they should have been virtually supplanted and

buried out of sight by the act of one General
Assembly, in a factious time convened; without
any observance of the Barrier Act, which
requireth every act of legislature to pass slowly
and patiently through the Presbyteries;—while,
I say, I lament this other instance of Scottish
haste, I am far from disavowing the Westminster Confession, to which I have set my hand,
or even disallowing it as an excellent composition upon the whole. But for many reasons I
greatly postpone it to our original standards;
under which it ranks, and is subordinated, not
they under it. The Westminster Confession is
subject to the censure of the original Confession,
being adopted under this proviso, that it was
found by the Assembly of 1647 to be "most agreeable to the word of God, and in nothing contrary
to the received doctrine, worship, discipline, and
government of this kirk." The truth is, that
the Church of Scotland was working with head
and hand to proselytize or to beat England
into the Presbyterian form of church government, and therefore adopted these books of
the English Presbyterians, thinking there could
be no unity without uniformity; a cruel mistake which was woefully retaliated upon them
in the reigns of the Second Charles and the
Second James. It is not with any particular
expressions or doctrines of the Westminster
Confession that I find fault, but with the general
structure of it. It is really an imposition upon
a man's conscience to ask him to subscribe
such a minute document: it is also a call upon
his previous knowledge of ecclesiastical con-

troversy, which very few can honestly answer; and, being digested on a systematic principle, it is rather an exact code of doctrine, than the declaration of a person's faith in a personal God, Father, Son, and Holy Ghost. I find it to be a great snare to tender consciences, a great trial to honest men ;—insomuch that as a pastor I have often been greatly perplexed to reconcile men, both elders and preachers, to the subscription of it. They seem to feel that it is rather an instrument for catching dishonest, than a rule for guiding honest, people ; that it presupposeth men knavish, and prepareth gyves upon their legs, and shackles for their hands. I have a great objection to it, moreover, for mixing up the form of church government and ecclesiastical discipline, with the matter of a man's confession of faith, seeing these are surely not necessary to salvation. In one word, there is a great deal too much of it for rightly serving the ends of a confession ; I greatly prefer the old Confession, and the Apostle's Creed to both. There is no use in hard-fasting men at such a rate ; although it be very necessary to exhibit a distinct standard of faith for them to rally under.

While I say these things of this book as of a human composition, I do solemnly protest against those who maintain that it declares the doctrine, That Christ died only for the elect, and redeemed them, and them only, from the curse and bondage and misery of the Fall; which were to contradict the truth, that he redeemed every thing which was created upon the earth, and every being who inherits the nature of Adam. This truth is not sufficiently declared, because it was not much called in question: about that time, indeed, it began to be called in question; and the contrary doctrine, according to Archbishop Usher, in his judgment upon the subject, was introduced into England by Ames: and, I suppose, because there were some in the assembly who were given to that error the subject was avoided. But surely it *was avoided*, and neither decreed for nor decreed against; and, being so, it remains in the state in which they found it, as expressed in our Standards and in the Articles of the Church of England. If I believed that the doctrine of particular redemption were embodied in the Westminster Confession, I would speak of it in very different language than I have used above; I would denounce it as an ungodly book, and move the church to have it condemned of heresy, instead of exalting it as a standard of orthodoxy.

The two passages which they quote in support of their pernicious error are these: "As God hath appointed the elect unto glory, so hath he, by the eternal and most free purpose of his will, fore-ordained all the means thereunto. Wherefore they who are elected, being fallen in Adam, are redeemed by Christ,—are effectually called unto faith in Christ, by his Spirit working in due season,—are justified, adopted, sanctified, and kept by his power through faith unto salvation. Neither are any other redeemed by Christ, effectually called, justified, adopted, sanctified, and saved, but

1

the elect only." The last sentence is what
they strain at, saying, that it declareth redemption by Christ to be only for the elect.
If the particle had been disjunctive instead of
conjunctive, *or* instead of *and*, I would have
allowed the conclusion; but being as it is, I
deny it utterly. The thing asserted is, that
only the elect have that done for them which
is described by the combined and united force
of these words, "redeemed, called, justified,
adopted, sanctified, and saved." This is the
true interpretation of the document. And
that it is the one intended is manifest by this,
that the whole section is affirmative of the
elect; inclusive of them, and when it hath included them within the proper definition, it
negatives all others from that chosen dignity.
And of the rest of mankind, it asserteth that
they are not so included in the decree of election, but passed by and ordained to dishonour
and wrath, without mentioning whether God
hath done any thing for them or not. And
why this silence? Because the subject treated
of is " God's eternal decree," and not the work
of Christ the Mediator.—The second passage
occurs under this latter head, and is as follows:
"To all those, for whom Christ hath purchased
redemption, he doth certainly and effectually
apply and communicate the same, making intercession for them, and revealing unto them
in and by the word the mysteries of salvation;
effectually persuading them by his Spirit to
believe and obey; and governing their hearts
by his word and Spirit; overcoming all their

enemies by his almighty power and wisdom, in such manner and ways as are most consonant to his wonderful and unsearchable dispensation." If the word *redemption* here used mean purchased from under the curse and bondage of sin, then this passage would be conclusive against the truth; which, in the catechism of the Church of England, is expressed thus, " redeemed me and all mankind; " but, because that word hath no meaning in itself save as is defined by the words with which it is connected, and by which the condition of the bondage is expressed, we must always ascertain this before we can judge of its import. In Rev. vi. 9, it is used of the church and them only, who are purchased for priests and kings unto God; in 2 Pet. ii. 1, it is used of the reprobate who deny the Lord that bought them, being before ordained unto condemnation. If now we go into the context to ascertain what is the exact thing signified by the word *redemption*, we find it to be, " purchased not only reconciliation, but an everlasting inheritance in the kingdom of heaven, for all those whom the Father hath given unto him; " that is the same sense in which it is used in Rev. vi. 9; and in which we have already seen it used in the iii d chapter of the Confession above referred to. Now to the redeemed in this sense, we are all agreed that Christ doth certainly and effectually apply the same, &c.

While, therefore, we do exceedingly blame the Westminster divines for being silent on the great head of orthodox doctrine, the redemption of all mankind and of all the material creation, out of the hands of Satan and his wicked angels, which is the very basis of all orthodox truth, the ground whereon God and the sinner meet, we will not allow these divines to be stigmatized by their indiscreet admirers, as if they had gainsaid the most precious of all the truths of Holy Scripture, denied the love of God to all men and every man, denied the work of Christ for all men and every man. No; the Westminster divines have enough to bear already for bringing in such a dogmatical confession of faith, and for seeking agreement at the expense of being silent on a great fundamental truth of the Gospel: let them not be accused of overturning the foundation.

Along with the Confession, the Westminster divines drew up two Catechisms, The Larger, and The Shorter, intended to embody the faith and duty of a Christian. Of these, I have reprinted the former with the references to Scripture, as containing a full and sufficient code of Christian doctrine and morality. Taken as a whole, I approve of it very highly, especially the latter part concerning duty which is about three fourths of the whole. As a compendium of Christian morals I know of nothing better, and do most earnestly commend it to my flock, and indeed to the whole church. With respect to the doctrine, I think it sufficient in all that concerneth the offices and work of Christ for the elect people of God, and very deficient in all that respects God's goodness and grace to the rest of mankind and to the whole world. In all which concerneth the application of the Gospel unto the sinner by the Holy Ghost, through faith, with the benefits thereby conveyed and enjoyed, it is also good; but, in shewing forth the dealing of God with men in their unconverted state, and their wickedness in resisting him, it cometh far short. If it be understood as a Church Catechism, for making the members of Christ acquainted with their privileges and obligations, it is one of the most perfect which was ever penned; but if it be considered as a complete exhibition of the character of God and his actings towards his creatures, it cometh far short indeed. I have always contemplated it in the former sense, and in that sense I do now give it forth to the church. It is not faultless even as a Church Catechism, but its faults are few compared with its excellencies. One constant and common fault of this and all the Reformation standards that I have seen, is to palliate and even to provide for the short-comings, imperfections, and positive transgressions of the regenerate; which is clean contrary to Scripture, where the regenerate state is presented as a state of holiness, and all men are urged with diligence to attain unto sinless perfection. I agree as to the fact of the remainders of sin in the saints; but I disagree as to the necessity of their being there, and I charge them upon myself and upon all saints as a direct and wilful sin against the Spirit of Christ, which is given to us for complete and not for partial holiness. The time is come to meet this deficiency of the Reformation doctrine, directly and fully in the face, for by this door hath come in the most abominable heresy that Christ had not the law of the flesh to deal with and to destroy. For they say, if this were so, then he must have been sinful; for to have flesh with the law of flesh in it, is to be a sinner. We deny this, and assert that all Scripture regardeth the regenerate man as holy, as having ceased from sin, the law of the flesh notwithstanding. And this it truly is, not by an artifice of language or a fiction of theology, but of very truth; because of regeneration it is the native force and property to take the flesh out of its bondage to sin, and give it liberty and power to all holiness. But having argued this matter when treating of Craig's Catechism, I refrain from saying any thing more upon it in this place. While I have lamented, and will ever lament, over the deficiency of these Westminster standards, and the short-coming of all the Reformation divinity upon the subject of God's goodness and grace to every creature which doth on earth abide, I am far from signifying that they are without notices and distinct declarations thereof; but I mean that this, the character of our good Father, doth not appear every where shining out on sinners through these writings, which are often not a transparency, but a veil cast over the face of God; the veil indeed beautifully embroidered, but still a veil. Therefore the writings of men, and even the best standards of the most orthodox church, are to be put in an infinitely inferior place to the Holy Scriptures, in every word of which God lives, and breathes, and feels, and acts. And being thus persuaded, I have had my own scruples about re-publishing these standards of the church, much as I admire and love them. But, perceiving how entirely the judges of the ecclesiastical courts have forsaken both the letter and the spirit of the laws under which they are beholden to act, I thought it better to proceed with the publication than to delay it any longer.

One word more before I close this labour of love for the almost desperate Church of Scotland, which we would have healed, but healed she would not be. If those ministers who, in the last General Assembly, condemned the characteristic and essential features of the three persons of the Godhead, the love of the Father, the flesh of the Son, the assurance of the Holy Ghost, will go and in their several parishes preach as they dared to judge; if they repent not of their deeds, but go on in their ignorance and error, to preach that God loveth not every man, and that Christ hath not atoned for the sins of every man by taking the common flesh of every man, and prevailing over all its temptations to present it holy, and that the Holy Ghost doth not work assurance of God's love wherever he worketh faith, they are to be denounced by all God-fearing people as the enemies of souls, and as ministers whose doctrine is not according to godliness. And come what will, every God-fearing man is to separate himself from such a ministry, accord-

ing to the canons of the Lord and all the Apostles, to "come out from among them, and be
separate, and touch not the unclean thing."
But where any minister of the church is faithful, the people are to draw around him and to
support his hands, and by all means to separate from those crafty men who are bringing
in such heresies; nor to wish them God-speed:
for otherwise God will not dwell amongst them,
neither will be their God. They have denounced
"the orthodox and catholic Doctrine of our
Lord's Human Nature" as heresy, and have
thus proved themselves to be heretical judges;
and their ministry must be characterised as
unfaithful and contrary to sound doctrine, so
long as they adhere to those sentiments which
were unanimously expressed and applauded in
the condemnatory acts of that Assembly. Let
the church once more save Scotland from the
curse of wicked shepherds by their faithfulness
unto Christ, and their firm reliance upon the
preaching of the Gospel. But more of this in
another form, if God give me opportunity. This
I now send forth, under the charge of the great
Head of the church; to whom I solemnly devote it by prayer and fasting, entreating Him
to make it a blessing to the poor Church of
Scotland just ready to perish.

EDWARD IRVING.

THE

CONFESSION

OF

THE FAITH AND DOCTRINE,

believed and professed by the

PROTESTANTS OF SCOTLAND,

Exhibited to the Estates of the same in Parliament, and by their public votes authorized, as a Doctrine grounded upon the infallible Word of God, August 1560;

And ratified and established by Act of Parliament 1567, as the public and avowed

Confession of Faith of the Church of Scotland;

And afterwards

Further established and publicly confirmed by sundry Acts of Parliaments and of lawful General Assemblies.

WITH PROOFS FROM THE SCRIPTURE.

" And this Gospel of the kingdom shall be preached in all the world, for a witness unto all nations ; and then shall the end come."— MATT. xxiv. 14.

" For other foundation can no man lay than that is laid, which is Jesus Christ."—1 COR. iii. 11.

B

CONTENTS.

PREFACE.

The States of Scotland, with the Inhabitants of the same, professing Christ Jesus his holy Gospel, to their natural Countrymen, and unto all other Realms and Nations professing the same Lord Jesus with them; wish grace, mercy, and peace, from God the Father of our Lord Jesus Christ, with the spirit of righteous judgment, for salvation.

LONG have we thirsted, dear brethren, to have notified unto the world the sum of that doctrine which we profess, and for the which we have sustained infamy and danger; but such hath been the rage of Satan against us, and against Christ Jesus his eternal verity, lately now again born amongst us, that to this day no time hath been granted unto us to clear our consciences, as most gladly we would have done; for now we have been tossed a whole year past, as the most part of Europe, as we do suppose, doth understand. But seeing that of the infinite goodness of our God, who never suffereth his afflicted utterly to be confounded, above expectation, we have obtained some rest and liberty, we could not but set forth this brief and plain Confession of such doctrine as is proposed unto us, and as we believe and profess; partly for satisfaction of our brethren, whose hearts, we doubt not, have been, and yet are, wounded by the despiteful railing of such as yet have not learned to speak well; and partly for stopping the mouths of impudent blasphemers, who boldly condemn

B 2

that which they neither heard nor understood : not that
we judge that the cankered malice of such is able to be
cured by this simple Confession; no, we know that the
sweet savour of the Gospel is and shall be death unto
the sons of perdition: But we have chief respect to our
weak and infirm brethren, to whom we would communicate the bottom of our hearts, lest that they be troubled
or carried away by diversity of rumours, which Satan
spreadeth against us to the defeating of this our most
godly enterprise; protesting, that, if any man will note
in this our Confession any article or sentence repugning
to God's holy word, that it would please him of his
gentleness, and for Christian charity's sake, admonish
us of the same in writing; and we, upon our honour
and fidelity, do promise unto him satisfaction from the
mouth of God (that is, from his holy Scriptures) or
else reformation of that which he shall prove to be
amiss. For God we take to record in our consciences,
that from our hearts we abhor all sects of heresy, and
all teachers of erroneous doctrine; and that with all humility we embrace the purity of Christ's Gospel, which
is the only food of our souls; and therefore so precious
unto us, that we are determined to suffer. the extremest
of worldly danger, rather than that we will suffer ourselves to be defrauded of the same. For hereof we are
most certainly persuaded, that whosoever denieth Christ
Jesus, or is ashamed of him in presence of men, shall
be denied before the Father and before his holy angels.
And therefore, by the assistance of the mighty Spirit of
the same our Lord Jesus Christ, we firmly purpose to
abide to the end in the confession of this our faith.

THE

CONFESSION OF THE FAITH

OF THE

CHURCH OF SCOTLAND.

"And this Gospel of the kingdom shall be preached in all
the world, for a witness unto all nations; and then
shall the end come."—MATT. xxiv. 14.

ARTICLE I. *Of God.*

WE confess and acknowledge one only God,
to whom only we must cleave, whom only
we must serve, whom only we must worship,
and in him whom only we must put our
trust (*a*), who is eternal, infinite, unmea-
sureable, incomprehensible, omnipotent, invisible (*b*); one in substance, and yet in
three persons, the Father, the Son, and the
Holy Ghost (*c*); by whom we confess and
believe all things in heaven and earth, as
well visible as invisible, to have been created,

(*a*) Deut. vi. 4; 1 Cor. viii. 6; Deut. iv. 35; Isa. xliv.
5, 6.   (*b*) 1 Tim. i. 17; 1 Kings viii. 27; 2 Chron.
vi. 18; Psal. cxxxix. 7, 8; Gen. xvii. 1; 1 Tim. vi. 15,
16; Exod. iii. 14, 15.   (*c*) Matt. xxviii. 19;
1 John v. 7.

to be retained in their being, and to be ruled and guided by his inscrutable providence, to such ends as his eternal wisdom, goodness, and justice hath appointed them, to the manifestation of his own glory (*d*).

(*d*) Gen. i. 1; Heb. xi. 3; Acts xvii. 28; Prov. xvi. 4.

ART. II. *Of the Creation of Man.*

We confess and acknowledge this our God to have created man, *to wit*, our first father Adam, to his own image and similitude; to whom he gave wisdom, lordship, justice, free will, and clear knowledge of himself, so that in the whole nature of man there could be noted no imperfection (*e*): from which honour and perfection man and woman did both fall; the woman being deceived by the serpent, and man obeying the voice of the woman; both conspiring against the sovereign Majesty of God, who, in express words, had before threatened death if they presumed to eat of the forbidden tree. (*f*).

(*e*) Gen. i. 26—28, &c.; Coloss. iii. 10; Ephes. iv. 24.
(*f*) Gen iii. 6; ii. 17.

ART. III. *Of Original Sin.*

By which transgression, commonly called original sin, was the image of God utterly defaced in man, and he and his posterity of nature become enemies to God, slaves to

Satan, and servants to sin (g); insomuch that death everlasting hath had and shall have power and dominion over all that have not been, are not, or shall not be, regenerated from above; which regeneration is wrought by the power of the Holy Ghost working in the hearts of the elect of God an assured faith in the promise of God, revealed to us in his word; by which faith we apprehend Christ Jesus with the graces and benefits promised in him (h).

(g) Psal. li. 5; Rom. v. 10; vii. 5; 2 Tim. ii. 26; Eph. ii. 1—3.　　(h) Rom. v. 14, 21; Rom. vi. 23; John iii. 5; Rom. v. 1; Phil. i. 29.

ART. IV. *Of the Revelation of the Promise.*

For this we constantly believe, that God, after the fearful and horrible defection of man from his obedience, did seek Adam again, call upon him, rebuke his sin, convict him of the same, and in the end made unto him a most joyful promise, *to wit*, 'That the Seed of the woman should break down the serpent's head;' that is, he should destroy the work of the devil; which promise, as it was repeated, and made more clear from time to time, so was it embraced with joy, and most constantly received of all the faithful from Adam to Noah, from Noah to Abraham, from Abraham to David, and so forth to the incarnation of Christ Jesus. All (we mean the faithful fathers under the law) did see the joyful day of Christ Jesus, and did rejoice (*i*).

(*i*) Gen. iii. 9, 15; xii. 3; xv. 5, 6; 2 Sam. vii. 14; Isai. vii. 14; ix. 6; Hag. ii. 7, 9; John viii. 56.

ART. V. *Of the Continuance, Increase, and Preservation of the Kirk.*

We most constantly believe, that God preserved, instructed, multiplied, honoured, decored, and from death called to life his Kirk in all ages, from Adam till the coming of Christ Jesus in the flesh (*k*); for Abraham he called from his Father's country, him he instructed, his seed he multiplied (*l*); the same he marvelously preserved and more marvelously delivered from the bondage and tyranny of Pharaoh (*m*); to them he gave his laws, constitutions, and ceremonies (*n*); them he possessed in the land of Canaan (*o*); to them, after Judges (*p*), and after Saul (*q*), he gave David to be king (*r*), to whom he made promise that of the fruit of his loins, should one sit for ever upon his regal seat (*s*); to this same people, from time to time, he sent prophets to reduce them to the right way of their God (*t*), from the which often times they declined by idolatry (*u*). And

(*k*) Ezek. xvi. 6, 14. (*l*) Gen. xii. &c. (*m*) Exod. i. &c. (*n*) Exod. xx. &c. (*o*) Josh. i. 3; xxiii. 4. (*p*) Judg. i. &c. (*q*) 1 Sam. 10. (*r*) 1 Sam. xvi. 13. (*s*) 2 Sam. vii. 12. (*t*) 2 Kings xvii. 13. (*u*) 2 Kings xvii. 14, 15, &c.

albeit that, for their stubborn contempt of
justice, he was compelled to give them into
the hands of their enemies (*x*), as before was
threatened by the mouth of Moses (*y*), insomuch that the holy city was destroyed, the
temple burnt with fire (*z*), and the whole
land left desolate the space of seventy years (*a*);
yet of mercy did he reduce them again to
Jerusalem, where the city and temple were
re-edified, and they, against all temptations
and assaults of Satan, did abide till the Messias came according to the promise (*b*).

(*x*) 2 Kings xxiv. 3, 4.   (*y*) Deut. xxviii. 36; 48, &c.
(*z*) 2 Kings xxv.   (*a*) Dan. ix. 2.   (*b*) Jer. xxx;
Ezra i. &c.; Hag. i. 14; ii. 7—9; Zech. iii. 8.

ART. VI. *Of the Incarnation of Christ Jesus.*

When the fulness of time came, God sent
his Son, his eternal wisdom, the substance
of his own glory into this world, who took
the nature of manhead, of the substance of
woman, *to wit,* of a Virgin, and that by operation of the Holy Ghost, and so was born
the just Seed of David, the Angel of the
great counsel of God, the very Messias promised, whom we confess and acknowledge
Immanuel, very God, and very man, two
perfect natures, united and joined in one
person (*c*); by which our confession, we

(*c*) Gal. iv. 4; Luke i. 31; Matt. i. 18; ii. 1; Rom. i.
3; Matt. i. 23; John i. 45; 1 Tim. ii. 5.

condemn the damnable and pestilent heresies of Arius, Marcion, Eutyches, Nestorius, and such others, as either did deny the eternity of his Godhead, or the verity of his human nature, or confounded them, or yet divided them.

Art. VII. *Why it behoved the Mediator to be very God, and very Man.*

We acknowledge and confess, that this most wondrous conjunction between the God-head and the man-head in Christ Jesus, did proceed from the eternal and immutable decree of God, from which all our salvation springs and depends (*d*).

(*d*) Ephes. i. 3—6.

Art. VIII. *Of Election.*

For that same eternal God and Father, who of mere grace elected us in Christ Jesus his Son, before the foundation of the world was laid (*e*), appointed him to be our head (*f*), our brother (*g*), our pastor, and great bishop of our souls (*h*); but, because that the enmity between the justice of God and our sins was such that no flesh by itself could or might have attained unto God (*i*), it behoved that the Son of God should descend unto us, and take to himself a body of our body,

(*e*) Ephes. i. 11; Matt. xxv. 34. (*f*) Ephes. i. 22, 23. (*g*) Heb. ii. 7, 8, 11, 12; Psal. xxii. 22.   (*h*) Heb. xiii. 20; 1 Pet. ii. 25; v. 4. (*i*) Psal. cxxx. 3; cxliii. 2.

flesh of our flesh, and bone of our bones, and so become the Mediator between God and man (k); giving power to so many as believe in him, to be the sons of God (l), as himself doth witness, "I pass up to my Father, and unto your Father; to my God, and your God (m):" by which most holy fraternity, whatsoever we have lost in Adam is restored unto us again (n); and, for this cause are we not afraid to call God our Father (o): not so much because he hath created us, which we have common with the reprobates (p), as for that he hath given to us his only Son to be our brother (q), and given unto us grace to acknowledge and embrace him for our only Mediator, as before is said. It behoved, further, the Messias and Redeemer to be very God and very man, because he was to underly the punishment due for our transgressions; and to present himself in the presence of his Father's judgment as in our person, to suffer for our transgression and inobedience (r), by death to overcome him that was the author of death; but, because the only God-head could not suffer death (s), neither yet could the only man-head overcome the same, he joined both together in one person, that the

(k) 1 Tim. ii. 5.   (l) John i. 12.   (m) John xx. 17.
(n) Rom. v. 17—19.   (o) Rom. viii. 15; Gal. iv. 5, 6.
(p) Acts xvii. 26.   (q) Heb. ii. 11, 12.   (r) 1 Pet.
iii. 18; Isai. liii. 8.   (s) Acts ii. 24.

imbecility of the one should suffer, and be subject to death (which we had deserved) and the infinite and invincible power of the other, *to wit*, of the God-head should triumph and purchase to us life, liberty, and perpetual victory (*t*); and so we confess, and most undoubtedly believe.

(*t*) 1 John i. 2; Acts xx. 28; 1 Tim. iii. 16; John iii. 16.

Art. IX. *Of Christ's Death, Passion, and Burial.*

That our Lord Jesus offered himself a voluntary sacrifice unto his Father for us (*u*); that he suffered contradiction of sinners; that he was wounded and plagued for our transgressions (*w*); that he, being the clean innocent Lamb of God (*x*), was condemned in the presence of an earthly judge (*y*), that we should be absolved before the tribunal seat of our God (*z*); that he suffered not only the cruel death of the cross (which was accursed by the sentence of God) (*a*), but also that he suffered for a season the wrath of his Father (*b*), which sinners had deserved; but yet we avow that he remained the only well-beloved and blessed Son of his Father, even in the midst of his anguish and tor-

(*u*) Heb. x. 4—12.   (*w*) Isai. liii. 5; Heb. xii. 3.
(*x*) John i. 29.   (*y*) Matt. xxvii. 11, 26; Mark xv.;
Luke xxiii.   (*z*) Gal. iii. 13.   (*a*) Deut. xxi. 23.
(*b*) Matt. xxvi. 38, 39.

ment, which he suffered in body and soul to make the full satisfaction for the sins of the people (c); after the which we confess and avow that there remaineth no other sacrifice for sin (d); which, if any affirm, we nothing doubt to avow that they are blasphemous against Christ's death, and the everlasting purgation and satisfaction purchased to us by the same.

(c) 2 Cor. v. 21.　　(d) Heb. ix. 12; x. 14.

ART. X. *Of his Resurrection.*

We undoubtedly believe, that insomuch as it was impossible that the dolours of death should retain in bondage the Author of life (e); that our Lord Jesus, crucified, dead and buried, who descended into hell, did rise again for our justification (f); and destroying of him who was the author of death, brought life again to us that were subject to death, and to the bondage of the same (g); we know that his resurrection was confirmed by the testimony of his very enemies (h), by the resurrection of the dead, whose sepulchres did open, and they did rise, and appear to many without the city of Jerusalem (i); it was also confirmed by the testimony of his angels (k), and by the senses and judgments of his Apostles, and of others who had con-

(e) Acts ii. 24.　　(f) Acts iii. 26; Rom. vi. 5, 9; Rom. iv. 25. (g) Heb. ii. 14, 15. (h) Matt. xxviii. 4. (i) Matt. xxvii. 52, 53.　　(k) Matt. xxviii. 5, 6.

versation, and did eat and drink with him after his resurrection (*l*).

(*l*) John xx. 27 ; xxi. 7 ; xii. 13 ; Luke xxiv. 41—43.

Art. XI. *Of his Ascension.*

We nothing doubt, but the self-same body, which was born of the Virgin, was crucified, dead and buried, and which did rise again, did ascend into the heavens for the accomplishment of all things (*m*), where, in our names, and for our comfort, he had received all power in heaven and earth (*n*), where he sitteth at the right hand of the Father, inaugurate in his kingdom, Advocate and only Mediator for us (*o*); which glory, honour, and prerogative, he alone, amongst the brethren, shall possess till that all his enemies be made his footstool (*p*), as that we undoubtedly believe that they shall be in the final judgment, to the execution whereof, we certainly believe, that the same our Lord Jesus shall as visibly return as that he was seen to ascend (*q*); and then we firmly believe that the time of refreshing and restitution of all things shall come (*r*), insomuch that these that from the beginning have suffered violence, injury, and wrong, for righteousness sake, shall inherit that blessed im-

(*m*) Luke xxiv. 51 ; Acts i. 9.   (*n*) Matt. xxviii. 18. (*o*) 1 John ii. 1 ; 1 Tim. ii. 5.   (*p*) Psal. cx. 1 ; Matt. xxii. 44 ; Mark xii. 36 ; Luke xx. 42, 43.   (*q*) Acts i. 11.   (*r*) Acts iii. 19.

mortality promised from the beginning (*s*) ; but contrariwise, the stubborn, inobedient, cruel oppressors, filthy persons, idolaters, and all such sorts of unfaithful, shall be cast into the dungeon of utter darkness, where the worm shall not die, neither yet shall their fire be extinguished (*t*) : the remembrance of which day, and of the judgment to be executed in the same, is not only to us a bridle whereby our carnal lusts are restrained, but also such inestimable comfort, that neither may the threatening of worldly princes, neither yet the fear of temporal death, and present danger, move us to renounce and forsake that blessed society, which we, the members, have with our Head and only Mediator Christ Jesus (*u*), whom we confess and avow to be the Messias promised, the only Head of his Kirk, our just Law-giver, our only High Priest, Advocate, and Mediator (*w*). In which honours and offices, if man or angel presume to intrude themselves, we utterly detest and abhor them, as blasphemous to our Sovereign and supreme Governor Christ Jesus.

(*s*) Matt. xxv. 34 ; 2 Thess. i. 4, &c. (*t*) Rev. xxi. 27; Isai. lxvi. 24; Matt. xxv. 41; Mark ix. 44, 46, 48; Matt. xxii. 13. (*u*) 2 Pet. iii. 11 ; 2 Cor. v. 9—11 ; Luke xxi. 27, 28; John xiv. 1, &c. (*w*) Isai. vii. 14; Ephes. i. 22 ; Col. i. 18 ; Heb. ix. 11, 15 ; x. 21 ; 1 John ii. 1 ; 1 Tim. ii. 5.

ART. XII. *Of Faith in the Holy Ghost.*

This our faith, and assurance of the same, proceeds not from flesh and blood, that is to say, from no natural powers within us, but is the inspiration of the Holy Ghost (*x*); whom we confess God equal with the Father and with his Son (*y*); who sanctifieth us, and bringeth us into all verity by his own operation, without whom we should remain for ever enemies to God, and ignorant of his Son Christ Jesus. For of nature we are so dead, so blind, and so perverse, that neither can we feel when we are pricked, see the light when it shines, nor assent to the will of God when it is revealed, except the Spirit of the Lord Jesus quicken that which is dead, remove the darkness from our minds, and bow our stubborn hearts to the obedience of his blessed will (*z*). And so, as we confess, that God the Father created us when we were not (*a*); as his Son our Lord Jesus redeemed us when we were enemies to him (*b*); so also do we confess that the Holy Ghost doth sanctify and regenerate us, without all respect of any merit proceeding from us, be it before, or be it after our rege-

(*x*) Matt. xvi. 17; John xiv. 26; xv. 26; xvi. 13. (*y*) Acts v. 3, 4.   (*z*) Col. ii. 13; Ephes. ii. 1; John ix. 39; Rev. iii. 17; Matt. xvii. 17; Mark ix. 19; Luke ix. 41; John vi. 63; Micah vii. 8; 1 Kings viii. 57, 58.   (*a*) Psal. c. 3.   (*b*) Rom. v. 10.

neration (*c*). To speak this one thing yet in more plain words, as we willingly spoil ourselves of all honour and glory of our own creation and redemption (*d*), so do we also of our regeneration and sanctification (*e*): for of ourselves we are not sufficient to think a good thought; but he who hath begun the work in us, is only he that continues us in the same, to the praise and glory of his undeserved grace (*f*).

(*c*) John iii. 5; Tit. iii. 5; Rom. v. 8.   (*d*) Phil iii. 9.
(*e*) Phil i. 6; 2 Cor. iii. 5.   (*f*) Ephes. i. 6.

ART. XIII. *Of the Cause of Good Works.*

So that the cause of good works we confess to be, not our free-will, but the Lord Jesus, who, dwelling in our hearts by true faith, bringeth forth such works as God hath prepared for us to walk in. For this we most boldly affirm, that it is blasphemy to say, that Christ abides in the hearts of such, in whom there is no spirit of sanctification (*g*); and therefore we fear not to affirm that murderers, oppressors, cruel persecutors, adulterers, whoremongers, filthy persons, idolaters, drunkards, thieves, and all workers of iniquity, have neither true faith, nor any portion of the Spirit of the Lord Jesus, so long as obstinately they continue in their wickedness; for, so soon as the Spirit of the

(*g*) Ephes. ii. 20; Phil. ii. 13; Rom. viii. 9.

c

Lord Jesus (which God's elect children receive by true faith) taketh possession in the
heart of any man, so soon doth he regenerate
and renew the same man; so that he beginneth to hate that which before he loved;
and beginneth to love that which before he
hated; and from thence cometh that continual battle which is between the flesh and
the spirit in God's children : still the flesh
and natural man, according to their own
corruption, lusteth for things pleasant and
delectable unto itself, and grudgeth in adversity, is lifted up in prosperity, and at
every moment is prone and ready to offend
the Majesty of God (h). But the Spirit of
God, which giveth witnessing to our spirit
that we are the sons of God (i), maketh us
to resist filthy pleasures, and to groan in
God's presence for deliverance from this
bondage of corruption (k); and, finally, to
triumph over sin, that it reign not in our
mortal bodies (l). This battle hath not the
carnal man, being destitute of God's Spirit,
but doth follow and obey sin with greediness,
and without repentance, even as the devil
and their corrupt lusts do prick them (m);
but the sons of God, as before is said, do
fight against sin, do sob and mourn when
they perceive themselves tempted to iniquity;

(h) Rom. vii. 15, *ad ult.*; Gal. v. 17.   (i) Rom. viii. 16.
(k) Rom. vii. 24; viii. 22.   (l) Rom. vi. 12.
(m) Ephes. iv. 17, &c.

and if they fall, they rise again with earnest
and unfeigned repentance (*n*); and these
things they do not by their own power, but
by the power of the Lord Jesus, without
whom they were able to do nothing (*o*).

(*n*) 2 Tim. ii. 26.   (*o*) John xv. 5.

ART. XIV. *What Works are reputed good before God.*

WE confess and acknowledge, that God
hath given man his holy law, in which not
only are forbidden all such works as displease
and offend his godly Majesty, but also are
commanded all such as please him and as
he hath promised to reward (*p*): and these
works be of two sorts; the one is done to
the honour of God, the other to the profit of
our neighbours, and both have the revealed
will of God for their assurance. To have
one God, to worship and honour him, to
call upon him in all our troubles, to reverence
his holy name, to hear his word, to believe
the same, to communicate with his holy sacraments (*q*), are the works of the first table.
To honour father, mother, princes, rulers,
and superior powers; to love them, to support
them, yea, to obey their charges (not repugning to the commandment of God); to
save the lives of innocents, to repress ty-

(*p*) Exod. xx. 1, 6; Deut. v. 6, &c.; iv. 8.   (*q*) Luke
i. 74, 75; Micah vi. 8.

ranny, to defend the oppressed, to keep our bodies clean and holy, to live in soberness and temperance, to deal justly with all men, both in word and deed ; and, finally, to repress all appetite of our neighbour's hurt (r); are the good works of the second table, which are most pleasing and acceptable unto God, as these works that are commanded by himself. The contrary whereof is sin most odious, which always displeaseth him and provoketh him to anger ; as not to call upon him alone when we have need, nor to hear his word with reverence, to contemn and despise it; to have or to worship idols; to maintain and defend idolatry ; lightly to esteem the reverend name of God ; to profane, abuse, or contemn the sacraments of Christ Jesus; to disobey or resist any that God hath placed in authority (while they pass not over the bounds of their office) (s); to murder, or to consent thereto ; to bear hatred, or to suffer innocent blood to be shed, if we may withstand it (t); and, finally, the transgression of any other commandment in the first or second table, we confess and affirm to be sin (u), whereby God's anger and displeasure is kindled against the proud unthankful world, so that good works we

(r) Ephes. vi. 1, 7 ; Ezek. xxii. 1, &c. ; 1 Cor. vi. 19, 20 ; 1 Thess. iv. 3, 7 ; Jer. xxii. 3, &c. ; Isai. l. 1. (s) 1 Thess. iv. 6 ; Rom. xiii. 2. (t) Ezek. xxii. 13, &c. (u) 1 John iii. 4.

affirm to be these only that are done in faith (*w*), and at God's commandment (*x*), who in his law hath expressed what the things be that please him; and evil works, we affirm, not only these that expressly are done against God's commandment (*y*), but these also that in matters of religion and worshipping of God, have no other assurance but the invention and opinion of man; which God from the beginning hath ever rejected, as by the Prophet Isaiah (*z*), and by our Master Christ Jesus we are taught in these words, "In vain do they worship me, teaching for doctrine the precepts of men" (*a*).

(*w*) Rom xiv. 23; Heb. xi. 6.   (*x*) 1 Sam. xv. 22; 1 Cor. x. 31.   (*y*) 1 John iii. 4.   (*z*) Isai. xxix. 13. (*a*) Matt. xv. 9; Mark vii. 7.

Art. XV. *Of the Perfection of the Law, and the Imperfection of Man.*

The law of God, we confess and acknowledge most just, most equal, most holy, and most perfect; commanding those things which, being wrought in perfection, were able to give life, and able to bring man to eternal felicity (*b*); but our nature is so corrupt, so weak, and so imperfect, that we are never able to fulfil the works of the law in perfection (*c*); yea, if we say we have no

(*b*) Lev. xviii. 5; Gal. iii. 12; 1 Tim. i. 8; Rom. vii. 12; Psal. xix. 7—11.   (*c*) Deut. v. 29; Rom. x. 3.

sin, even after we are regenerated, we deceive ourselves, and the verity of God is not in us (*d*). And, therefore, it behoveth us to apprehend Christ Jesus with his justice and satisfaction, who is the end and accomplishment of the law, by whom we are set at this liberty, that the curse and malediction of God fall not upon us, albeit we fulfil not the same in all points (*e*); for God the Father, beholding us in the body of his Son Christ Jesus, accepteth our imperfect obedience as it were perfect (*f*); and covers our works, which are defiled with many spots (*g*), with the justice of his Son. We do not mean that we are so set at liberty that we owe no obedience to the law; (for that before we have plainly confessed;) but this we affirm, that no man in earth (Christ Jesus only excepted) hath given, gives, or shall give in work, that obedience to the law, which the law requires; but, when we have done all things, we must fall down and unfeignedly confess that we are unprofitable servants (*h*); and, therefore, whosoever boast themselves of merits of their own works, or put their trust in the works of supererogation, boast themselves in that which is nought, and put their trust in damnable idolatry.

(*d*) 1 Kings viii. 46; 2 Chron. vi. 36; Prov. xx. 9; Eccles. vii. 22; 1 John i. 8:   (*e*) Rom. x. iv; Gal. iii. 13; Deut. xxvii. 26.   (*f*) Phil. ii. 15. (*g*) Isai. lxiv. 6.   (*h*) Luke xvii. 10.

Art. XVI. *Of the Kirk.*

As we believe in one God, Father, Son, and Holy Ghost, so do we most constantly believe, that from the beginning there hath been, and now is, and to the end of the world shall be, one kirk; that is to say, one company and multitude of men chosen of God, who rightly worship and embrace him by true faith in Christ Jesus (*i*), who is the only head of the same kirk, which also is the body and spouse of Christ Jesus: which kirk is catholic—that is, universal, because it containeth the elect of all ages, of all realms, nations, and tongues, be they of the Jews, or be they of the Gentiles, who have communion and society with God the Father, and with his Son Christ Jesus, through the sanctification of his Holy Spirit (*k*); and therefore it is called the communion, not of profane persons, but of saints, who, as citizens of the heavenly Jerusalem (*l*), have the fruition of the most inestimable benefits; to wit, of one God, our Lord Jesus, one faith, and one baptism (*m*); out of which kirk there is neither life nor eternal felicity: and therefore we utterly abhor the blasphemy of them, that affirm, that men, which live according to equity and justice, shall be saved, what

(*i*) Matt. xxviii. 20; Ephes. i. 4. (*k*) Col. i. 18;
Ephes. v. 23, 24, &c.; Rev. vii. 9. (*l*) Ephes. ii. 19.
(*m*) Ephes. iv. 5.

religion that ever they have professed. For, as without Christ Jesus there is neither life nor salvation (*n*) ; so shall there none be participant thereof, but such as the Father hath given unto his Son Christ Jesus, and these that in time come unto him, avow his doctrine, and believe in him (*o*) : we comprehend the children with the faithful parents (*p*). This kirk is invisible, known only to God, who alone knoweth whom he hath chosen (*q*), and comprehendeth as well (as. said is) the elect that be departed, commonly called the church triumphant, as those that yet live and fight against sin and Satan, and shall live hereafter (*r*).

(*n*) John iii. 36.　　(*o*) John vi. 37, 39, 65 ; xvii. 6.
(*p*) Acts ii. 39.　　(*q*) 2 Tim. ii. 19; John xiii. 18.
(*r*) Ephes. i. 10; Col. i. 20 ; Heb. xii. 4.

Art. XVII. *Of the Immortality of the Soul.*

The elect departed are in peace, and rest from their labours (*s*); not that they sleep, and come to a certain oblivion, as some phantastics do affirm, but that they are delivered from all fear and torment, and all temptation, to which we, and all God's elect, are subject in this life (*t*), and therefore do bear the name of the church militant : as, contrariwise, the reprobate and unfaithful

(*s*) Rev. xiv. 13.　　(*t*) Isai. xxv. 8; Rev. vii. 14—17; xxi. 4.

departed have anguish, torment, and pain,
that cannot be expressed (*u*); so that neither
are the one nor the other in such a sleep,
that they feel not their torment, as the pa-
rable of Christ Jesus in the xvi th of Luke (*w*),
his words to the thief (*x*), and these words of
the souls crying under the altar (*y*), O Lord,
thou that art righteous and just, how long
shalt thou not revenge our blood upon those
that dwell on the earth ? do testify.

(*u*) Rev. xvi. 10, 11; Isai. lxvi. 24; Mark ix. 44, 46,
48.   (*w*) Luke xvi. 23—25.   (*x*) Luke xxiii. 43.
(*y*) Rev. vi. 9, 10.

Art. XVIII. *Of the Notes whereby the true
Kirk is discerned from the false; and
who shall judge of the Doctrine.*

Because that Satan from the beginning
hath laboured to deck his pestilent synagogue with the title of the church of God,
and hath inflamed the hearts of cruel murderers, to persecute, trouble, and molest the
true kirk, and members thereof; as Cain
did Abel (*a*); Ishmael, Isaac (*b*); Esau,
Jacob (*c*); and the whole priesthood of the
Jews, Christ Jesus himself, and his Apostles
after him (*d*): it is one thing most requisite,
that the true kirk be discerned from the
filthy synagogues, by clear and perfect notes,
lest we, being deceived, receive and embrace,

(*a*) Gen. iv. 8.   (*b*) Gen. xxi. 9.   (*c*) Gen.
xxvii. 41.   (*d*) Matt. xxiii. 34; John xv. 18—20,
24; xi. 47, 53; Acts iv. 1—3; v. 17, 18.

to our own condemnation, the one for the other. The notes, signs, and assured tokens, whereby the immaculate spouse of Christ Jesus is known from the horrible harlot, the kirk malignant, we affirm, are neither antiquity, title usurped, lineal descent, place appointed, nor multitude of men approving an error; for Cain in age and title was preferred to Abel and Seth (e); Jerusalem had prerogative above all places of the earth (f), where also were the priests lineally descended from Aaron: and greater number followed the Scribes, Pharisees, and priests, than unfeignedly believed and approved Christ Jesus and his doctrine (g); and yet, as we suppose, no man of sound judgment will grant, that any of the forenamed were the church of God. The notes, therefore, of the true church of God we believe, confess, and avow to be, First, the true preaching of the word of God, wherein God hath revealed himself unto us, as the writings of the Prophets and Apostles do declare. Secondly, The right administration of the sacraments of Christ Jesus, which must be annexed unto the word and promise of God to seal and confirm the same in our hearts (h). Last, Ecclesiastical discipline uprightly ministered as God's word

(e) Gen. iv.　　　(f) Psal. xlviii. 2, 3; Matt. v. 35. (g) John xii. 42.　　　(h) Ephes. ii. 20; Acts ii. 42; John x. 27; xviii. 37; 1 Cor. i. 23, 24; Matt. xxviii. 19, 20; Mark xvi. 15, 16; 1 Cor. xi. 23—26; Rom. iv. 11.

prescribeth, whereby vice is repressed, and
virtue nourished (*i*). Wheresoever, then,
these former notes are seen, and of any
time continue (be the number never so few,
about two or three), there, without all doubt,
is the true church of Christ, who, according
to his promise, is in the midst of them (*k*) :
not that universal of which we have before
spoken, but particular, such as were in Corinthus (*l*), Galatia (*m*), Ephesus (*n*), and
other places, wherein the ministry was planted
by Paul, and were of himself named the
churches of God : and such churches, we
the inhabitants of the realm of Scotland,
professors of Christ Jesus, profess ourselves
to have in our cities, towns, and places reformed, for the doctrine taught in our
churches, contained in the written word of
God ; to wit, in the books of the Old and
New Testaments : in these books we mean,
which of the ancients have been reputed
canonical, in the which we affirm, that all
things necessary to be believed for the salvation of mankind, are sufficiently expressed (*o*). The interpretation whereof, we confess, neither appertaineth to private nor public
person ; neither yet to any kirk for any
pre-eminence, or prerogative, personally or

(*i*) Matt. xviii. 15—18 ; 1 Cor. v. 4, 5.   (*k*) Matt.
xviii. 19, 20.   (*l*) 1 Cor. i. 2 ; 2 Cor. i. 2.
(*m*) Gal. i. 2.   (*n*) Acts xx. 17.   (*o*) John xx. 31 ;
2 Tim. iii. 16, 17.

locally, which one hath above another, but appertaineth to the Spirit.of God, by whom also the Scripture was written (*p*). When controversy, then, happeneth, for the right understanding of any place or sentence in Scripture, or for the reformation of any abuse within the church of God, we ought not so much to look what men before us have said or done, as unto that which the Holy Ghost uniformly speaketh,.within the body.of the Scriptures; and unto that which Jesus Christ himself did, and commanded to be done (*q*). For this is a thing universally granted, that the Spirit of God, who is the Spirit of unity, is nothing contrarious unto himself (*r*). If, then, the interpretation, determination, or sentence, of any doctor, church, or council, be repugnant to the plain word of God, written in any other place of Scripture, it is a thing most certain, that there is not the true understanding and meaning of the Holy Ghost, although that councils, and realms, and nations have approved and received the same. For we dare not admit any interpretation, which repugneth to any principal point of our faith, or to any other plain text of Scripture, or yet unto the rule of charity.

(*p*) 2 Pet. i. 20, 21.   (*q*) John v. 39.   (*r*) Ephes. iii. 4.

ART. XIX. *Of the Authority of the Scriptures.*

As we believe and confess the Scriptures of God sufficient to instruct, and make the man of-God perfect, so do we affirm and avow the authority of the same to be of God, and neither to depend on men nor angels (*s*). We affirm, therefore, that such as allege the Scripture to have no other authority, but that which it hath received from the church, to be blasphemous against God, and injurious to the true church, which always heareth and obeyeth the voice of her own Spouse and Pastor (*t*), but taketh not upon her to be mistress over the same.

(*s*) 2 Tim. iii. 16, 17.　　　(*t*) John x. 27.

ART. XX. *Of General Councils, of their Power, Authority, and Cause of their Convention.*

As we do not rashly condemn that which godly men assembled together in general councils, lawfully gathered, have proponed unto us, so, without just examination, dare we not receive whatsoever is obtruded unto men, under the name of general councils: for plain it is, as they were men, so have some of them manifestly erred, and that in matters of great weight and importance (*u*).

(*u*) Gal. ii. 11—14.

So far, then, as the council proveth the determination and commandment that it giveth, by the plain word of God, so soon do we reverence and embrace the same; but if men, under the name of a council, pretend to forge unto us new articles of our faith, or to make constitutions repugning to the word of God, then utterly we must refuse the same, as the doctrine of devils, which draweth our souls from the voice of our only God, to follow the doctrines and constitutions of men (w). The cause, then, why that general councils convened, were neither to make any perpetual law, which God had not before made, neither yet to forge new articles of our belief, nor to give the word of God authority; much less to make that to be his word, or yet the true interpretation of the same, which was not before by his holy will expressed in his word (x): but the cause of councils (we mean, of such as merit the name of councils) was partly for confutation of heresies (y), and for giving public confession of their faith to the posterity following; which both they did by the authority of God's written word, and not by any opinion, or prerogative, that they could not err, by reason of their general assembly: and this we judge to have been the chief cause of general councils.

(w) 1 Tim. iv. 1—3.   (x) Col. ii. 16, 18, 22.
(y) Acts xv.

The other was for good policy and order, to be constitute and observed in the kirk, which (as in the house of God)(z) it becometh all things to be done decently and in order (a). Not that we think, that any policy, or an order in ceremonies, can be appointed for all ages, times, and places: for as ceremonies, such as men have devised, are but temporal; so may and ought they to be changed, when they rather foster superstition, than edify the church, using the same.

(z) 2 Tim. iii. 15; Heb. iii. 2.   (a) 1 Cor. xiv. 40.

Art. XXI. *Of the Sacraments.*

As the fathers, under the law, besides the verity of the sacrifices, had two chief sacraments; to wit, circumcision and the passover, the despisers and contemners whereof were not reputed of God's people (b), so do we acknowledge and confess, that we now, in time of the Evangel, have two chief sacraments only, instituted by the Lord Jesus, and commanded to be used of all those that will be reputed members of his body; to wit, Baptism, and the Supper or Table of the Lord Jesus, called the communion of his body and blood (c): and these sacraments,

(b) Gen. xvii. 10—14; Exod. xxi.; Numb. ix. 13, 14.
(c) Matt. xxviii. 19; Mark xvi. 15, 16; Matt. xxvi. 26—28; Mark xiv. 22—24; Luke xxii. 19, 20; 1 Cor. xi. 23—26.

as well of the Old as of the New Testament, now instituted of God, not only to make a visible difference betwixt his people, and these that were without his league, but also to exercise the faith of his children, and by participation of the same sacraments, to seal in their hearts the assurance of his promise and of that most blessed conjunction, union, and society, which the elect have with their Head, Christ Jesus. And thus we utterly condemn the vanity of these that affirm sacraments to be nothing else but naked and bare signs ; no, we assuredly believe, that by Baptism we are engrafted in Christ Jesus, to be made partakers of his justice, whereby our sins are covered and remitted : and also, that in the Supper, rightly used, Christ Jesus is so joined with us, that he becometh very nourishment and food to our souls (*d*) : not that we imagine any transubstantiation of bread into Christ's natural body, and of wine into his natural blood, as the Papists have perniciously taught, and damnably believed; but this union and conjunction, which we have with the body and blood of Christ Jesus, in the right use of the sacraments, wrought by operation of the Holy Ghost, who by true faith carrieth us above all things that are visible, carnal, and earthly, and maketh us to feed upon the body and blood

(*d*) 1 Cor. x. 16 ; Rom. ii. 3—5 ; Gal. iii. 27.

of Christ Jesus, which was once broken and shed for us, which now is in heaven, and appeareth in the presence of his Father for us (e) : and yet, notwithstanding the far distance of place which is between his body now glorified in heaven, and us now mortal on this earth ; yet we most assuredly believe, that the bread which we break is the communion of Christ's body, and the cup which we bless is the communion of his blood (f). So that we confess, and undoubtedly believe, that the faithful, in the right use of the Lord's table, do so eat the body and drink the blood of the Lord Jesus, that he remaineth in them, and they in him ; yea, they are so made flesh of his flesh, and bone of his bones (g), that as the eternal Godhead hath given to the flesh of Christ Jesus (which of its own nature was mortal and corruptible) (h) life and immortality ; so doth Christ Jesus his flesh and blood, eaten and drunken by us, give unto us the same prerogatives. Which albeit, we confess, are neither given unto us at this time only, neither yet by the proper power and virtue of the sacrament only ; yet we affirm, that the faithful, in the right use of the Lord's table, have such conjunction with Christ Jesus (i), as the natural man

(e) Mark xvi. 19; Luke xxiv. 51; Acts i. 11, iii. 21.
(f) 1 Cor. x. 16.   (g) Eph. v. 30.   (h) Matt xxvii.
50; Mark xv. 37; Luke xxiii. 46; John xix. 30.
(i) John vi. 51, &c.

D

cannot apprehend : yea, and further we affirm, that albeit the faithful, oppressed by negligence and manly infirmity, do not profit so much as they would, in the very instant action of the supper, yet shall it after bring fruit forth, as lively seed sown in good ground : for the Holy Spirit, which can never be divided from the right institution of the Lord Jesus, will not frustrate the faithful of the fruit of that mystical action; but all these, we say, come of true faith, which apprehendeth Christ Jesus, who only maketh his sacraments effectual unto us. And therefore, whosoever slandereth us, that we affirm and believe sacraments to be naked and bare signs, do injury unto us, and speak against the manifest truth. But this liberally and frankly we confess, that we make a distinction between Christ Jesus in his eternal substance, and between the elements in the sacramental signs; so that we will neither worship the signs, in place of that which is signified by them; neither yet do we despise and interpret them as unprofitable and vain, but do use them with all reverence, examining ourselves diligently before that we so do; because we are assured by the mouth of the Apostle, that such as "eat of that bread and drink of that cup unworthily, are guilty of the body and blood of Christ Jesus (*k*)."

(*k*) 1 Cor. xi. 28, 29.

Art. XXII. *Of the Right Administration of the Sacraments.*

That sacraments be rightly ministrate, we judge two things are requisite: the one, that they be ministrate by lawful ministers, whom we affirm to be only they that are appointed to the preaching of the word, into whose mouth God hath put some sermon of exhortation, they being men lawfully chosen thereto by some church. The other, that they be ministrate in such elements, and in such sort, as God hath appointed: else we affirm, that they cease to be the right sacraments of Christ Jesus. And therefore it is, that we flee the doctrine of the papistical church in participation of their sacraments: first, because their ministers are no ministers of Christ Jesus; yea (which is more horrible) they suffer women, whom the Holy Ghost will not suffer to teach in the congregation, to baptize. And secondly, because they have so adulterated both the one sacrament and the other with their own inventions, that no part of Christ's actions abides in the original purity; for oil, salt, spittle, and such like in baptism, are but men's inventions. Adoration, veneration, bearing throughout streets and towns, and keeping of bread in boxes or buists, are profanation of Christ's sacraments, and no use of the same. For Christ Jesus said, "Take eat, &c. Do this in remembrance of me (*l*) :". by which words and charge, he sanctified bread and wine, to be the sacrament of his holy body and blood, to the end that the one should be eaten; and that all should drink of the other : and not that they should be keeped to be worshipped and honoured as God, as the Papists have done herebefore, who also have committed sacrilege, stealing from the people the one part of the sacrament, to wit, the blessed cup. Moreover, that the sacraments be rightly used, it is required that the end and cause why the sacraments were institute be understood and observed, as well of the minister as by the receivers : for if the opinion be changed in the receiver, the right use ceaseth; which is most evident by the rejection of the sacrifices : as also, if the teacher plainly teach false doctrine, which were odious and abominable before God, (albeit they were his own ordinances) because that wicked men use them to another end than God hath ordained. The same affirm we of the sacraments in the papistical church, wherein we affirm the whole action of the Lord Jesus to be adulterated, as well in the external form, as in the end and opinion. What Christ Jesus did, and commanded to be done, is evident by the Evangelists, and by St. Paul : what the priest doth at his

(*l*) Matt xxvi. 26; Mark xiv. 22 ; Luke xxii. 19 ; 1 Cor. xi. 24.

altar, we need not rehearse. The end and cause of Christ's institution, and why the same should be used, is expressed in these words, " Do ye this in remembrance of me; so oft as ye shall eat of this bread, and drink of this cup, ye shall shew forth," that is, extol, preach, and magnify and praise, "the Lord's death till he come again (m)." But to what end and in what opinion their priests say their mass, let the words of the same, their own doctors and writings, witness; to wit, that they, as mediators between Christ and his church, do offer unto God the Father a sacrifice propitiatory for the sins of the quick and dead; which doctrine, as blasphemous to Jesus Christ, and making derogation to the sufficiency of his only sacrifice, once offered, for purgation of all those that shall be sanctified (n), we utterly abhor, detest, and renounce.

(m) 1 Cor. xi. 25, 26.　　　(n) Heb. ix. 28; x. 13.

Art. XXIII. *To whom Sacraments appertain.*

We confess and acknowledge, that baptism appertaineth as well to the infants of the faithful, as unto them that be of age and discretion; and so we condemn the error of Anabaptists, who deny baptism to appertain to children; before they have faith and understanding (*o*). But the supper of the Lord, we confess to appertain to such only as be of the household of faith, and can try and examine themselves, as well in their faith, as in their duty towards their neighbours : such as eat and drink at the holy table without faith, or being at dissension or division with their brethren, do eat unworthily (*p*) : and therefore it is, that in our kirk our ministers take public and particular examination of the knowledge and conversation of such as are to be admitted to the table of the Lord Jesus.

(*o*) Col. ii. 11, 12 ; Rom iv. 11 ; Gen. xvii. 10 ; Matt. xxviii. 19.   (*p*) 1 Cor. xi. 28, 29.

ART. XXIV. *Of the Civil Magistrate.*

We confess and acknowledge empires, kingdoms, dominions, and cities, to be distincted and ordained by God ; the power and authority in the same, be it of emperors in their empires, of kings in their realms, dukes and princes in their dominions, and of other magistrates in the cities, to be God's holy ordinance, ordained for manifestation of his own glory and for the singular profit and commodity of mankind (*q*) : so that whosoever goeth about to take away or to confound the whole state of civil policies, now long established, we affirm the same men,

(*q*) Rom. xiii. 1 ; Tit. iii. 1 ; 1 Pet. ii. 12, 14.

not only to be enemies to mankind, but
wickedly to fight against God's expressed
will (*r*). We further confess and acknowledge, that such persons, as are placed in
authority, are to be loved, honoured, feared,
and holden in most reverent estimation (*s*),
because that they are the lieutenants of God,
in whose sessions God himself doth sit, and
judge (*t*); yea, even the judges and princes
themselves, to whom by God is given the
sword to the praise and defence of good
men, and to revenge and punish all open
malefactors (*u*). Moreover, to kings, princes,
rulers, and magistrates, we affirm, that
chiefly, and most principally, the conserva-
tion and purgation of the religion appertain;
so that not only they are appointed for civil
policy, but also for maintenance of the true
religion, and for suppressing of idolatry, and
superstition whatsoever : as in David (*w*),
Jehoshaphat (*x*), Hezekias (*y*), Josias (*z*), and
others highly commended for their zeal in
that case, may be espied. And therefore we
confess and avow, that such as resist the
supreme power, doing that thing which appertaineth to his charge, do resist God's ordinance; and therefore cannot be guiltless.

(*r*) Rom. xiii. 1, 2.　　(*s*) Rom. xiii. 7; 1 Pet. ii. 17.
(*t*) Psal. lxxxii. 1.　(*u*) 1 Pet. ii. 14.　(*w*) 1 Chron.
xxii. xxiii. xxiv. xxv. xxvi.　　　　(*x*) 2 Chron. xvii.
6, &c.; xix. 8, &c.　　(*y*) 2 Chron. xxix. xxx. xxxi.
(*z*) 2 Chron. xxxiv. xxxv.

And further we affirm, that whosoever deny
unto them aid, their counsel and comfort,
whiles the princes and rulers vigilantly travel
in execution of their office, that the same
men deny their help, support, and counsel
to God, who by the presence of his lieutenant
doth crave it of them.

Art. XXV. *Of the Gifts freely given to the Church.*

Albeit the word of God truly preached,
and the sacraments rightly ministrated, and
discipline executed according to the word of
God, be the certain and infallible signs of
the true church; we mean not, that every
particular person joined with such company
be an elect member of Christ Jesus (*a*): for
we acknowledge and confess, that darnel,
cockle and chaff may be sown, grow, and in
great abundance lie in the midst of the wheat;
that is, the reprobate may be joined in the
society of the elect, and may externally use
with them the benefits of the word and sacraments. But such being but temporal
professors in mouth, but not in heart, do fall
back, and continue not to the end (*b*); and
therefore have they no fruit of Christ's
death, resurrection, nor ascension. But
such as with heart unfeignedly believe,
and with mouth boldly confess the Lord Jesus,

(*a*) Matt. xiii. 24, &c.   (*b*) Matt. xiii. 20, 21.

as before we have said, shall most assuredly
receive these gifts (c):—First, in this life, remission of sins, and that only by faith in
Christ's blood, insomuch, that albeit sin
remain, and continually abide in these our
mortal bodies, yet it is not imputed to us,
but is remitted, and covered with Christ's
justice (d). Secondly, in the general judgment, there shall be given to every man and
woman, resurrection of the flesh (e): for the
sea shall give her dead, the earth those that
therein be enclosed : yea, the Eternal, our
God, shall stretch out his hand on the dust,
and the dead shall rise incorruptible (f), and
that in the substance of the self-same flesh
that every man now beareth (g), to receive
according to their works, glory or punishment (h): for such as now delight in vanity,
cruelty, filthiness, superstition, or idolatry,
shall be adjudged to the fire unquenchable,
wherein they shall be tormented for ever,
as well in their own bodies, as in their souls,
which now they give to serve the devil in all
abominations. But such as continue in well
doing to the end, boldly professing the Lord
Jesus, we constantly believe, that they shall
receive glory, honour, and immortality, to
reign for ever in life everlasting with Christ

(c) Rom. x. 9, 13.   (d) Rom. vii; 2 Cor. v. 21.
(e) John v. 28, 29.   (f) Rev. xx. 13; 1 Cor. xv.
25—54.   (g) Job xix. 25—27.   (h) Matt. xxv.
31, &c.

Jesus (*i*): to whose glorified body all his elect shall be made like (*k*), when he shall appear again in judgment, and shall render up the kingdom to God his Father, who then shall be, and ever shall remain in all things, God blessed for ever (*l*): to whom, with the Son, and with the Holy Ghost, be all honour and glory for now and ever. So be it.

(*i*) Rev. xiv. 10; Rom. ii. 6—10.   (*k*) Phil. iii. 21.
(*l*) 1 Cor. xv. 24, 28.

" Arise, O Lord, and let thy enemies be confounded : let them flee from thy presence, that hate thy godly Name. Give thy servants strength to speak thy word in boldness, and let all nations cleave to thy true knowledge." Amen. (Num. ix. 35 ; Psal. lxviii. 15; Acts iv. 29.)

These acts and articles were read in the face of Parliament, and ratified by the three estates of this realm, at Edinburgh, the 17th day of August, in the year of our Lord 1560. And again ratified, established, and repeated in the fourth act of King James VI. first Parliament, at Edinburgh, December 15th, 1567. (And in several other acts.) And all acts against the truth, in any Parliament before whatsoever, abolished.

A

SHORT SUM

OF THE

FIRST BOOK OF DISCIPLINE,

FOR THE

INSTRUCTION OF MINISTERS AND READERS
IN THEIR OFFICE.

"According to all that I shewed thee, after the pattern of
the tabernacle, and the pattern of all the instruments
thereof, even so shall ye make it."—Exod. xxv. 9.

THE SUM

OF THE

FIRST BOOK OF DISCIPLINE.

I. *Doctrine.*

THE word of God only, which is the New and Old Testament, shall be taught in every kirk within this realm; and all contrary doctrine to the same shall be impugned and utterly suppressed.

We affirm that to be contrary doctrine to the word, that man has invented, and imposed on the consciences of men, by laws, councils, and constitutions, without the express command of God's word.

Of this kind are vows of chastity, disguised apparel, superstitious observation of fasting-days, difference of meats for conscience sake, prayer for the dead, calling upon saints, with such other inventions of men. In this rank, the holy-days invented by men, such as Christmas, Circumcision, Epiphany,

Purification, and other fond feasts of our Lady; with the feasts of the Apostles, martyrs, and virgins, with others; which we judge utterly to be abolished forth of this realm, because they have no assurance in God's word. All maintainers of such abominations should be punished with the civil sword.

The word is sufficient for our salvation; and therefore all things needful for us are contained in it. The Scriptures shall be read in private houses, for removing of this gross ignorance.

II. *Sacraments.*

The sacraments, of necessity, are joined with the word, which are two only, baptism and the table of the Lord. The preaching of the word must precède the ministration of the sacraments. In the due administration of the sacraments, all things should be done according to the word, nothing being added, nor yet diminished. The sacraments should be ministered after the order of the Kirk of Geneva. All ceremonies and rites invented by men should be abolished, and the simple word followed in all points.

The ministration of the sacraments in no ways should be given him in whose mouth God has not put the word of exhortation. In the ministration of the table, some comfortable places may be read of the Scriptures.

III. *Idolatry.*

All kind of idolatry and monuments of idolatry should be abolished, such as places dedicate to idolatry and relics. Idolatry is all kind of worshipping of God not contained in the word, as the mass, invocation of saints, adoration of images, and all other such things invented by man.

IV. *The Ministry.*

No man should enter in the ministry, without a lawful vocation. The lawful vocation standeth in the election of the people, examination of the ministry, and admission by them both. The extraordinary vocation has another consideration, seeing it is wrought only by God inwardly in men's hearts.

No minister should be intruded upon any particular kirk without their consent; but if any kirk be negligent to elect, then the superintendant, with his council, should provide a qualified man within forty days.

Neither for rarity of men, necessity of teaching, nor for any corruption of time, should unable persons be admitted to the ministry. Better it is to have the room vacant, than to have unqualified persons, to the scandal of the ministry, and hurt of the kirk : in the rarity of qualified men, we should call unto the Lord, that he of his goodness would send forth true labourers to his harvest. The kirk and faithful magistrate should compel such as have the gifts, to take the office of teaching upon them.

We should consider, first, whether God has given the gifts to him whom we would choose; for God calls no man to the ministry, whom he arms not with necessary gifts.

Persons noted with infamy, or unable to edify the kirk by wholesome doctrine, or of a corrupt judgment, should not be admitted, nor yet retained in the ministry: the prince's pardon, nor reconciliation with the kirk, takes not away the infamy before men : therefore public edicts should be set forth in all places where the person is known, and strict charge given to all men to reveal, if they know any capital crime committed by him, or if he be scandalous in his life.

Persons proponed by the kirk shall be examined publicly by the superintendant and brethren, in the principal kirk of the diocese or province.

They shall give public declaration of their gifts, by the interpretation of some places of Scripture.

They shall be examined openly, in all the principal points that now are in controversy. When they are approven by the judgment of the brethren, they should make sundry sermons before their congregations, before they be admitted.

In their admission, the office and duty of

ministers and people should be declared by some godly and learned minister; and so publicly, before the people, should they be placed in their kirks, and joined to their flocks at the desire of the samen: other ceremonies, except fasting with prayer, such as laying on of hands, we judge not necessary in the institution of the ministry.

Ministers, so placed, may not for their own pleasure leave their own kirks, nor yet their kirks refuse them, without some weighty causes tried and known: but the general assembly, for good causes, may remove ministers from place to place, without the consent of the particular kirks.

Such as are preachers, already placed, and not found qualified after this form of trial, shall be made readers; and so for no sort of men shall this rigour of examination be omitted.

V. Readers.

Readers are but for a time, till, through reading of the Scriptures, they may come to further knowledge and exercise of the kirk, in exhorting and explaining of the Scriptures. No reader shall be admitted within twenty-one years of age; and unless there be an hope, that by reading he should shortly come to exhorting. Readers found unable, after two years' exercise, for the ministry, should be removed, and others as long put in their room.

E

No reader shall attempt to minister the sacraments until he be able to exhort and persuade by wholesome doctrine. Readers in landwart shall teach the youth of the parochines. :

Ministers and readers shall begin ever some book of the Old or New Testament, and continue upon it unto the end, and not to hip from place to place as the Papists did.

VI. *Provision for Ministers.*

The ministers' stipend should be moderated, that neither they have occasion to be careful for the world, nor yet wanton, nor insolent anywise: their wives and children should be sustained, not only in their time, but also after their death.

VII. *Elders and Deacons.*

Men of the best knowledge, judgment, and conversation, should be chosen for elders and deacons. Their election shall be yearly, where it may be conveniently observed. How the votes and suffrages may be best received with every man's freedom in voting, we leave to the judgment of every particular kirk. They shall be publicly admitted and admonished of their office ; and also the people of their duty to them, at their first admission.

Their office is, to assist the ministers in

their execution of discipline, in all great and weighty matters.

The elders shall watch upon all men's manners, religion, and conversation, that are within their charge, correct all licentious livers, or else accuse them before the session.

They should take heed to the doctrine, diligence, and behaviour of their minister and his household; and, if need be, admonish and correct them accordingly.

It is undecent for ministers, to be boarded in an ale-house or tavern; or to haunt much the court, or to be occupied in council of civil affairs.

The office of deacons is, to gather and distribute the alms of the poor, according to the direction of the session: the deacons should assist the assembly in judgment, and may read publicly, if need requires.

Elders and deacons, being judges of other men's manners, must, with their household, live godly, and be subject to the censure of the kirk.

It is not necessary to appoint a public stipend for elders and deacons, seeing they are changed yearly, and may wait upon their own vocation with the charge of the kirk.

VIII. *Superintendants.*

The necessity, nomination, examination, and institution of superintendants, are at large contained in the Book of Discipline, and in many things do agree with the examination and admission of ministers: principal towns shall not be spoiled of their ministers, to be appointed superintendants: superintendants, once admitted, shall not be changed, without great causes and considerations.

Superintendants shall have their own special kirks, beside the common charge of others : they shall not remain in one place, until their kirks be provided of ministers or readers : they shall not remain above twenty days in one place in their visitation, till they pass through their bounds; they shall preach themselves thrice in the week at the least : when they come home again to their own kirk, they must be occupied in preaching and edifying of the kirk; they shall not remain at their chief kirk above three or four months, but shall pass again to their visitation.

In their visitation, they shall not only preach, but also examine the doctrine, life, diligence, and behaviour of the ministers, readers, elders, and deacons. They shall consider the order of the kirk, the manners of the people, how the poor are provided, how the youth are instructed, how the discipline and policy of the kirk are keeped, how heinous and horrible crimes are corrected : they shall admonish and dress things out of order with their counsel, as they may best.

Superintendants are subject to the censure and correction, not only of the synodal convention, but also of their own kirk, and others within their jurisdiction. Whatsomeever crime deserves correction or deposition in any other minister, the same deserves the like in the superintendant : their stipend would be considered and augmented above other ministers, by reason of their great charges and travel.

IX. *Discipline.*

As no commonwealth can be governed without execution of good laws, no more can the kirk be retained in purity without discipline.

Discipline standeth in the correction of those things that are contrary to God's law, for the edifying of the kirk. All estates within the realm are subject to the discipline of the kirk, as well rulers and preachers, as the common people.

In secret and private faults, the order prescribed by our Master should be observed, whereof we need not to write at length, seeing it is largely declared in the Book of Excommunication*.

Before the sentence proceed, labour should be taken with the guilty by his friends, and

---

* The Book of Excommunication was written in the year 1567. So this Summary was not written till some time after.

public prayer made for his conversion unto
God. When all is done, the minister should
ask, if any man will assure the kirk of his
obedience; and if any man promise, then
the sentence shall stay for that time.

If, after public proclaiming of their names,
they promise obedience, that should be declared to the kirk, who heard their former
rebellion.

The sentence being once pronounced, no
member of the kirk should have company
with them, under pain of excommunication,
except such persons as are exeemed by the
law; their children should not be received
to baptism in their name, but by some
member of the kirk, who shall promise for
the children, and detest the parent's impiety.

Committers of horrible crimes worthy of
death, if the civil sword spare them, they
should be holden as dead to us, and cursed
in their facts.

If God move their hearts to repentance,
the kirk cannot deny them conciliation,
their repentance being tried and found true.
Some of the elders should receive such persons publicly in the kirk, in token of reconciliation.

X. *Marriage.*

Persons, under care of others, shall not
marry without their consent lawfully required.

When the parents and others are hard

and stubborn, then the kirk and magistrates should enter in the parents' room, and discern upon the equity of the cause, without affection : the kirk and magistrate shall not sute for them that commit fornication, before they sute the kirk.

Promises of bairns within age are null, except they be ratified after they come to age. Band of marriage should be proclaimed upon three several Sabbaths, to take away all excuse of impediment.

Committers of adultery should not be overseen by the kirk, albeit the civil sword oversee them, but should be esteemed as dead and excommunicate in their wicked fact. If such offenders desire earnestly to be reconciled to the kirk, we dare not refuse them, nor excommunicate them, whom God has brought to repentance.

The party, that is proven to be innocent, should be admitted to marriage again. As for the party offending, all doubt of marriage would be removed, if the civil sword would strike according to God's word.

XI. *Policy.*

Policy is an exercise of the kirk, serving for instruction of the ignorant, inflaming of the learned to greater service, and for retaining of the kirk of God in good order.

Of the parts of policy, some are necessary, and some not necessary absolutely. Necessary is the true preaching of the word, the right ministration of the sacraments, the common-prayers, the instruction of the youth, the support of the poor, and the punishment of vice : but singing of psalms certain days of the conventions in the week, thrice or twice preaching on week days, certain places of Scripture to be read when there is no sermon, with such things, are not necessary.

In towns, we require every day, either sermon or public prayers, with some reading of the Scriptures ; public prayers are not needful in the days of preaching, lest thereby we should nourish the people in superstition, causing them to understand that the public prayers succeed to the papistical mass. In every notable town, we require, that at least once in the week, beside the Sabbath, the whole people convene to the preaching.

The Sabbath must be kept strictly in all towns, both forenoon and afternoon for hearing of the word ; at afternoon upon the Sabbath, the Catechism shall be taught, the children examined, and the baptism ministered. Public prayers shall be used upon the Sabbath, as well afternoon as before, when sermons cannot be had.

It appertains to the policy of every particular kirk, to appoint the time when the sacraments shall be ministered.

XII. *Baptism.*

Baptism may be ministered whensoever the word is preached, but we think it most expedient that it be ministered upon Sabbathday, or upon the day of common-prayers: thus we take away that error of the Papists, concerning the estate of the infants departing without baptism; we bring the ministration of baptism to the presence of the people, to be kept in greater reverence, and to put every one in remembrance of the promises of baptism, in the which now many wax faint and cold.

XIII. *The Table.*

The table of the Lord shall be ministered four times in the year, and out of the times of superstition. We judge the first Sabbath of March, June, September, and December, to be meetest: but this we leave to the judgment of the particular kirks.

Let all ministers be diligent, rather to instruct the ignorant, and to suppress superstition, than to serve the vain appetites of men. The ministration of the table should never be without sharp examination going before, chiefly of them whose life, ignorance, or religion is suspected. Who cannot say the Lord's prayer, the articles of the faith, and declare the sum of the law, should not be admitted. Whoso will stubbornly remain ignorant of the principal points of our salvation, should be excommunicate, with their parents and masters that keep them in that ignorance. Every master of a household should be commanded either to instruct his children and servants, or cause them to be instructed; and, if they will not, the kirk should proceed against them.

It is very needful, that public examination of every person be made, at least once in the year, by the ministers and elders.

Every master and masters of household should come with their household and family, to give confession of their faith, and answer to the principal points of our religion.

We think it very expedient, that prayers be had daily in private houses, at morning and at night, for the comfort and instruction of others; and this to be done by the most grave and discreet person of the house.

XIV. *The Exercise.*

In towns where learned men are, the exercise of the Scriptures should be weekly. In this exercise, three only shall speak to the opening of the text, and edifying of the people. This exercise shall be upon some places of Scripture, and openly, that all that will, may hear, and speak their judgment, to the edifying of the kirk. In this kind of exercise, the text is only opened without any digressing or exhortation, following the file and dependence of the text, confuting all errors, as occasion shall · be given. No man should move a question, the which himself is not able to solve.

The exercise being ended, the ministers and elders present should convene apart, and correct the things that have been done or spoken without order, and not to the edifying of the kirk. In this public exercise, all affectation and vain curiosity must be above all things eschewed, lest for edifying we should slander the kirk of God.

Ministers within six miles about, should come in willingly; and also, readers that would profit, should come, both to teach others, and to learn : other learned men, to whom God has given the gift of interpretation, should be charged to join themselves.

XV. *Schools.*

Because schools are the seed of the ministry, diligent care should be taken over them, that they be ordered in religion and conversation according to the word. Every town should have a school-master : and in landwart, the minister or reader should teach the children that come to them. Men should be compelled by the kirk and magistrates to send their bairns to the schools : poor men's children should be helped.

XVI. *Universities.*

The Universities should be erected in this realm, St. Andrews, Glasgow, and Aberdeen. Their order of proceeding, provision, and degrees, with their readers and officers, are at length declared in the Book of Discipline; how many colleges, how many classes in every college, and what should be taught in every class, is there expressed.

A contribution shall be made at the entry of the students, for the upholding of the place, and a sufficient stipend is ordained for every member of the university, according to their degrees.

XVII. *Rents of the Kirk.*

The whole rents of the kirk, abused in papistry, shall be referred again to the kirk, that thereby the ministry, schools, and the poor, may be maintained within this realm, according to their first institution.

Every man should be suffered to lead and use his own tithes, and no man should lead another man's tithes. The uppermost cloth, the cors-present, the clerk-mail, the pasch-offerings, tithe-ale, and all other such things should be discharged.

The deacons should take up the whole rents of the kirk, disponing them to the ministry, the schools, and poor within their bounds, according to the appointment of the kirk.

All friaries, nunries, chantries, chaplainries, annual rents, and all things doted * to the hospitality, shall be reduced to the help of the kirk. Merchants and craftsmen in burgh, should contribute to the support of the kirk.

XVIII. *Burial.*

We desire, that burial be so honourably handled, that the hope of our resurrection may be nourished; and all kind of superstition, idolatry, and whatsomever thing proceedeth of the false opinion, may be avoided.

At the burial, neither singing of psalms, nor reading, shall be used, lest the people should be nourished thereby in that old superstition of praying for the dead : but this we remit to the judgment of the particular kirks, with advice of the ministers. All superstition being removed, ministers shall not be burdened with funeral sermons; seeing that daily sermons are sufficient enough for ministering of the living. Burial should be without the kirk, in a fine air, and place walled and kept honourably.

XIX. *Repairing of Kirks.*

The kirk does crave most earnestly the lords their assistance, for hasty repairing of all parish-kirks, where the people should

* Gifted.

convene for the hearing of the word, and receiving of the sacraments : this reparation should not only be in the walls and fabric, but also in all things needful within, for the people, and decencies of the place appointed for God's service.

XX. *Punishment of Profaners of the Sacraments.*

We desire strict laws to be made, for punishment of them that abuse the sacraments, as well the ministers as readers. The holy sacraments are abused, when the minister is not lawfully called, or when they are given to open injurers of the truth, or to profane livers ; or when they are ministered in a private place, without the word preached.

The examples of Scripture do plainly declare, that the abusers of the sacraments, and contemners of the word, are worthy of death.

This our judgment, for reformation of the kirk, shall bear witness both before God and man, what we have craved of the nobility, and how they have obeyed our loving admonitions.

Thus far out of the Book of Discipline, which was subscribed by the Kirk and Lords.

THE

SECOND BOOK OF DISCIPLINE,

OR

HEADS AND CONCLUSIONS OF THE
POLICY OF THE KIRK;

Agreed upon in the General Assembly 1578; inserted in
the Registers of Assembly 1581; sworn to in the
NATIONAL COVENANT; revived and ratified by the
Assembly 1638, and by many other Acts of Assembly:
and according to which the Church Government is established by Law, anno 1592 and 1640.

———

"Let all things be done decently, and in order."—1 COR. xiv. 40.

Act of the General Assembly, concerning the Book of Policy.

April 1581, Sess. 9.

Forasmuch as travels have been taken in the framing of the policy of the Kirk, and divers suits have been made to the magistrate for the approbation thereof, which yet. hath not taken the happy effect that good men would wish; yet, that the posterity may judge well of this present age, and of the meaning of the Kirk, the Assembly hath concluded, that the Book of Policy, agreed to in divers assemblies before, should be registered in the acts of the Kirk, and remain there *ad perpetuam rei memoriam*, and the copies thereof to be taken by every presbytery. Of which book the tenor followetn.

THE

SECOND BOOK OF DISCIPLINE,

OR

HEADS AND CONCLUSIONS OF THE
POLICY OF THE KIRK.

CHAP. I. *Of the Kirk, and Policy thereof
in general, and wherein it is different from
the Civil Policy.*

THE kirk of God sometimes is largely taken,
for all them that profess the Evangel of Jesus
Christ: and so it is a company and fellowship, not only of the godly, but also of hypo-
crites, professing always outwardly the true
religion.

Other times it is taken for the godly and
elect only; and sometimes for them that exercise spiritual function in the congregation
of them that profess the truth.

The kirk in this last sense hath a certain
power granted by God, according to the
which it uses a proper jurisdiction and go-

F

vernment, exercised to the comfort of the whole kirk.

This power ecclesiastical is an authority granted by God the Father, through the Mediator Jesus Christ, unto his kirk gathered; and having ground in the word of God, to be put in execution by them, unto whom the spiritual government of the kirk, by lawful calling, is committed.

The policy of the kirk, flowing from this power, is an order or form of spiritual government, which is exercised by the members appointed thereto by the word of God; and therefore is given immediately to the office bearers, by whom it is exercised, to the good of the whole body.

This power is diversely used: for sometime it is severally exercised, chiefly by the teachers; sometime conjunctly, by mutual consent of them that bear the office and charge, after the form of judgment. The former is commonly called *potestas ordinis*, and the other *potestas jurisdictionis*.

These two kinds of power have both one authority, one ground, one final cause; but are different in the manner and form of execution, as is evident by the speaking of our Master in the xvith and xviiith of Matthew.

This power and policy ecclesiastical is different and distinct, in their own nature, from that power and policy which is called civil power, and appertaineth to the civil government of the commonwealth : albeit they be both of God, and tend to one end, if they be rightly used—viz. to advance the glory of God, and to have godly and good subjects.

For this power ecclesiastical floweth immediately from God, and the Mediator Jesus Christ, and is spiritual, not having a temporal head on the earth, but only Christ, the only spiritual King and Governor of his kirk.

It is a title falsely usurped by Antichrist, to call himself head of the kirk; and ought nor to be attributed to angel, nor man, of what estate soever he be, saving to Christ, the only head and monarch in the kirk.

Therefore this power and policy of the kirk should lean upon the word immediately, as the only ground thereof, and should be taken from the pure fountains of the Scriptures, the kirk hearing the voice of Christ, the only spiritual King, and being ruled by his laws.

It is proper to kings, princes, and magistrates to be called lords, and dominators over their subjects, whom they govern civilly; but it is proper to Christ only to be called Lord and Master, in the spiritual government of the kirk; and all others, that bear office therein, ought not to usurp dominion therein, nor be called lords, but only ministers, disciples, and servants; for it is Christ's proper office to command and rule his kirk

universally, and every particular kirk, through
his Spirit and word, by the ministry of men.

Notwithstanding, as the ministers, and
others of the ecclesiastical estate, are subject
to the magistrate civil, so ought the person
of the magistrate be subject to the kirk
spiritually, and in ecclesiastical government.
And the exercise of both these jurisdictions
cannot stand in one person ordinarily.

The civil power is called the power of the
sword, and the other the power of the keys.

The civil power should command the spiritual to exercise, and to do their office according to the word of God ; the spiritual
rulers should require the Christian magistrate
to minister justice and punish vice, and to
maintain the liberty and quietness of the
kirk within their bounds.

The magistrate commandeth external
things, for external peace and quietness
amongst the subjects ; the minister handleth
external things only for conscience cause.

The magistrate handleth external things
only, and actions done before men ; but the
spiritual ruler judgeth both inward affections, and external actions in respect of conscience, by the word of God.

The civil magistrate craves and gets obedience by the sword, and other external
means ; but the ministry by the spiritual
sword, and spiritual means.

The magistrate neither ought to preach,

minister the sacraments, nor execute the censures of the kirk, nor yet prescribe any rule. how it should be done, but command the ministers to observe the rule commanded in the word, and punish the transgressors by civil means. The ministers exercise not the civil. jurisdiction, but teach the magistrate how it should be exercised according to the word.

The magistrate. ought to assist, maintain, and fortify the jurisdiction of the kirk. The ministers should assist their princes in all things agreeable to the word, providing they neglect not their own charge, by involving themselves in civil affairs.

Finally, as ministers are subject to the judgment and punishment of the magistrate, in external things, if they offend; so ought the magistrates to submit themselves to the discipline of the kirk, if they transgress in matters of conscience and religion.

CHAP. II.   *Of the Policy of the Kirk, and Persons or Office-bearers to whom the administration is committed.*

As in the civil policy, the whole commonwealth consisteth in them that are governors, or magistrates ; and them that are governed, or subjects : so in the policy of the kirk, some are appointed to be rulers, and the rest. of the members thereof to be ruled, and obey according to the word of God, and inspiration of his Spirit, always under one head and chief governor, Jesus Christ.

Again, the whole policy of the kirk consisteth in three things—viz. in doctrine, discipline, and distribution. With doctrine is annexed the administration of sacraments; and, according to the parts of this division, ariseth a threefold sort of officers in the kirk; *to wit*, of ministers or preachers, elders or governors, and deacons or distributors: and all these may be called by a general word, ministers of the kirk: for albeit the kirk of God be ruled and governed by Jesus Christ, who is the only King, High-Priest, and Head thereof, yet he useth the ministry of men, as the most necessary mids for this purpose.

For so he hath, from time to time, before the Law, under the Law, and in the time of the Evangel, for our great comfort, raised up men endued with the gifts of the Spirit, for the spiritual government of his kirk, exercising by them his own power, through his Spirit and word, to the building up of the same.

And, to take away all occasion of tyranny, he willeth that they should rule with mutual consent, as brethren, and with equality of power, every one according to their functions.

In the New Testament, and time of the Evangel, he hath used the ministry of the Apostles, Prophets, Evangelists, Pastors and Doctors, in administration of the word; the

Eldership for good order, and administration of discipline; the Deaconship to have the care of the ecclesiastical goods.

Some of these ecclesiastical functions are ordinary, and some extraordinary, or tem-porary. There be three extraordinary functions,—the office of the Apostle, of the Evangelist, and of the Prophet; which are not perpetual, and now have ceased in the kirk of God; except when it pleased God extraordinarily for a time to stir some of them up again.

There are four ordinary functions or offices in the kirk of God,—the office of the Pastor, Minister, or Bishop; the Doctor; the Presbyter, or Elder; and the Deacon.

These offices are ordinary, and ought to continue perpetually in the kirk, as necessary for the government and policy thereof: and no more offices ought to be received or suffered in the true kirk of God, established according to his word.

Therefore all the ambitious titles, invented in the kingdom of Antichrist, and in his usurped hierarchy, which are not of one of these four sorts, together with the offices depending thereupon, in one word, ought to be rejected.

CHAP. III. *How the Persons that bear Ecclesiastical Functions are to be admitted to their Office.*

Vocation, or calling, is common to all that should bear office within the kirk; which is a lawful way, by the which qualified persons are promoted to any spiritual office within the kirk of God.

Without this lawful calling it was never leisom to any person to meddle with any function ecclesiastical.

There are two sorts of calling: one extraordinary, by God immediately; as was that of the Prophets and Apostles, which, in kirks established, and already well reformed, hath no place.

The other calling is ordinary, which, besides the calling of God, and inward testimony of a good conscience, hath the lawful approbation and outward judgment of men, according to God's word, and order established in his kirk.

None ought to presume to enter into any office ecclesiastical, without this testimony of a good conscience before God, who only knows the hearts of men.

This ordinary and outward calling hath two parts, election and ordination. Election is the choosing out of a person or persons, most able, to the office that vakes, by the judgment of the eldership, and consent of the congregation, to which the person or persons shall be appointed.

The qualifications requisite in all them who should bear charge in the kirk, consist of soundness of religion, and godliness of life, according as they are sufficiently set forth in the word.

In the order of election is to be eschewed, that any person be intruded in any offices of the kirk, contrary to the will of the congregation to which they are appointed, or without the voice of the eldership.

None ought to be intruded, or placed in the places already planted, or in any place that vakes not, for any worldly respect: and that, which is called the benefice, ought to be nothing else but the stipend of the ministers that are lawfully called.

Ordination is the separation and sanctifying of the person appointed, to God and his kirk, after he is well tried and found qualified.

The ceremonies of ordination are fasting, earnest prayer, and imposition of hands of the eldership.

All these, as they must be raised up by God, and by him made able for the work whereto they are called; so ought they to know their message to be limited within God's word, without the bounds of the which they ought not to pass.

All these should take those titles and names only (lest they be exalted and puffed up in themselves) which the Scriptures give unto them, as those which import labour, travel, and work, and are names of offices and service, and not of idleness, dignity, worldly honour or pre-eminence, which by Christ our Master is expressly reproved and forbidden.

All these office-bearers should have their own particular flocks, amongst whom they exercise their charge: and should make residence with them, and take the inspection and oversight of them, every one in his vocation.

And generally these two things ought they all to respect, the glory of God, and edifying of his kirk, in discharging their duties in their calling.

CHAP. IV. *Of the Office-bearers in particular, and first of the Pastors or Ministers.*

Pastors, Bishops, or Ministers, are they who are appointed to particular congregations, which they rule by the word of God, and over the which they watch: in respect whereof, sometime they are called pastors, because they feed their congregation; sometime *episcopi,* or bishops, because they watch over their flock; sometime ministers, because of their service and office; sometime also presbyters, or seniors, for the gravity in manners which they ought to have in taking care of their spiritual government, which ought to be most dear unto them.

They that are called unto the ministry, or that offer themselves thereunto, ought not to be elected, without some certain flock assigned unto them.

No man ought to ingyre himself, or usurp this office, without a lawful calling.

They who are once called by God, and duly elected by man, after that they have once accepted the charge of the ministry, may not leave their functions.

The deserters should be admonished; and, in case of obstinacy, finally excommunicated.

No pastor may leave his flock without licence of the provincial or national assembly; which if he do, after admonitions not obeyed, let the censures of the kirk strike upon him.

Unto the pastor appertains teaching of the word of God, in season and out of season, publicly and privately, always travelling to edify, and to discharge his conscience, as God's word prescribes to him.

Unto the pastors only appertains the administration of the sacraments, in like manner as the administration of the word; for both are appointed by God, as means to teach us, the one by the ear, and the other by the eyes and other senses; that by both, knowledge may be transferred to the mind.

It appertains, by the same reason, to the

pastor, to pray for the people, and namely for the flock committed to his charge; and to bless them in the name of the Lord, who will not suffer the blessings of his faithful servants to be frustrate.

He ought also to watch over the manners of his flock, that he may the better apply the doctrine to them, in reprehending the dissolute persons, and exhorting the godly to continue in the fear of the Lord.

It appertains to the minister, after lawful proceeding by the eldership, to pronounce the sentence of binding and loosing upon any person, according unto the power of the keys granted unto the kirk.

It belongs to him likewise, after lawful proceeding in the matter by the eldership, to solemnize marriage betwixt them that are to be joined therein; and to pronounce the blessing of the Lord upon them that enter into that holy band in the fear of God.

And generally all public denunciations, that are to be made in the kirk, before the congregation, concerning the ecclesiastical affairs, belong to the office of a minister: for he is as a messenger and herald betwixt God and the people, in all these affairs.

CHAP. V. *Of Doctors, and their Office; and of the Schools.*

One of the two ordinary and perpetual functions that travel in the word, is the office of the doctor, who may be also called a prophet, bishop, elder, catechiser; that is, teacher of the catechism, and rudiments of religion.

His office is, to open up the mind of the Spirit of God in the Scriptures, simply, without such applications as the ministers use, to the end that the faithful may be instructed, and sound doctrine taught; and that the purity of the Gospel be not corrupted through ignorance or evil opinions.

He is different from the pastor, not only in name, but in diversity of gifts : for to the doctor is given the word of knowledge, to open up, by simple teaching, the mysteries of faith; to the pastor the gift of wisdom, to apply the same by exhortation to the manners of the flock, as occasion craveth.

Under the name and office of a doctor, we comprehend also the order of schools, colleges, and universities, which hath been from time to time carefully maintained, as well among the Jews and Christians, as among the profane nations.

The doctor being an elder, as said is, should assist the pastor in the government of the kirk, and concur with the elders, his brethren, in all assemblies, by reason the interpretation of the word, which is only judge in ecclesiastical matters, is committed to his charge.

But to preach unto the people, to minister the sacraments, and to celebrate marriages, pertain not to the doctor, unless he be otherwise called ordinarily : howbeit, the pastor may teach in the schools, as he who hath the gift of knowledge oftentimes meet for that end, as the examples of Polycarpus and others testify, &c.

CHAP. VI. *Of Elders, and their Office.*

The word Elder, in the Scripture, sometime is the name of age, sometime of office. When it is the name of any office, sometime it is taken largely, comprehending as well the pastors and doctors, as them who are called seniors and elders.

In this our division, we call those elders, whom the Apostles call presidents, or governors : their office, as it is ordinary, so it is perpetual, and always necessary in the kirk of God. The eldership is a spiritual function, as is the ministry.

Elders, once lawfully called to the office, and having gifts from God meet to exercise the same, may not leave it again. Albeit such a number of elders may be chosen in certain congregations, that one part of them may relieve another for a reasonable time, as was among the Levites under the Law, in serving of the temple.

The number of the elders, in every congregation, cannot well be limited, but should be according to the bounds and necessity of the people.

It is not necessary that all elders be also teachers of the word, albeit the chief ought to be such; and so are worthy of double honour.

What manner of persons they ought to be, we refer it to the express word, and namely, to the canons written by the Apostle Paul.

Their office is, as well severally as conjunctly, to watch diligently over the flock committed to their charge, both publicly and privately, that no corruption of religion or manners enter therein.

As the pastors and doctors should be diligent in teaching, and sowing the seed of the word; so the elders should be careful in seeking after the fruit of the same in the people.

It appertains to them to assist the pastor in examination of them that come to the Lord's table.   *Item,* in visiting the sick.

They should cause the acts of the assemblies, as well particular as general, to be put in execution carefully.

They should be diligent in admonishing all men of their duty, according to the rule of the Evangel.

Things that they cannot correct by private admonitions, they should bring to the eldership.

Their principal office is, to hold assemblies with the pastors and doctors, who are also of their number, for establishing of good order, and execution of discipline; unto the which assemblies all persons are subject, that remain within their bounds.

CHAP. VII.   *Of the Elderships, Assemblies, and Discipline.*

Elderships and assemblies are commonly constitute of pastors, doctors, and such as we commonly call elders, that labour not in the word and doctrine; of whom, and of whose several power, hath been spoken.

Assemblies are of four sorts. For either they are of particular kirks and congregations one or mo, or of a province, or of a whole nation, or of all and divers nations, professing one Jesus Christ.

All the ecclesiastical assemblies have power to convene lawfully together, for treating of things concerning the kirk, and pertaining to their charge.

They have power to appoint times and places to that effect; and at one meeting, to appoint the diet, time, and place for another.

In all assemblies, a moderator should be chosen, by common consent of the whole brethren convened, who should propone matters, gather the votes, and cause good order to be kept in the assemblies.

Diligence should be taken, chiefly by the moderator, that only ecclesiastical things be handled in the assemblies; and that there be no meddling with any thing pertaining to the civil jurisdiction.

Every assembly hath power to send forth from them, of their own number, one or more visitors, to see how all things be ruled in the bounds of their jurisdiction.

Visitation of more kirks, is no ordinary office ecclesiastic, in the person of one man; neither may the name of a bishop be attributed to the visitor only, neither is it necessary to abide always in one man's person; but it is the part of the eldership to send out qualified persons to visit *pro re nata*.

The final end of assemblies is, first, To keep religion and doctrine in purity, without error and corruption. Next, To keep comeliness and good order in the kirk.

For this order's cause, they may make certain rules and constitutions, appertaining to the good behaviour of all the members of the kirk, in their vocation.

They have power also to abrogate and abolish all statutes and ordinances, concerning ecclesiastical matters, that are found noisome and unprofitable, and agree not with the time, or are abused by the people.

They have power to execute ecclesiastical discipline and punishment upon all transgressors, and proud contemners of the good order and policy of the kirk; and so the whole discipline is in their hands.

The first kind and sort of assemblies,

G

although they be within particular congregations, yet they exerce the power and jurisdiction of the kirk with mutual consent, and
therefore bear sometime the name of the kirk..

When we speak of the elders of the particular congregations, we mean not that every
particular parish-kirk can, or may, have their
own particular elderships, especially in landward; but we think three, four, more or fewer
particular kirks, may have one eldership,
common to them all, to judge their ecclesiastical causes.

Yet this is meet, that some of the elders
be chosen out of every particular congregation, to concur with the rest of their brethren
in the common assembly, and to take up the
delations of offences within their own kirks,
and bring them to the assembly.

This we gather out of the practice of the
primitive kirk, where elders, or colleges of
seniors, were constitute in cities and famous
places.

The power of these particular elderships,
is to use diligent labours in the bounds committed to their charge, that the kirks be
kept in good order; to inquire diligently of
naughty and unruly persons, and travel to
bring them in the way again, either by admonition or threatening of God's judgments,
or by correction.

It pertains to the eldership, to take heed
that the word of God be purely preached

within their bounds, the sacraments rightly
ministered, the discipline rightly maintained,
and the ecclesiastical goods uncorruptly distributed.

It belongs to this kind of assembly, to cause
the ordinances made by the assemblies provincial, national, and general, to be kept,
and put in execution.

To make constitutions, which concern το
πρεπον in the kirk, for the decent order of
those particular kirks where they govern :
providing they alter no rules made by the
general or provincial assemblies; and that
they make the provincial assemblies foreseen
of those rules that they shall make, and abolish them that tend to the hurt of the same.

It hath power to excommunicate the obstinate.

The power of election of them who bear
ecclesiastical charges, pertains to this kind
of assembly, within their own bounds, being
well erected, and constitute of many pastors,
and elders of sufficient ability.

By the like reason, their deposition also
pertains to this kind of assembly ; as of them
that teach erroneous and corrupt doctrine ;
that be of scandalous life, and after admonitions desist not; that be given to schism,
or rebellion against the kirk ; manifest blasphemy, simony, corruption of bribes, falsehood, perjury, whoredom, theft, drunkenness,
fighting worthy of punishment by the law,

usury, dancing, infamy, and all others, that
deserve separation from the kirk.

Those also, who are altogether found insufficient to execute their charge, should be
deposed; whereof other kirks should be ad-
vertised, that they receive not the persons
deposed.

Yet they ought not to be deposed, who
through age, sickness, or other accidents,
become unmeet to do their office; in which
case, their honour should remain to them,
their kirk should maintain them, and others
ought to be provided to do their office.

Provincial assemblies, we call lawful conventions of the pastors, doctors, and other
elders of a province gathered, for the common
affairs of the kirks thereof; which also may
be called the conference of the kirk and
brethren.

These assemblies are institute for weighty
matters, to be handled by mutual consent
and assistance of the brethren within that
province, as need requires.

This assembly hath power to handle, order,
and redress all things, omitted or done amiss
in the particular assemblies.

It hath power to depose the office-bearers
of that province, for good and just causes
deserving deprivation.

And, generally, these assemblies have the
whole power of the particular elderships,
whereof they are collected.

The national assembly, which is general to us, is a lawful convention of the whole kirks of the realm, or nation, where it is used and gathered, for the common affairs of the kirk, and may be called the general eldership of the whole kirks in the realm. None are subject to repair to this assembly to vote, but ecclesiastical persons, to such a number as shall be thought good by the same assembly, not excluding other persons, that will repair to the said assembly to propone, hear, and reason.

This assembly is instituted, that all things, either omitted or done amiss in the provincial assemblies, may be redressed and handled; and things, generally serving for the good of the whole body of the kirk within the realm, may be foreseen, treated, and set forth, to God's glory.

It should take care, that kirks be planted in places where they are not planted.

It should prescribe the rule, how the other two kinds of assemblies should proceed in all things.

This assembly should take heed that the spiritual jurisdiction and civil be not confounded, to the hurt of the kirk; that the patrimony of the kirk be not consumed nor abused; and generally concerning all weighty affairs, that concern the well and good order of the whole kirks of the realm, it ought to interpone authority thereto.

There is, beside these, another more general kind of assembly, which is, of all nations, and all estates of persons within the kirk, representing the universal kirk of Christ, which may be called properly the general assembly, or general council, of the whole kirk of God.

: These assemblies were appointed and called together, especially, when any great schism or controversy in doctrine did arise in the kirk; and were convocate at command of godly emperors being for the time, for avoiding of schisms within the universal kirk of God; which, because they pertain not to the particular estate of any realm, we cease further to speak of them.

CHAP. VIII.   *Of the Deacons and their Office, the last ordinary Function in the Kirk.*

The word *Diakanos* sometimes is largely taken, comprehending all them that bear office in the ministry, and spiritual function in the kirk.

But now, as we speak, it is taken only for them unto whom the collection and distribution of the alms of the faithful, and ecclesiastical goods, doth belong.

The office of the deacons, so taken, is an ordinary and perpetual ecclesiastical function in the kirk of Christ.

Of what properties and duties he ought

to be, that is called to this function, we remit
it to the manifest Scriptures.

The deacon ought to be called and elected,
as the rest of the spiritual officers, of the
which election was spoken before.

Their office and power is to receive and
to distribute the whole ecclesiastical goods
unto them to whom they are appointed.

This they ought to do, according to the
judgment and appointment of the presbyteries, or elderships (of the which the deacons
are not members), that the patrimony of the
kirk and poor be not converted to private
men's uses, nor wrongfully distribute.

CHAP. IX. *Of the Patrimony of the Kirk, and Distribution thereof.*

By the patrimony of the kirk, we mean,
whatsoever thing hath been at any time before, or shall be in times coming, given, or
by consent or universal custom of countries
professing the Christian religion applied to,
the public use and utility of the kirk.

So that under the patrimony we comprehend all things given, or to be given, to the
kirk and service of God; as lands, buildings,
possessions, annual rents, and all such like,
wherewith the kirk is doted, either by dona-
tions, foundations, mortifications, or any
other lawful titles, of kings, princes, or any
persons inferior to them, together with the
continual oblations of the faithful.

We comprehend also all such things, as by laws or custom, or use of countries, have been applied to the use and utility of the kirk; of the which sort are tiends, means, [manses], glebe, and such like, which by common and municipal laws, and universal custom, are possessed by the kirk.

To take any of this patrimony by unlawful means, and convert it to the particular and profane use of any person, we hold it a detestable sacrilege before God.

The goods ecclesiastical ought to be collected and distributed by the deacons, as the word of God appoints, that they who bear office in the kirk be provided for, without care or solicitude.

In the apostolical kirk, the deacons were appointed to collect and distribute what sum soever was collected of the faithful, to distribute unto the necessity of the saints; so that none lacked among the faithful.

These collections were, not only of that which was collected in manner of alms, as some suppose, but of other goods, moveable and immoveable, of lands and possessions, the price whereof was brought to the feet of the Apostles.

This office continued in the deacon's hands; who intromitted with the whole goods of the kirk, aye, and while the estate thereof was corrupted by Antichrist, as the ancient canons bear witness.

The same canons make mention of a four-fold distribution of the patrimony of the kirk, whereof one part was applied to the pastor, or bishop, for his sustentation and hospitality; another to the elders and deacons, and all the clergy; the third to the poor, sick persons, and strangers; the fourth to the upholding of other affairs of the kirk, especially extraordinary.

We add hereunto the schools and schoolmasters also, which ought and may be well sustained of the same goods, and are comprehended under the clergy. To whom we join also clerks of assemblies, as well particular as general, syndics, or procurators of the kirk affairs, takers-up of psalms, and such like other ordinary officers of the kirk, so far as they are necessary.

CHAP. X. *Of the Office of a Christian Magistrate in the Kirk.*

Although all the members of the kirk be holden, every one in their vocation, and according thereto, to advance the kingdom of Jesus Christ, so far as lieth in their power; yet chiefly Christian princes, and other magistrates, are holden to do the same.

For they are called in the Scripture, nourishers of the kirk; for so much as by them it is, or at least ought to be, maintained, fostered, upholden, and defended, against all that would procure the hurt thereof.

So it pertains to the office of a Christian magistrate, to assist and fortify the godly proceedings of the kirk, in all behalfs; and namely, to see that the public estate and ministry thereof be maintained and sustained, as it appertains, according to God's word.

To see that the kirk be not invaded, nor hurt by false teachers and hirelings; nor the rooms thereof occupied by dumb dogs, or idle bellies.

To assist and maintain the discipline of the kirk, and punish them civilly that will not obey the censure of the same, without confounding always the one jurisdiction with the other.

To see that sufficient provision be made for the ministry, the schools, and the poor: and, if they have not sufficient to await upon their charges, to supply their indigence even with their own rents, if need require.

To hold hand as well to the saving of their persons from injury and open violence, as to their rents and possessions, that they be not defrauded, robbed, nor spoiled thereof.

Not to suffer the patrimony of the kirk to be applied to profane and unlawful uses, or to be devoured by idle bellies, and such as have no lawful function in the kirk, to the hurt of the ministry, schools, poor, and other godly uses, whereupon the same ought to be bestowed.

To make laws and constitutions, agreeable

to God's word, for advancement of the kirk, and policy thereof, without usurping any thing that pertains not to the civil sword, but belongs to the offices that are merely ecclesiastical, as is the ministry of the word and sacraments, using ecclesiastical discipline, and the spiritual execution thereof, or any part of the power of the spiritual keys, which our Master gave to the Apostles, and to their true successors.

And although kings and princes that be godly, sometimes by their own authority, when the kirk is corrupted, and all things out of order, place ministers, and restore the true service of the Lord, after the example of some godly kings of Judah, and divers godly emperors, and kings also, in the light of the New Testament; yet, where the ministry of the kirk is once lawfully constitute, and they that are placed do their office faithfully, all godly princes and magistrates ought to hear and obey their voice, and reverence the majesty of the Son of God speaking in them.

CHAP. XI. *Of the present Abuses remaining in the Kirk, which we desire to be reformed.*

As it is the duty of the godly magistrate to maintain the present liberty, which God hath granted to the preaching of his word, and the true administration of the sacraments within this realm; so it is to provide, that all abuses which yet remain in the kirk be removed, and utterly taken away.

Therefore, first, the admission of men to papistical titles of benefices, such as serve not, nor have no function in the reformed kirk of Christ, as abbots, commendators, priors, prioresses, and other titles of abbacies, whose places are now for the most part, by the just judgment of God, demolished, and purged of idolatry, is a plain abuse, and is not to receive the kingdom of Christ among us, but rather to refuse it.

Such like, that they that of old were called the chapters and convents of abbeys, cathedral kirks, and like places, serve for nothing now but to set feus and tacks, if any thing be left of the kirk lands and tiends, in hurt and prejudice thereof, as daily experience teacheth; and therefore ought to be utterly abrogate and abolished.

Of the like nature are the deans, archdeacons, chanters, subchanters, treasurers, chancellors, and others having the like titles, flowing from the pope and canon law only, who have no place in the reformed kirk.

The kirks also which are united together, and joined by annexation to their benefices, ought to be separated and divided, and given to qualified ministers, as God's word craves.

Neither ought such abusers of the kirk patrimony to have vote in parliament, nor sit in council, under the name of the kirk and kirkmen, to the hurt and prejudice of the liberty thereof, and laws of the realm, made in favour of the reformed kirk.

Much less is it lawful, that any person amongst these men should have five, sixteen, twenty, or more kirks, all having the charge of souls, and enjoy the patrimony thereof, either by admission of the prince, or of the kirk, in this light of the Evangel. For it is but a mockage, to crave reformation where such like have place.

And in so far as, in the order taken at Leith in the year of our Lord 1571, it appears that such may be admitted, being found qualified : either that pretended order is against all good order, or else it must be understood, not of them that be qualified in worldly affairs, or to serve in court; but of such as are qualified to teach God's word, having their lawful admission of the kirk.

As to bishops, if the name *Episkopos* be properly taken, they are all one with the ministers, as was before declared. For it is not a name of superiority and lordship, but of office and watching.

Yet, because in the corruption of the kirk, this name (as others) hath been abused, and yet is likely to be, we cannot allow the fashion of these new chosen bishops, neither of the chapters, that are electors of them to such an office as they are chosen unto.

True bishops should addict themselves to a particular flock, which sundry of them refuse; neither should they usurp lordship over their brethren, and over the inheritance of Christ, as these men do.

Pastors, in so far as they are pastors, have not the office of visitation of more kirks joined to the pastorship, without it be given to them.

It is a corruption, that bishops should have further bounds to visit nor they may lawfully.

No man ought to have the office of visitation, but he that is lawfully chosen thereunto.

The elderships, being well established, have power to send out visitors, one or more, with commission to visit the bounds within their their eldership; and likewise, after account taken of them, either continue them, or remove them from time to time, to the which elderships they should be always subject.

The civil jurisdiction in the person of a pastor, is a corruption. It agreeth not with the word of God, that bishops should be pastors of pastors, pastors of many flocks, and yet without a certain flock, and without ordinary teaching.

It agreeth not with the Scriptures, that they should be exeemed from the correction of their brethren, and discipline of the particular eldership of the kirk where they shall serve; neither that they usurp the office of

visitation of other kirks, nor any other function beside other ministers, but so far as
shall be committed to them by the kirk.

Wherefore we desire the bishops that now
are, either to agree to that order that God's
word requires in them, as the general kirk
will prescribe unto them, not passing their
bounds either in ecclesiastical or civil affairs,
or else to be deposed from all function in the
kirk.

We deny not, in the mean time, but ministers may and should assist their princes,
when they are required, in all things agreeable to the word, whether it be in council
or parliament, or otherwise ; providing always
they neither neglect their own charges, nor,
through flattery of princes, hurt the public
estate of the kirk.

But generally we say, no person, under
whatsomever title of the kirk, and specially
the abused titles in papistry, of prelates, convents, and chapters, ought to attempt any
act in the kirk's name, either in council or
parliament, or out of council, having no commission of the reformed kirk within this
realm.

And by act of parliament it is provided,
that the papistical kirk and jurisdiction
should have no place within the same ; and
no bishop nor other prelate, in times coming,
should use any jurisdiction flowing from his
authority.

And again, that no other ecclesiastical jurisdiction should be acknowledged within this realm, but that which is and shall be in the reformed kirk, and flowing therefrom.

So we esteem holding of chapters in a papistical manner, either in cathedral kirks, abbeys, colleges, or other conventual places, usurping the name and authority of the kirk, to hurt the patrimony thereof, or use any other act to the prejudice of the same, since the year of our Lord 1560, to be an abuse and corruption, contrary to the liberty of the true kirk and laws of the realm; and therefore ought to be annulled, reduced, and, in times coming, utterly discharged.

The dependencies also of the papistical jurisdiction are to be abolished; of the which sort is the mixed jurisdiction of the commissars, in so far as they meddle with ecclesiastical matters, and have no commission of the kirk thereto, but were elected in time of our sovereign's mother, when things were out of order. It is an absurd thing, that several of them, having no function of the kirk, should be judges to ministers, and depose them from their places. Therefore they either should be discharged to meddle with ecclesiastical matters; or it should be limited to them in what matters they might be judges, and not hurt the liberty of the kirk.

They also that formerly were of the ecclesiastic estate in the pope's kirk, or that are admitted of new to the papistical titles, and now are tolerate by the laws of the realm to possess the two parts of their ecclesiastical rents, ought not to have any further liberty, but to intromit with the portion assigned and granted to them for their life-times, and not, under the abused titles which they had, to dispone the kirk-rents, set tacks and feus thereof at their pleasure, to the great hurt of the kirk, and poor labourers that dwell upon the kirk-lands, contrary to all good conscience and order.

CHAP. XII. *Certain special Heads of Reformation which we crave.*

Whatsoever hath been spoken of the offices of the kirk, of the several power of the office-bearers, of their conjunct power also, and lastly, of the patrimony of the kirk, we understand it to be the right reformation which God craves at our hands, that the kirk be ordered according thereto, as with that order which is most agreeable to the word.

But, because something should be touched in particular concerning the estate of the country, and that which we principally seek to be reformed in the same, we have collected them in these heads following.

Seeing the whole country is divided in provinces, and these provinces again are divided in parishes, as well in landward as in towns; in every parish and reasonable con-

H

gregation, there should be placed one or more
pastors, to feed the flock; and no pastor or
minister always be burdened with the particular charge of more kirks or flocks than
one alone.

And because it would be thought hard to
find out pastors or ministers to all the parish
kirks of the realm, as well in landward as in
towns; we think, by the advice of such as
commission may be given to by the kirk and
prince, parishes in landward, or small villages, may be joined, two or three, or more
in some places, together, and the principal
and most commodious kirks to stand, and be
repaired sufficiently, and qualified ministers
placed thereat; and the other kirks, which
are not found necessary, may be suffered to
decay, their kirk-yards always being kept for
burial places; and in some places, where
need requires, a parish, where the congregation is over great for one kirk, may be divided
in two or more.

Doctors should be appointed in universities,
colleges, and in other places needful, and
sufficiently provided for, to open up the
meaning of the Scriptures, and to have the
charge of schools, and teach the rudiments
of religion.

As for elders, there should be some to be
censurers of the manners of the people, one
or more in every congregation, but not an
assembly of elders in every particular kirk,

but only in towns and famous places, where resort of men of judgment and ability, to that effect, may be had ; where the elders of the particular kirks about may convene together, and have a common eldership, and assembly-place among them, to treat of all things that concern the congregations of which they have the oversight.

And as there ought to be men appointed to unite and divide the parishes, as necessity and commodity requires ; so there should be appointed by the general kirk, with the assent of the prince, such men as fear God, and know the estate of the countries, that were able to nominate and design the places where the particular elderships should convene, taking consideration of the dioceses, as they were divided of old, and of the estate of the countries and provinces of the realm.

Likewise, concerning provincial and synodal assemblies, consideration were easy to be taken ; how many, and in what places they were to be holden, and how oft they should convene, ought to be referred to the liberty of the general kirk, and order to be appointed therein.

The national assemblies of this country, called commonly the general assemblies, ought always to be retained in their own liberty, and have their own place ; with power to the kirk to appoint times and places convenient for the same ; and all men, as well magistrates as inferiors, to be subject to the judgment of the same, in ecclesiastical causes, without any reclamation or appellation to any judge, civil or ecclesiastical, within the realm.

The liberty of the election of persons called to the ecclesiastical functions, and observed without interruption, so long as the kirk was not corrupted by Antichrist, we desire to be restored and retained within this realm; so that none be intruded upon any congregation, either by the prince, or any inferior person, without lawful election, and the assent of the people over whom the person is placed; as the practice of the apostolical and primitive kirk, and good order, crave.

And because this order, which God's word craves, cannot stand with patronages and presentations to benefices used in the pope's kirk, we desire all them that truly fear God, earnestly to consider, that forasmuch as the names of patronages and benefices, together with the effect thereof, have flowed from the pope, and corruption of the canon law only, in so far as thereby any person was intruded or placed over kirks, having *curam anima-rum;* and forasmuch as that manner of proceeding hath no ground in the word of God, but is contrary to the same, and to the said liberty of election, they ought not now to have place in this light of reformation : and therefore, whosoever will embrace God's word, and desire the kingdom of his Son

Christ Jesus to be advanced, they will also embrace and receive that policy and order, which the word of God, and upright estate of his kirk, crave: otherwise it is in vain that they have professed the same.

Notwithstanding, as concerning other patronages of benefices, that have not *curam animarum*, as they speak, such as are chaplainries, prebendaries, founded upon temporal lands, annuals, and such like, may be reserved unto the ancient patrons, to dispone hereupon, when they vaike, to scholars and bursars, as they are required by act of parliament.

As for the kirk-rents in general, we desire that order be admitted and maintained amongst us, that may stand with the sincerity of God's word, and practice of the kirk of Christ:

To wit; That, as was before spoken, the whole rent and patrimony of the kirk, excepting the patronages before mentioned, may be divided in four portions: one thereof to be assigned to the pastor for his entertainment and hospitality; another to the elders, deacons, and other officers of the kirk, such as clerks of assemblies, takers-up of the psalms, bedals, and keepers of the kirk, so far as is necessary; joining with them also the doctors and schools, to help the ancient foundations where need requires: the third portion to be bestowed upon the poor members of the faithful, and on hospitals: the fourth for reparation of the kirks, and other extraordinary charges, as are profitable for the kirk; and also for the commonwealth, if need require.

We desire therefore the ecclesiastical goods to be uplifted, and distributed faithfully to whom they appertain; and that by the ministry of the deacons, to whose office properly the collection and distribution thereof belongs; that the poor may be answered of their portion thereof, and they of the ministry live without care and solicitude: as also, the rest of the treasure of the kirk may be reserved and bestowed to their right uses.

If these deacons be elected with such qualities as God's word craves to be in them, there is no fear that they shall abuse themselves in their office, as the profane collectors did before.

Yet, because this vocation appeareth to many to be dangerous, let them be obliged, as they were of old, to give a yearly account to the pastors and eldership; and, if the kirk and prince think expedient, let cautioners be obliged for their fidelity, that the kirk-rents nowise be dilapidate.

And, to the effect this order may take place, it is to be provided, that all other intromitters with the kirk-rent, collectors general or special, whether it be by appointment of the prince or otherwise, may be denuded of further intromission therewith, and suffer the kirk-rents, in time coming, to be wholly intromitted with by the ministry of the deacons, and distribute to the use before mentioned.

And also, to the effect that the ecclesiastical rents may suffice to those uses for the which they are to be appointed, we think it necessary to be desired, that all alienations, setting of feus, or tacks of the rents of the kirk, as well lands as tiends, in hurt and diminution of the old rentals, be reduced and annulled, and the patrimony of the kirk restored to the former old liberty.

And likewise, that in times coming the tiends be set to none but to the labourers of the ground, or else not set at all; as was agreed upon, and subscribed by the nobility before.

CHAP. XIII. *The Utility that shall flow from this Reformation to all Estates.*

Seeing the end of this spiritual government and policy, whereof we speak, is, that God may be glorified, the kingdom of Jesus Christ advanced, and all who are of his mystical body may live peaceably in conscience; therefore we dare boldly affirm, that all those who have true respect to these ends, will, even for conscience cause, gladly agree and conform themselves to this order, and advance the same, so far as lieth in them, that, their conscience being set at rest, they may be replenished with spiritual gladness, in giving full obedience to that which God's word and the testimony of their own conscience do crave, and in refusing all corruption contrary to the same.

Next; We shall become an example and pattern of good and godly order to other nations, countries, and kirks, professing the same religion with us; that as they have glorified God, in our continuing in the sincerity of the word hitherto, without any errors (praise to his Name!), so they may have the like occasion in our conversation, whenas we conform ourselves to that discipline, policy, and good order which the same word and purity of reformation crave at our hands. Otherwise that fearful sentence may be justly said to us, "The servant knowing the will of his master, and not doing it," &c.

Moreover, if we have any pity or respect to the poor members of Jesus Christ, who so greatly increase and multiply amongst us, we will not suffer them to be longer defrauded of that part of the patrimony of the kirk which justly belongs unto them: and by this order, if it be duly put to execution, the burden of them shall be taken off us, to our great comfort; the streets shall be cleansed of the cryings and murmurings of them, so as we shall no more be any scandal to other

nations, as we have hitherto been, for not
taking order with the poor amongst us, and
causing the word which we profess to be evil
spoken of, giving an occasion of slander to
the enemies, and offending the consciences
of the simple and godly.

Besides this, it shall be a great ease and
commodity to the whole common people, in
relieving them of the building and upholding
their kirks, in building of bridges and other
like public works; to the labourers of the
ground, in payment of their tiends; and,
shortly, in all those things whereinto they
have been hitherto rigorously handled by
them that were falsely called kirk-men, their
tacksmen, factors, chamberlains, and extor-
tioners.

Finally; To the king's majesty, and commonwealth of the country, this profit shall
redound, that, the other affairs of the kirk
being sufficiently provided, according to the
distribution, of the which hath been spoken,
the superplus, being collected in the treasure
of the kirk, may be profitably employed, and
liberally bestowed upon the extraordinary
support of the affairs of the prince and commonwealth; and especially of that part which
is appointed for reparation of kirks.

So, to conclude; all being willing to apply
themselves to this order; the people suffering
themselves to be ruled according thereto;
the prince and magistrates not being ex-

eemed, and they that are placed in the ecclesiastical estate rightly ruling and governing; God shall be glorified, the kirk edified, and the bounds thereof enlarged; Christ Jesus and his kingdom set up; Satan and his kingdom subverted; and God shall dwell in the midst of us, to our comfort, through Jesus Christ; who, together with the Father and the Holy Ghost, abides blessed in all eternity. *Amen.*

Assembly at Edinburgh, 4th August 1590. Sess. 10.

Forasmuch as it is certain that the word of God cannot be kept in its own sincerity without the holy discipline be had in observance; it is therefore, by common consent of the whole brethren and commissioners present, concluded, that whosoever hath borne office in the ministry of the kirk within this realm, or that presently bears, or shall hereafter bear office herein, shall be charged by every particular presbytery where their residence is, to subscribe the heads of discipline of the kirk of this realm, at length set down, and allowed by act of the whole assembly, in the book of policy, which is registrate in the assembly books; and namely, the heads, controverted by enemies of the discipline of the reformed kirk of this realm, betwixt and the next synodal assemblies of the provinces, under the pain of excommunication, to be executed against the non-subscribers; and the presbyteries which shall be found remiss or negligent herein, to receive public rebuke of the whole assembly: and to the effect the said discipline may be known, as it ought to be, to the whole brethren, it is ordained, that the moderator of each presbytery shall receive, from the clerk of the assembly, a copy of the said book under his subscription, upon the expenses of the presbytery, betwixt and the 1st day of September next to come, under the pain to be openly accused in face of the whole assembly.

A FORM

OF

EXAMINATION *before the* COMMUNION.

APPROVED BY THE

GENERAL ASSEMBLY OF THE KIRK
OF SCOTLAND;

AND

𝕬𝖕𝖕𝖔𝖎𝖓𝖙𝖊𝖉 𝖙𝖔 𝖇𝖊 𝖚𝖘𝖊𝖉 𝖎𝖓 𝔉𝖆𝖒𝖎𝖑𝖎𝖊𝖘 𝖆𝖓𝖉 𝕾𝖈𝖍𝖔𝖔𝖑𝖘.

WITH PROOFS FROM THE SCRIPTURE.

Assembly 1590. *Sess.* 12. *August* 10.

Anent the examination before the communion, it is thought meet for the common profit of the whole people, that ane uniforme order be keepit in examination, and that ane schort forme of examination be set down, be their breither, Mess. John Craig, Robert Pont, Thomas Buchanan, and Andrew Melvine, to be presentit to the next Assembly.

Assembly 1591. *Sess.* 17. *July* 13.

Anent the forme of examination before the communion, pennit be their brother Mr. Craig, the Assembly thought it meet to be imprintit, being be the author thairof contractit in some schorter bounds.

Assembly 1592. *Sess.* 10. *May* 30.

For swa meikle as, at the special desire of the kirk, ane forme of examination before the communion was pennit and formit be their brother Mr. John Craig, quhilk is now imprintit, and allowit be the voyce of the Assembly: Therefore it is thought needful that every pastor travel with his flock, that they may buy the samen buik, and read it in their families, quhereby they may be better instructit; and that the samen be read and learnit in lectors' schools, in place of the Little Catechism *.

* That is, The Manner to examine Children, at the end of Calvin's Catechism.

A FORM

OF

EXAMINATION BEFORE THE COMMUNION.

I. *Of our miserable Bondage through Adam.*

Q. 1. WHAT are we by nature?—A. The children of God's wrath, Eph. ii. 3.

Q. 2. Were we thus created of God?—A. No: for he made us to his own image, Gen. i. 26.

Q. 3. How came we to this misery?—A. Through the fall of Adam from God, Gen. iii.

Q. 4. What things came to us by that fall?—A. Original sin, and natural corruption, Rom. v. 12, 18, 19.

Q. 5. What power have we to turn to God?—A. None at all; for we are dead in sin, Eph. ii. 1.

Q. 6. What is the punishment of our sin?—A. Death eternal, both in body and soul, Rom. vi. 23.

II. *Of our Redemption by Christ.*

Q. 7. Who may deliver us from this bondage?—A. God only, who bringeth life out of death.

Q. 8. How know we that he will do it?—A. By his promise, and sending his Son Christ Jesus in our flesh, John iii. 16, 17.

Q. 9. What kind of person is Christ?—A. Perfect God and perfect man, without sin, Matt. i. 23, Luke i. 31.

Q. 10. What needed this wonderful union?—A. That he might be a meet Mediator for us.

Q. 11. How did he redeem us?—A. Through his obedience to the law, and death of the cross, Phil. ii. 8.

Q. 12. Suffered he only natural death?—A. No: but he suffered also the curse of God, in body and soul, Gal. iii. 13.

Q. 13. How know we that his death brought life to us?—A. By his glorious resurrection and ascension.

Q. 14. Wherefore that?—A. For if he hath not satisfied for all our sins perfectly, he hath not risen, nor we by him, 1 Cor. xv. 14, 17.

Q. 15. Is it needful that we believe these mysteries?—A. No doubt, but yet that is not enough, Jam. ii. 17, 20.

Q. 16. What more is required?—A. That we be made partakers of Christ and his merits, John xv. 4—7.

III. *Of our Participation with Christ.*

Q. 17. How is that wrought?—A. Through his continual intercession for us in heaven Heb. vii. 25.

Q. 18. Declare how that is done?—A. Hereby the Holy Spirit is sent, John xiv. 16, 26.

Q. 19. What doth the Spirit in this work?—A. He offereth Christ and his graces to us, and moveth us to receive him.

Q. 20. How doth he offer Christ to us?—A. By the preaching of the Evangel, Rom. x. 13—15.

Q. 21. How doth he move us to receive him?—A. Through printing in our hearts true faith in Christ, Acts xvi. 14.

Q. 22. What thing is faith in Christ?—A. A sure persuasion that he is the only Saviour of the world, but ours in special, who believe in him, John vi.

Q. 23. What doth this faith work?—A. Our inseparable union with Christ in his graces, Eph. iii. 16—19.

Q. 24. What is the first fruit of this union?—A. Remission of our sins, and imputation of justice, Rom. vi. 19.

Q. 25. Which is the next fruit of our union with him?—A. Our sanctification and regeneration to the image of God, John iii. 3, 5.

Q. 26. Who doth this, and how?—A. The

Holy Spirit, through our union with Christ, in his death, burial, and resurrection, Rom. vi.

Q. 27. What are the chief parts of our regeneration ?—A. Mortification of sin, and rising to righteousness, Rom. vi.

Q. 28. How know we sin and righteousness ?—A. By the just and perfect law of God, Rom. vii.

IV. *Of the Word.*

Q. 29. Where shall we find the word of God ?—A. Only in the Holy Scriptures, Rom. xv. 4.

Q. 30. Are the Scriptures sufficient for our instruction ?—A. No doubt, as the Apostles do testify, John xx. 31, Gal. i. 8, 2 Tim. iii. 16.

Q. 31. How should we receive and use the word ?—A. We should read it privately and publicly with all reverence, Deut. xxxi. 21.

Q. 32. Is this sufficient for our instruction ?—A. No, if public teaching may be had, Eph. iv. 11, 12.

Q. 33. Wherefore that ?—A. For as God raiseth public teachers and pastors, so he hath commanded us to hear them, Mal. ii. 7.

Q. 34. How long should we continue in this school ?—A. All the days of our lives, seeing we are ignorant, forgetful, and easy to be deceived, Col. iii. 16.

Q. 35. What then serve the sacraments for ?—A. They are added for our further

comfort and admonition, as a visible word,
Gen. xvii. 9—11, Exod. xii.

V. *Of our Liberty to serve God.*

Q. 36. What good things may we do now,
being thus regenerated?—A. We may serve
our God freely and uprightly, Rom. xii.

Q. 37. May we do it perfectly according
to the Law?—A. No truly, for our regeneration is not perfect, Gal. v. 17, Eccles. vii. 22.

Q. 38. What followeth upon that?—A.
A certain rebellion of the flesh against the
Spirit, Rom. vii. 15—25.

Q. 39. Is not this rebellion cursed by the
Law?—A. Yea, truly; but yet it is not imputed to us, 2 Cor. v. 19.

Q. 40. Wherefore that, seeing it is sin,
and the root of all our sins?—A. Because
Christ satisfied all the points of the Law for
us, Rom. iii. 21, &c.

Q. 41. What are we, then, who believe in
Christ?—A. Just in him, but sinners in ourselves, Rom. viii.

Q. 42. What craveth this confession of
us?—A. A constant faith in Christ, and
continual repentance.

Q. 43. What then is our only joy in life
and death?—A. That all our sins bypast,
present, and to come, are buried; and Christ
only is made our wisdom, justification, sanctification, and redemption, 1 Cor. i. 30.

Q. 44. What fruit cometh of this faith?—

A. Peace of conscience, and joy in the Spirit, in all our troubles within and without, Rom. v. 2, 2 Cor. vi. 4.

Q. 45. What shall we gather of this whole discourse?—A. How miserable we are through Adam, and how blessed through Christ, Phil. iii. 8.

Q. 46. When should we remember of this doctrine?—A. At all times, but chiefly when we are touched with a proud opinion of our own worthiness, or are troubled in conscience for sin, Luke xviii. 19.

Q. 47. Then this meditation serveth for a preparation to the holy sacraments?—A. Yea truly, if they be rightly considered.

VI. *Of the Sacraments.*

Q. 48. Declare that in Baptism.—A. We see there the seal of our spiritual filthiness through our communion with Adam, and our purgation by our communion with Christ.

Q. 49. Declare the same in the Supper.— A. We see, feel, and taste there also, the seal of our spiritual wants, and death through Adam; and likewise of our spiritual treasures, and life through Christ only.

Q. 50. How contract we our spiritual filthiness from Adam?—A. Through our natural communion with him, Rom. v. 12, &c.

Q. 51. How came we to our spiritual purgation, and life by Christ?—A. Through our spiritual communion with our second Adam, Head and Spouse, Eph. v. 30.

Q. 52. Do the word and the sacraments work this communion?—A. No: for it is the work of the Spirit only; Eph. iii. 16.

Q. 53. Whereunto do the word and sacraments lead us?—A. Directly to the cross and death of Christ, 1 Cor. i. 17, 18, 23, 24.

Q. 54. Wherefore that?—A. Because through his cross and death the wrath of God was quenched, and all his blessings made ours, Gal. iii. 13, 14.

Q. 55. Why was this high mystery represented by these weak and common elements?—A. Because they express most lively our spiritual purging and feeding, which we have by Christ, John vi. 32, &c.

Q. 56. When doth he these things to us in very deed?—A. When he is so joined with us, and we with him, that he abideth in us, and we in him spiritually, John xv. 4, 5.

Q. 57. How is this union and abiding expressed here?—A. By natural washing, eating, drinking, digesting, feeding, and abiding in us.

Q. 58. How may we feel and know this spiritual abiding in us?—A. By the testimony of the Spirit in us, and external actions agreeable to Christ in us, Matt. vii. 6, Rom. viii. 16.

Q. 59. Then Christ is not an idle guest in us?—A. No, truly; for he came not only with water and blood, but also with the Spirit, to assure us, in some measure, of his presence in us, 1 John v. 6.

VII. *Of Baptism.*

Q. 60. What signifieth Baptism unto us ?— A. That we are filthy by nature, and are purged by the blood of Christ, Titus iii. 5.

Q. 61. What meaneth this our union with the water?—A. Our spiritual union with Jesus Christ, Rom. vi. 3, 8, Gal. iii. 27.

Q. 62. What followeth upon this our union with him?—A. Remission of sins and regeneration, Rom. vi. 4, 18, 22.

Q. 63. From whence cometh our regeneration?—A. From the communion with the death, burial, and resurrection of Christ, Rom. vi. 4, 5, 8.

Q. 64. How long, and by what way doth Baptism work in us?—A. All the days of our life, through faith and repentance, 1 Cor. vi. 19, 20.

Q. 65. How then are infants baptized?— A. Upon the promise made to the faithful and their seed, Gen. xvii. 7, 10.

Q. 66. How doth Baptism differ from the Supper?—A. In the elements, action, rites, signification, and use.

Q. 67. Wherefore is Baptism but once ministered?—A. It is enough to be received once in the house of God, Rom. viii. 16.

Q. 68. Declare the cause of that?—A. For

they are never casten out, who are once truly received in his society, John vi. 37.

Q. 69. Why is the Supper so oft ministered?—A. We have need to be fed continually, John vi. 55.

Q. 70. Why is not the Supper ministered to infants?—A. Because they cannot examine themselves, 1 Cor. xi. 28.

VIII. *Of the Supper.*

Q. 71. What signifieth the action of the Supper?—A. That our souls are fed spiritually, by the body and blood of Jesus Christ, John vi. 54.

Q. 72. When is this done?—A. When we feel the efficacy of his death in our conscience by the spirit of faith, John vi. 63.

Q. 73. Why is this sacrament given in meat and drink?—A. To seal up our near conjunction with Christ.

Q. 74. Wherefore is both meat and drink given?—A. To testify that Christ is the whole food of our souls, John vi.

Q. 75. Is Christ's body in the elements? A. No; but it is in heaven, Acts i. 11.

Q. 76. Why then is the element called his body?—A. Because it is a sure seal of his body given to our souls.

Q. 77. To whom should this sacrament be given?—A. To the faithful only, who can examine themselves.

Q. 78. Wherein should they examine themselves?—A. In faith and repentance, with their fruits.

Q. 79. What should pastors do, when men are negligent, and abuse the sacraments?—A. They should use the order of discipline established in the word.

IX. *Of Discipline.*

Q. 80. Who should use this discipline?—A. The pastors and elders, by their mutual consent and judgment.

Q. 81. What is the office of the eldership?—A. To watch upon their flock, and exercise the discipline.

Q. 82. How is this done?—A. By private and public admonition, and other censures of the kirk, as need requireth.

Q. 83. Who ought to be excluded from the sacraments?—A. All infidels and public slanderers.

Q. 84. Wherefore are these excluded?—A. Lest they should hurt themselves, slander the kirk, and dishonour God.

X. *Of the Magistrate.*

Q. 85. What is the office of the Christian magistrate in the kirk?—A. He should defend the true religion and discipline, and punish all troublers and contemners of the same.

XI. *Of the Table in special.*

Q. 86. Why use we a table here, and not an altar, as the fathers did at God's commandment?—A. Because we convene, not to offer a sacrifice for sin, but to eat and drink of that sacrifice, which Christ once offered upon the cross for us, Heb. vii. 23, 24, 27, and x. 11, 12, 14, 18.

Q. 87. What profess we when we come to the table?—A. That we are dead in ourselves, and seek our life only in Christ.

Q. 88. Shall this confession of our unworthiness be a stay to come to the communion?—A. No, truly; but rather a preparation to the same, if faith and repentance be with it, Mark ii. 17.

Q. 89. Wherefore is there mention made here of Christ's body and blood severally?—A. To testify his death, by the which only he was made our spiritual meat and drink, John vi. 51, 55.

Q. 90. For what cause is this action called the communion?—A. Because it is the true cause of our mutual society with Christ in all things, good and evil.

Q. 91. Declare how that is performed?—A. Hereby he removeth all evil things from us, which we have by nature; and we receive of him all good things, which we want by nature.

Q. 92. Declare these things more plainly?—A. The wrath of God and sin is removed, which we have by nature; and the favour of God, and adoption, with the joy of heaven is restored to us, the which things we have not by nature, Rom. viii.

Q. 93. What things then may the faithful soul say?—A. Now live I; not I, but Christ liveth in me: it is God that justifieth, who shall condemn?

Q. 94. Let us therefore give thanks, and pass to this holy action, every one of us saying and singing in his heart, "The Lord is the portion of mine inheritance and of my cup; thou shalt maintain my lot: the lines are fallen unto me in pleasant places; yea, I have a fair heritage," Psal. xvi. 5, 6.—A. Let it be done so with heart and mouth, to the confusion of all idolaters, and glory of our God.

XII. *The End of our Redemption.*

Q. 95. To what end are we thus redeemed, and brought in hope of that endless joy to come?—A. To move us effectually to deny all ungodliness, worldly lusts, and unrighteousness, and so live godly, soberly, and righteously in this present world, looking for the coming of Christ for our full redemption, Tit. ii. 11—13.

Q. 96. What shall be the final end of all these graces?—A. God shall be glorified for ever in mercy, and we shall enjoy that endless life with Christ our Head, to whom, with the Father, and the Holy Spirit, be all honour and glory for ever. *Amen.*

APPENDIX,

APPENDIX.

The Confession of Faith used in the English Congregation at Geneva;

Received and approved by the Church of Scotland in the Beginning of the Reformation.

I.

I BELIEVE and confess (*a*) my Lord God *I believe in* eternal, infinite, unmeasurable, incompre- *God the* hensible, and invisible(*b*), one in substance(*c*), *Father Al-* and three in persons, Father, Son, and Holy *mighty,* Ghost (*d*): who by his almighty power and *Maker of* wisdom (*e*), hath not only of nothing created *heaven and* heaven, earth, and all things therein con- *earth;* tained (*f*), and man after his own image (*g*), that he might in him be glorified (*h*); but also by his fatherly providence governeth, maintaineth, and preserveth the same(*i*), according to the purpose of his will (*k*).

(*a*) Rom. x. 10.   (*b*) Gen. xvii. 1 ; Psal. lxiii. 1, xc. 2, cxxxix. 1, 16 ; 1 Tim. i. 17.   (*c*) Deut. vi. 4 ; Eph. iv. 6.   (*d*) Gen. i. 26 ; Matt. iii. 16, 17, xxviii. 19 ; 1 John v. 7.   (*e*) Heb. i. 2 ; Prov. viii. 22, 30. (*f*) Gen. i. 1 ; Jer. xxxii. 16 ; Psal. xxxiii. 6, 7. (*g*) Gen. i. 26 ; Eph. iv. 24 ; Col. iii. 10.   (*h*) Prov. xvi. 4 ; John xvii. 1 ; 1 Cor. vi. 20.   (*i*) Matt. vi. 26, 32 ; Luke xii. 24, 30 ; 1 Pet. v. 7 ; Phil. iv. 6. (*k*) Eph. i. 11.

II.

And in Je- I believe also and confess JESUS CHRIST,
sus Christ, the only Saviour and Messias (*l*), who, being
his only equal with God, made himself of no repu-
Son our tation; but took on him the shape of a ser-
Lord, vant (*m*), and became man, in all things like
unto us, sin excepted (*n*), to assure us of
mercy and forgiveness (*o*): for when through
our father Adam's transgression, we were
become children of perdition (*p*), there was
no means to bring us from that yoke of sin
and damnation, but only Jesus Christ our
Lord (*q*), who giving us that by grace which
was his by nature (*r*), made us through faith
the children of God (*s*).

Who was Who, when the fulness of time was
conceived come (*t*), was conceived by the power of the
by the Holy Holy Ghost, born of the Virgin Mary, accord-
Ghost, ing to the flesh (*u*), and preached in earth
born of the the Gospel of salvation (*w*), till at length, by
Virgin tyranny of the priests, he was guiltless con-
Mary, suf- demned under Pontius Pilate, then president
feredunder of Jewry, and most slanderously hanged on
Pontius the cross between two thieves, as a notorious
Pilate, trespasser (*x*); where, taking upon him the

(*l*) Matt. i. 21; Acts iv. 12; 1 Tim i. 15.   (*m*) John
i.; Phil. ii. 6, 7; 1 Tim. iii. 16; 1 John v. 20; Rom.
ix. 5.   (*n*) Heb. ii. 14, 16, 17; Phil. ii. 7, 8; 1 Pet.
ii. 22; 1 John iii. 5.   (*o*) Rom. viii. 31, &c.;
1 John ii. 1.   (*p*) Gen. iii.; Rom. v. 16—18;
Eph. ii. 3; Gal. iii. 10, 13.   (*q*) Acts iv. 12;
1 Pet. ii. 6; Isai. xxviii. 16; Rom. ix. 33.   (*r*) John
i. 1, 2; Heb. i. 5; Rom. i. 4; Psal. ii. 7.   (*s*) Gal.
iii. 26; Rom. viii. 14; John i. 12; Eph. i. 5.   (*t*) Gal.
iv. 4; Rom. i. 2, 3; Acts ii. 22.   (*u*) Isai. vii. 14;
Luke i. 31, 35; Rom. i. 3. (*w*) Acts x. 36; Heb. i. 1.
(*x*) John vii. 32, xi. 47, 48, 53, xii. 10, 11, 42; Matt. xii.
14, and xxvii.; Luke xxiii.; Mark xv.; John xviii. xix.

.punishment of our sins, he delivered us from *was cru-*
the curse of the law (*y*).   *cified,*

And forasmuch as he, being only God,
could not feel death; neither, being only *Dead and*
man, could overcome death; he joined both *buried.*
together, and suffered his humanity to be
punished with most cruel death (*z*), feeling in
himself the anger and, severe judgment of
God, even as if he had been in the extreme *He de-*
torments of hell, and therefore cried with a *scended*
loud voice, "My God, my God, why hast *into hell.*
thou forsaken me? (*a*) "

Thus of his free mercy, without compulsion, he offered up himself as the only sacrifice to purge the sins of all the world (*b*); so
that all other sacrifices for sin are blasphemous, and derogate from the sufficiency
hereof. ·

The which death, albeit it did sufficiently
reconcile us to God (*c*), yet the Scriptures
do commonly attribute our regeneration to *The third*
his resurrection (*d*): for as by rising again *day he rose*
from the grave the third day (*e*), he con- *again from*
quered death (*f*); even so the victory of our *death.*
faith standeth in his resurrection, and therefore without the one we cannot feel the benefit of the other: for as by his death sin was
taken away, so our righteousness was restored
by his resurrection (*g*).

And because he would accomplish all things,

(*y*) Gal. iii. 13; Isai. liii. 6, 8, 10.   (*z*) Acts ii. 24;
1 Pet. ii. 24; Isai. liii. 4, 5, 7, 10.   (*a*) Psal. xxii. 1;
Matt. xxvii. 46.   (*b*) Isai. liii.; Heb. ix. 12, 14, 25,
26, 28, and x. 10, 12, 14; Gal. i. 4; Rom. iv. 25, and
v. 8—10; 1 John i. 7.   (*c*) Col. i. 20.   (*d*) Rom.
vi. 4, 5; 1 Pet. i. 3.   (*e*) Matt. xxviii.; Acts x. 40;
1 Cor. xv. 4.   (*f*) Hos. xiii. 14; 1 Cor. xv. 26,
55—57:   (*g*) Rom. iv. 25.

He ascend- and take possession for us in his kingdom (*h*),
ed into he ascended into heaven (*i*), to enlarge that
heaven, same kingdom by the abundant power of
his Spirit (*k*), by whom we are most assured
of his continual intercession towards God the
And sitteth Father for us (*l*). And although he be in
at the right heaven, as touching his corporal presence (*m*),
hand of where the Father hath now set him at his
God the right hand (*n*), committing unto him the ad-
Father ministration of all things, as well in heaven
Almighty. above, as in the earth beneath (*o*); yet is he
present with us his members, even to the
end of the world (*p*), in preserving and governing us with his effectual power and grace.
Who (when all things are fulfilled which
God hath spoken by the mouth of all his pro-
From phets, since the world began, *q*) will come
thence he in the same visible form in the which he
shall come ascended (*r*), with an unspeakable majesty,
to judge power, and company, to separate the lambs
the quick from the goats, the elect from the repro-
and the bate (*s*); so that none, whether he be alive
dead. then, or dead before, shall escape his judgment (*t*).

III.

I believe : Moreover, I believe and confess the Holy

(*h*) Eph. iv. 10; John xiv. 2, 3; Heb. vi. 20. (*i*) Mark
xvi. 19; Luke xxiv. 51; Acts i. ix. 11. (*k*) Luke
xxiv. 49; John xiv. 16, 17, 26; Acts i. 4, and ii. 4.
(*l*) Rom. viii. 34; Heb. vii. 25, and ix. 24; 1 John
ii. 1. (*m*) Acts iii. 21. (*n*) Col. iii. 1; Rom.
viii. 34; Heb. i. 3, x. 11, and xii. 2. (*o*) Eph. i.
20—22; Phil. ii. 9; Col. ii. 10. (*p*) Matt. xxviii. 20.
(*q*) Acts iii. 21. (*r*) Acts i. 11. (*s*) Matt. xxv.
31, 46; Phil. iii. 20. (*t*) Matt. xxiv. 30, 31; Acts
x. 42, and xvii. 31; 1 Cor. xv. 51, 52; 1 Thess. iv. 16,
17; 2 Thess. i. 7, 10; 2 Tim. iv. 1, 8.

Ghost, God equal with the Father and the *in the Holy* Son, who regenerateth and sanctifieth us, *Ghost,* ruleth and guideth us into all truth (*u*), persuading us most assuredly in our consciences, that we are the children of God, brethren to Jesus Christ, and fellow-heirs with him of life everlasting (*w*).

Yet, notwithstanding, it is not sufficient to believe that God is omnipotent and merciful, that Christ hath made satisfaction, or that the Holy Ghost hath this power and effect, except we do apply the same benefits to ourselves (*x*), who are God's elect (*y*).

IV.

I believe therefore and confess one holy *The holy* only church (*z*), which (as members of Jesus *catholic* Christ, the only Head thereof, *a*) consent in *Church,* faith, hope, and charity (*b*), using the gifts *the com-* of God, whether they be temporal or spiri- *munion of* tual, to the profit and furtherance of the *Saints,* same (*c*). Which church is not seen to man's eye, but only known to God (*d*), who of the lost sons of Adam hath ordained some as vessels of wrath to damnation (*e*); and hath chosen others as vessels of his mercy to be

(*u*) Matt. iii. 16, 17; 1 John v. 7; 1 Pet. i. 2, 22; 1 Cor. vi 11, 19; John xvi. 7, 13; Eph. iii. 16; 2 Thess. ii. 13. (*w*) Rom. viii. 13, 17; Gal. iv. 6, 7. (*x*) Hab. ii. 4; Rom i. 17; and x. 9, &c.; 1 John iii. 23; John iii. 36. (*y*) John xvii. 2, 3. (*z*) Matt. xvi. 18; John x. 14—16; Eph. v. 25—27; Rom. viii. 28, &c.; Cant. ii. (*a*) 1 Cor. xii. 12, 13; Eph. i. 10, 22, 23, and iv. 15, 16; Col. i. 18. (*b*) Eph. iv. 3—5, 13; Phil. iii. 16; Col. ii. 19. (*c*) Acts ii. 41, &c, and iv. 32, &c.; Rom. xii. 4, &c.; 1 Cor. xii.; Eph. iv. 7, 11, 12. (*d*) Rom. xi. 33, 34; 2 Tim. ii. 19. (*e*) Rom. ix. 21, 22.

K

saved (*f*), the which also in due time he calleth to integrity of life and godly conversation, to make them a glorious church to himself (*g*).

But that church which is visible, and seen to the eye (*h*), hath three tokens or marks, whereby it may be known. First, the word of God, contained in the Old and New Testament (*i*), which, as it is above the authority of the same church (*k*); and only sufficient to instruct us in all things concerning salvation (*l*); so is it left for all degrees of men to read, and understand (*m*): for without this word, neither church, council, nor decree can establish any point touching salvation (*n*).

The second is the holy sacraments—*to wit*, of Baptism and the Lord's, Supper; which sacraments Christ hath left unto us, as holy signs and seals of God's promises (*o*). For as by baptism once received, is signified, that we (as well infants, as others of age and discretion) being strangers from God by original sin, are received into his family and congregation (*p*): with full assurance that although this root of sin lie hid in us, yet to the elect it shall not be imputed (*q*): so the Supper declareth that God, as a most pro-

(*f*) Rom. ix. 23; Eph. i. 4—6, 11, 12.   (*g*) Rom. viii. 30; Eph. v. 26, 27.   (*h*) Matt. xviii. 17; 1 Cor. xv. 9.   (*i*) Matt. xxviii. 19, 20; Rom. x. 14, 17; Luke xvi. 31, and xxiv. 27; Eph. ii. 20; John x. 16; 2 Tim. iii. 15, 16.   (*k*) 2 Pet. i. 20, 21.   (*l*) John xx. 31; 2 Tim. iii. 15—17.   (*m*) Deut. vi. 6, 7; Jos. i. 8; Psal. lxxviii. 5; John v. 39.   (*n*) Matt. xv. 3, 6, 9, and xxii. 29; Eph. v. 17. (*o*) Matt. xxviii. 19, and xxvi. 26, 30; Rom. iv. 11.   (*p*) Rom. vi. 3—5; Gal. iii. 27; Col. ii. 11, 12; Titus iii. 5. (*q*) Rom. iv.; Psal. xxxii. 1, 2.

vident Father, doth not only feéd our bodies, but also spiritually nourish our souls with the graces and benefits of Jesus Christ; which the Scripture calleth eating of his flesh, and drinking of his blood (*r*). Neither must we in the administration of these sacraments follow man's fancy, but as Christ himself hath ordained, so must they be ministred, and by such as by ordinary vocation are thereunto called (*s*): therefore whosoever revereth and worshippeth these sacraments, or, contrariwise, contemneth them in time and place, procureth to himself damnation.

The third mark of this church is ecclesiastical discipline, which standeth in admonition and correction of faults (*t*): the final end whereof is excommunication, by the consent of the church determined, if the offender be obstinate (*u*).

And, besides this ecclesiastical discipline, I acknowledge to belong to the church a politic magistrate, who ministreth to every man justice, defending the good, and punishing the evil, to whom we must render honour and obedience in all things (*w*) which are not contrary to the word of God (*x*).

And as Moses (*y*), Hezekias(*z*), Josias(*a*), and other godly rulers, purged the church of God from superstition and idolatry: so the defence of Christ's church appertaineth to the Christian magistrates, against all ido-

(*r*) 1 Cor. xi. 23—29; John vi. 8—58. (*s*) Deut. xii. 32; Heb. v. 4; John i. 33; 1 Cor. iv. 1. (*t*) Matt. xviii. 15—22; Luke xvii. 3, 4; Lev. xix. 17. (*u*) 1 Cor. v. (*w*) Rom. xiii. 1—7; Titus iii. 1; 1 Pet. ii. 13, 14. (*x*) Acts iv. 19, and v. 29. (*y*) Exod. xxxii. (*z*) 2 Kings xviii. 4; 2 Chron. xxix.—xxxi. (*a*) 2 Kings xxiii. 1—25; 2 Chron. xxxiv.

laters and heretics, as Papists, Anabaptists, with such like limbs of Antichrist; to root out all doctrine of devils and men, as the Mass, Purgatory, *Limbus Patrum*, prayers to saints and for the dead, free-will, distinction of meats, apparel, and days, vows of single life, presence at idol-service, man's merits, with such like (*b*): which draw us from the society of Christ's church, wherein *The for-* standeth only remission of sins, purchased by *giveness of* Christ's blood to all them that believe, whe-*sins,* ther they be Jews or Gentiles (*c*); and lead us to vain confidence in creatures, and trust in our own imaginations. The punishment whereof, although God oftentimes deferreth in this life (*d*), yet, after the general resur-*The resur-* rection, when our souls and bodies shall rise *rection of* again to immortality (*e*), they shall be damned *the body,* to unquenchable fire (*f*): and then we, who have forsaken all men's wisdom to cleave unto Christ, shall hear the joyful voice, Come, ye blessed of my Father, inherit ye the kingdom prepared to you from the beginning of the world (*g*); and so shall go tri-

(*b*) 2 Tim. iv. 2—4; Col. ii. 8, 16—23; Matt. xv. 1—9; Isai. xxix. 13; Heb. ix. 12, 14, 25, 26, 28, and x. 10, 12, 14; Acts x. 15; 1 John ii. 22; Rom. vii. 6; Gal. v. 1; Col. ii. 8, 16—23; Rom. xiv.; 1 Tim. iv. 1—8; Matt. xix. 10—12; 1 Cor. vii. 2, 9, viii., and x. 25; 2 Cor. vi. 16, 17; Luke xvii. 23; Rom. iii. 19—29; 1 Cor. iii. 11; Gal. iv. 9, 10. (*c*) Isai. xxxiii. 24; Matt. xviii. 18; John xx. 23; 2 Cor. v. 18; Rom. i. 16, and x. 11, 12; Eph. ii. 11, &c. (*d*) 2 Pet. ii.; Jude; Rom. ix. 22. (*e*) Acts xxiv. 15; 1 Cor. xv. 12, &c.; Phil. iii. 11, 21; 1 Thess. iv. 13, &c. (*f*) 2 Thess. i. 7—9, and ii. 12; Isai. xxx. 27; John iii. 36, and v. 28, 29; Matt. xxv. 30, 41, 46. (*g*) Matt. xxv. 21, 23, 34, 46.

umphing with him in body and soul, to remain everlastingly in glory (*h*), where we
shall see God face to face, and shall no more *And life*
need one to instruct another; for we shall *everlast-*
all know him, from the highest to the low- *ing.*
est (*i*).   To whom, with the Father and the
Holy Ghost, be all praise, honour, and glory,
now and ever.   So be it.

(*h*) 1 Thess. iv. 16, 17, and v. 9, 10; John v. 29; Isai.
xxvi. 19.   (*i*) 1 Cor. xiii. 12; 1 John iii. 2; Jer.
xxxi. 34; Heb. viii. 11.

=======

THE

NATIONAL COVENANT;

OR,

*The Confession of Faith: subscribed at first by the
King's Majesty and his houshold in the year 1580;
thereafter by persons of all ranks in the year 1581;
by ordinance of the Lords of secret Council, and acts
of the General Assembly; subscribed again by all
sorts of persons in the year 1590, by a new ordinance
of Council, at the desire of the General Assembly;
with a general bond for the maintaining of the true
Christian religion, and the King's person; and, together, with a resolution and promise for the causes
after expressed, to maintain the true religion, and the
King's Majesty, according to the foresaid Confession
and acts of Parliament, subscribed by Barons, Nobles, Gentlemen, Burgesses, Ministers, and Commons,
in the year 1638; approven by the General Assembly
1638 and 1639; and subscribed again by persons of
all ranks and qualities in the year 1639, by an or-*

dinance of Council, upon the supplication of the General Assembly, and Act of the General Assembly; ratified by an Act of Parliament 1640; and subscribed by King Charles II. at Spey, June 23, 1650; and at Scoon, January 1, 1651.

WE, all and every one of us underwritten, protest, that after long and due examination of our own consciences in matters of true and false religion, we are now thoroughly resolved in the truth by the word and Spirit of God; and therefore we believe with our hearts, confess with our mouths, subscribe with our hands, and constantly affirm before God and the whole world, that this only is the true Christian faith and religion, pleasing God and bringing salvation to man, which now is, by the mercy of God, revealed to the world by the preaching of the blessed Evangel; and is received, believed, and defended by many and sundry notable kirks and realms, but chiefly by the Kirk of Scotland, the king's majesty and three estates of this realm, as God's eternal truth, and only ground of our salvation; as more particularly is expressed in the Confession of our Faith, established and publicly confirmed by sundry acts of Parliament, and now of a long time hath been openly professed by the King's majesty, and whole body of this realm, both in burgh and land. To the which Confession and form of religion we willingly agree in our conscience in all points, as unto God's undoubted truth and verity, grounded only upon his written word. And therefore we abhor and detest all contrary religion and doctrine: but chiefly all kinds of Papistry in general and particular heads, even as they are now damned and confuted by the Word of God and Kirk of Scotland. But in special we detest and refuse the usurped authority of the Roman Antichrist upon the Scriptures of God, upon the kirk, the civil magistrate, and consciences of men: all his tyrannous laws made upon indifferent things against our Christian liberty; his erroneous doctrine against the sufficiency

of the written word, the perfection of the law, the
office of Christ and his blessed Evangel; his corrupted
doctrine concerning original sin, our natural inability
and rebellion to God's law, our justification by faith
only, our imperfect sanctification and obedience to the
law; the nature, number, and use of the holy sacraments; his five bastard sacraments; with all his rites,
ceremonies, and false doctrine, added to the ministration of the true sacraments without the word of God:
his cruel judgment against infants departing without
the sacrament: his absolute necessity of baptism: his
blasphemous opinion of transubstantiation, or real presence of Christ's body in the elements, and receiving
of the same by the wicked, or bodies of men: his dispensations with solemn oaths, perjuries, and degrees
of marriage forbidden in the word: his cruelty against
the innocent divorced: his devilish mass: his blasphemous priesthood: his profane sacrifice for the sins
of the dead and the quick: his canonization of men,
calling upon angels or saints departed; worshipping of
imagery, relics, and crosses; dedicating of kirks, altars,
days; vows to creatures: his purgatory; prayers for
the dead; praying or speaking in a strange language;
with his processions and blasphemous litany, and multitude of advocates or mediators: his manifold orders;
auricular confession: his * desperate and uncertain re-

---

* In the copy which is in the Harmony of Confessions,
printed 1586, it is " dispersed and uncertain repentance ;"
and in the Latin translation, which is in the Syntagma
Confessionum, it is " dispersam et incertam pœniten-
tiam :" but in the copy which is in the college of Edinburgh, written 1585, and subscribed by the graduates,
till the defection at the restoration of King Charles II.
and in the copies which were subscribed 1638 and 1639,
it is " desperate :" and in the original subscribed by the
King, &c., and in the copy printed by Robert Wald-
grave, 1581, it is " despered :" which is the old Scottish
word for " desperate."

pentance : his general and doubtsome faith : his satis-
factions of men for their sins : his justification by works,
opus operatum, works of supererogation, merits, par-
dons, peregrinations, and stations: his holy water, bap-
tizing of bells, conjuring of spirits, crossing, sayning,
anointing, conjuring, hallowing of God's good creatures,
with the superstitious opinion joined therewith : his
worldly monarchy, and wicked hierarchy * : his three
solemn vows, with all his shavellings of sundry sorts :
his erroneous and bloody decrees made at Trent, with
all the subscribers or approvers of that cruel and bloody
band, conjured against the kirk of God. And, finally,
we detest all his vain allegories, rites, signs, and traditions brought in the kirk, without or against the word
of God, and doctrine of this true reformed kirk ; to the
which we join ourselves willingly, in doctrine, faith,
religion, discipline, and use of the holy sacraments, as
lively members of the same in Christ our Head : promising and swearing by the great name of the LORD
our GOD, that we shall continue in the obedience of
the doctrine and discipline of this kirk †, and shall defend the same, according to our vocation and power,
all the days of our lives; under the pains contained in
the law, and danger both of body and soul in the day
of God's fearful judgment.

And, seeing that many are stirred up by Satan and
that Roman Antichrist, to promise, swear, subscribe,
and for a time use the holy sacraments in the kirk de-
ceitfully, against their own conscience; minding hereby,
first, under the external cloke of religion, to corrupt
and subvert secretly God's true religion within the kirk ;

---

* See the explication of hierarchy, in the 5th Act of
Assembly, after the form of Presbyterian government.

† The Confession which was subscribed at Halyrud-
house the 25th of February 1587-8, by the King, Len-
nox, Huntly, the Chancellor, and about ninety-five other
persons, hath here added, " agreeing to the word." Sir
John Maxwell, of Pollock, hath the original parchment.

and afterward, when time may serve, to become open enemies and persecutors of the same, under vain hope of the pope's dispensation, devised against the word of God, to his greater confusion, and their double condemnation in the day of the Lord Jesus; we therefore, willing to take away all suspicion of hypocrisy, and of such double dealing with God and his kirk, protest, and call the Searcher of all hearts to witness, that our minds and hearts do fully agree with this our confession, promise, oath, and subscription; so that we are not moved with any worldly respect, but are persuaded only in our conscience, through the knowledge and love of God's true religion, imprinted in our hearts by the Holy Spirit, as we shall answer to him in the day when the secrets of all hearts shall be disclosed.

And because we perceive, that the quietness and stability of our religion and kirk doth depend upon the safety and good behaviour of the king's majesty, as upon a comfortable instrument of God's mercy granted to this country, for the maintaining of his kirk and ministration of justice amongst us; we protest and promise with our hearts, under the same oath, hand-writ, and pains, that we shall defend his person and authority with our goods, bodies, and lives, in the defence of Christ's Evangel, liberties of our country, ministration of justice, and punishment of iniquity, against all enemies within this realm or without, as we desire our God to be a strong and merciful defender to us in the day of our death, and coming of our Lord Jesus Christ; to whom, with the Father and the Holy Spirit, be all honour and glory eternally.

———

LIKE as many acts of Parliament, not only in general do abrogate, annul, and rescind all laws, statutes, acts, constitutions, canons civil or municipal, with all other ordinances, and practique penalties * whatsoever, made in prejudice of the true religion and professors thereof:

---

* In the act of Parliament, it is practicks penal.

or of the true kirk discipline, jurisdiction, and freedom thereof; or in favours of idolatry and superstition; or of the Papistical Kirk; as Act 3, Act 31, Parl. 1; Act 23, Parl. 2; Act 114*, Parl. 12 of King James VI.; that Papistry and superstition may be utterly suppressed, according to the intention of the acts of Parliament, repeated in the 5th Act, Parl. 20 King James VI., and to that end they ordain all Papists and priests to be punished by manifold civil and ecclesiastical pains, as adversaries to God's true religion, preached†, and by law established within this realm, Act 24, Parl. 11, King James VI.; as common enemies to all Christian government, Act 18, Parl. 16, King James VI.; as rebellers and gainstanders of our sovereign lord's authority, Act 47, Parl. 3, King James VI.; and as idolaters, Act 104, Parl. 7, King James VI. But also in particular, by and attour the Confession of Faith, do abolish and condemn the pope's authority and jurisdiction out of this land, and ordains the maintainers thereof to be punished, Act 2, Parl. 1, Act 51, Parl. 3, Act 106, Parl. 7, Act 114‡, Parl. 12, King James VI., do condemn the pope's erroneous doctrine, or any other erroneous doctrine repugnant to any of the articles of the true and Christian religion publicly preached, and by law established in this realm; and ordains the spreaders and makers of books or libels, or letters or writs of that nature, to be punished, Act 46, Parl. 3, Act 106, Parl. 7, Act 24, Parl. 11, King James VI., do condemn all baptism conform to the pope's kirk, and the idolatry of the mass; and ordains all sayers, wilful hearers, and concealers of the mass, the maintainers and resetters of the priests, Jesuits, trafficking Papists, to be punished,

---

* 116. The Acts of Parliament are quoted according to Sir John Skeen's edition, in which the acts are in some places wrong numbered, as they are likewise in Glendock's folio edition: the numbers on the foot-margin are according to Glendock's edition in 12mo.

† Professed.   ‡ 116.

without any exception or restriction, Act 5, Parl. 1, Act 120*, Parl. 12, Act 164†, Parl. 13, Act 193‡, Parl. 14, Act 1, Parl. 19, Act 5, Parl. 20, King James VI., do condemn all erroneous books and writs, containing erroneous doctrine against the religion presently professed, or containing superstitious rites and ceremonies Papistical, whereby the people are greatly abused; and ordains the home-bringers of them to be punished, Act 25, Parl. 11, King James VI., do condemn the monuments and dregs of by-gone idolatry, as going to crosses, observing the festival-days of saints, and such other superstitious and Papistical rites, to the dishonour of God, contempt of true religion, and fostering of great error among the people; and ordains the users of them to be punished for the second fault, as idolaters, Act 104, Parl. 7, King James VI.

Like as many acts of Parliament are conceived for maintenance of God's true and Christian religion, and the purity thereof, in doctrine and sacraments; of the true church of God, the liberty and freedom thereof, in her national, synodal assemblies, presbyteries, sessions, policy, discipline, and jurisdiction thereof: as that purity of religion and liberty of the church was used, professed, exercised, preached, and confessed according to the reformation of religion in this realm. As, for instance, Act 99, Parl. 7, Act 23, Parl. 11, Act 114§, Parl. 12, Act 160, Parl. 13, of King James VI., ratified by Act 4 of King Charles. So that Act 6, Parl. 1, and Act 68, Parl. 6, of King James VI., in the year of God 1579, declares the ministers of the blessed Evangel whom God of his mercy had raised up, or hereafter should arise, agreeing with them that then lived, in doctrine and administration of the sacraments: and the people that professed Christ, as he was then offered in the Evangel, and doth communicate with the holy sacraments (as in the reformed kirks of this realm, they were presently administrate), according to the Con-

---

* 122.   † 168.   ‡ 196.   § 116.

fession of Faith, to be the true and holy kirk of Christ
Jesus within this realm. And decerns and declares all
and sundry, who either gainsays the word of the Evangel received and approved, as the heads of the Confession of Faith, professed in Parliament in the year of
God 1560, specified also in the first Parliament of King
James VI., and ratified in this present Parliament, more
particularly do express; or that refuses the administration of the holy sacraments, as they were then ministrated: to be no members of the said kirk within this
realm, and true religion presently professed, so long as
they keep themselves so divided from the society of
Christ's body. And the subsequent Act 69, Parl. 6, of
King James VI., declares, that there is no other face of
kirk, nor other face of religion, than was presently at
that time, by the favour of God, established within this
realm: which therefore is ever styled God's true religion,
Christ's true religion, the true and Christian religion, and
a perfect religion; which, by manifold acts of Parliament all within this realm are bound to profess, to subscribe the articles thereof, the Confession of Faith, to
recant all doctrine and errors repugnant to any of the
said articles, Acts 4 and 9, Parl. 1, Acts 45—47, Parl. 3,
Act 71, Parl. 6, Act 106, Parl. 7, Act 24, Parl. 11, Act
123*, Parl. 12, Act 194† and 197‡, Parl. 14, of King
James VI. And all magistrates, sheriffs, &c., on the
one part, are ordained to search, apprehend, and punish
all contraveners: for instance, Act 5, Parl. 1, Act 104,
Parl. 7, Act 25, Parl. 11, King James VI., and that
notwithstanding of the king's majesty's licences, on the
contrary, which are discharged, and declared to be of
no force, in so far as they tend, in any ways, to the
prejudice and hinder of the execution of the acts of
Parliament against Papists and adversaries of true religion, Act 106, Parl. 7, King James VI. On the other
part, in Act 47, Parl. 3, King James VI., it is declared
and ordained, seeing the cause of God's true religion,

* 125. † 197. ‡ 200.

and his highness' authority are so joined, as the hurt
of the one is common to both, that none shall be reputed
as loyal and faithful subjects to our sovereign lord or
his authority, but be punishable as rebellers and gainstanders of the same, who shall not give their confession,
and make their profession of the said true religion;
and that they who after defection shall give the confession of their faith of new, they shall promise to continue therein in time coming, to maintain our sovereign
lord's authority; and at the uttermost of their power,
to fortify, assist, and maintain the true preachers and
professors of Christ's religion *, against whatsover enemies and gainstanders of the same; and namely, against
all such, of whatsoever nation, estate, or degree they be
of, that have joined and bound themselves, or have
assisted, or assists to set forward and execute the cruel
decrees of the Council of Trent, contrary to the true
preachers and professors of the word of God. Which
is repeated word by word, in the Articles of Pacifica-
tion, at Perth, the 23d of Feb. 1572, approved by Parliament the last of April 1573, ratified in Parliament
1587, and related Act 123 †, Parl. 12, of King James
VI., with this addition, ' That they are bound to resist
' all treasonable uproars and hostilities raised against
' the true religion, the king's majesty, and the true pro-
' fessors.'

Like as all lieges are bound to maintain the king's
majesty's royal person and authority, the authority of
parliaments : without the which, neither any laws or
lawful judicatories can be established, Acts 130 and
131, Parl. 8, King James VI., and the subjects' liberties,
who ought only to live and be governed by the king's
laws, the common laws of this realm allenarly, Act 48,
Parl. 3, King James I., Act 79, Parl. 6, King James
IV., repeated in Act 131, Parl. 8, King James VI.
Which, if they be innovated or prejudged, the com-

---

* Some copies have " true religion," others have
" Evangel."   † 125.

mission anent the Union of the two kingdoms of Scotland and England, which is the sole Act of Parl. 17 of King James VI., declares, such confusion would ensue, as this realm could be no more a free monarchy; because, by the fundamental laws, ancient privileges, offices, and liberties of this kingdom, not only the princely authority of his majesty's royal descent hath been these many ages maintained; but also the people's security of their lands, livings, rights, offices, liberties, and dignities preserved. And therefore, for the preservation of the said true religion, laws, and liberties of this kingdom, it is statute by Act 8, Parl. 1, repeated in Act 99, Parl. 7, ratified in Act 23, Parl. 11, and Act 114 *, Parl. 12, of King James VI., and Act 4, Parl. 1, of King Charles I., That all kings and princes, at their coronation, and reception of their princely authority, shall make their faithful promise, by their solemn oath, in the presence of the eternal God, That, enduring the whole time of their lives, they shall serve the same eternal God, to the uttermost of their power, according as he hath required in his most holy word, contained in the Old and New Testaments And, according to the same word, shall maintain the true religion of Christ Jesus, the preaching of his holy word, the due and right ministration of the sacraments now received and preached within this realm (according to the Confession of Faith immediately preceding), and shall abolish and gainstand all false religion contrary to the same; and shall rule the people committed to their charge, according to the will and command of God, revealed in his foresaid word: and according to the laudable † laws and constitutions received in this realm, noways repugnant to the said will ‡ of the eternal God: and shall procure, to the uttermost of their power, to the kirk of God, and the whole Christian people, true and perfect peace in all time coming; and that they shall be careful to root out of their empire, all heretics and enemies to

---

* 116. † In the act it is " lovabil." ‡ Word.

the true worship of God, who shall be convicted by the true kirk of God of the foresaid crimes. Which was also observed by his majesty *, at his coronation in Edinburgh †, 1633, as may be seen in the order of the coronation.

In obedience to the commandment of God, conform to the practice of the godly in former times, and according to the laudable example of our worthy and religious progenitors, and of many yet living amongst us, which was warranted also by act of council, commanding a general band to be made and subscribed by his majesty's subjects of all ranks, for two causes: one was, for defending the true religion as it was then reformed, and is expressed in the Confession of Faith above written, and a former large confession ‡, established by sundry acts of lawful general assemblies and of parliaments, unto which it hath relation, set down in public catechisms; and which had been for many years, with a blessing from Heaven, preached and professed in this kirk and kingdom, as God's undoubted truth, grounded only upon his written word. The other cause was for maintaining the king's majesty, his person, and estate; the true worship of God and the king's authority being so straitly joined, as that they had the same friends and common enemies, and did stand and fall together. And finally, being convinced in our minds, and confessing with our mouths, that the present and succeeding generations in this land, are bound to keep the foresaid national oath and subscription inviolable;

We, noblemen, barons, gentlemen, burgesses, ministers, and commons under subscribing, considering divers times before, and especially at this time, the danger of the true reformed religion, of the king's honour, and of the public peace of the kingdom, by the manifold innovations and evils generally contained, and particularly mentioned in our late supplications,

---

* K. Charles I.   † June 18th.
‡ See above, pp. 1—42.

complaints, and protestations, do hereby profess, and before God, his angels, and the world, solemnly declare, That with our whole hearts we agree, and resolve all the days of our life constantly to adhere unto and to defend the foresaid true religion, and forbearing the practice of all novations already introduced in the matters of the worship of God, or approbation of the corruptions of the public government of the kirk, or civil places and power of kirkmen, till they be tried and allowed in free assemblies and in parliaments; to labour, by all means lawful, to recover the purity and liberty of the Gospel, as it was established and professed before the foresaid novations. And because, after due examination, we plainly perceive and undoubtedly believe, that the innovations and evils contained in our supplications, complaints, and protestations, have no warrant of the word of God; are contrary to the articles of the foresaid confessions, to the intention and meaning of the blessed reformers of religion in this land, to the above written acts of Parliament; and do sensibly tend to the re-establishing of the popish religion and tyranny, and to the subversion and ruin of the true reformed religion, and of our liberties, laws, and estates: we also declare, that the foresaid confessions are to be interpreted, and ought to be understood of the foresaid novations and evils, no less than if every one of them had been expressed in the foresaid confessions; and that we are obliged to detest and abhor them, amongst other particular heads of Papistry abjured therein. And therefore, from the knowledge and conscience of our duty to God, to our king and country, without any worldly respect or inducement, so far as human infirmity will suffer, wishing a further measure of the grace of God for this effect; we promise and swear by the GREAT NAME OF THE LORD OUR GOD, to continue in the profession and obedience of the foresaid religion; and that we shall defend the same, and resist all these contrary errors and corruptions, according to our vocation, and to the uttermost of that power that God hath put in our hands, all the days of our life.

And in like manner, with the same heart we declare before God and men, that we have no intention, nor desire to attempt any thing, that may turn to the dishonour of God, or to the diminution of the king's greatness and authority: but on the contrary, we promise and swear, that we shall to the uttermost of our power, with our means and lives, stand to the defence of our dread sovereign the king's majesty, his person, and authority, in the defence and preservation of the foresaid true religion, liberties, and laws of the kingdom: as also, to the mutual defence and assistance every one of us of another, in the same cause of maintaining, the true religion and his majesty's authority, with our best counsel, our bodies, means, and whole power, against all sorts of persons whatsoever; so that whatsoever shall be done to the least of us for that cause, shall be taken as done to us all in general, and to every one of us in particular. And that we shall neither directly nor indirectly suffer ourselves to be divided or withdrawen by whatsoever suggestion, combination, allurement, or terror, from this blessed and loyal conjunction; nor shall cast in any let or impediment that may stay or hinder any such resolution, as by common consent shall be found to conduce for so good ends: but, on the contrary, shall, by all lawful means, labour to further and promove the same; and if any such dangerous and divisive motion be made to us by word or writ, We, and every one of us, shall either suppress it, or, if need be, shall incontinent make the same known, that it may be timeously obviated. Neither do we fear the foul aspersions of rebellion, combination, or what else our adversaries, for their craft and malice, would put upon us; seeing what we do is so well warranted, and ariseth from an unfeigned desire to maintain the true worship of God, the majesty of our king, and the peace of the kingdom, for the common happiness of ourselves and the posterity:

L

. And because we cannot look for a blessing from God upon our proceedings, except with our profession and subscription we join such a life and conversation as beseemeth Christians, who have renewed their covenant with God; we therefore faithfully promise for ourselves, our followers, and all others under us, both in public, and in our particular families and personal carriage, to endeavour to keep ourselves within the bounds of * Christian liberty ; and to be good examples to others of all godliness, soberness, and righteousness, and of every duty we owe to God and man.

And that this our union and conjunction may be observed without violation, we call the LIVING GOD, THE SEARCHER OF OUR HEARTS, to witness, who knoweth this to be our sincere desire and unfeigned resolution, as we shall answer to JESUS CHRIST in the great day; and under the pain of GOD's everlasting wrath, and of infamy and loss of all honour and respect in this world: most humbly beseeching the Lord to strengthen us by his HOLY SPIRIT for this end, and to bless our desires and proceedings with a happy success; that religion and righteousness may flourish in the land, to the glory of GOD, the honour of our king, and peace and comfort of us all. In witness whereof, we have subscribed with our hands all the premises.

The article of this covenant, which was at the first subscription referred to the determination of the General Assembly, being now determined : and thereby the five Articles of Perth, the government of the kirk by bishops, and the civil places and power of kirkmen, upon the reasons and grounds contained in the acts of the General Assembly, declared to be unlawful within this kirk ; we subscribe according to the determination foresaid.

How King Charles II. took this covenant, see Collection of Acts, &c., No. 25.

---

* In the copy subscribed anno 1638, by noblemen, &c., there is here added " our."

There are also several copies of this covenant, on parchment, with the original subscriptions of several congregations, ministers, elders, and people, yet extant, to be seen in divers hands.

THE

DIRECTORY *for* FAMILY WORSHIP,

Approved by the General Assembly of the Church of Scotland, and, by Act, Anno 1647, ordered to be observed, for Piety and Uniformity in Secret and Private Worship, and mutual Edification.

BESIDES the public worship in congregations, mercifully established in this land in great purity, it is expedient and necessary, that secret worship of each person alone, and private worship of families, be pressed and set up; that with national reformation, the profession and power of godliness, both personal and domestic, be advanced.

I. And, First, for secret Worship, it is most necessary, that every one apart, and by themselves, be given to prayer and meditation, the unspeakable benefit whereof is best known to them who are most exercised therein; this being the mean whereby, in a special way, communion with God is entertained, and right preparation for all other duties obtained: and therefore it becometh not only pastors, within their several charges, to press persons of all sorts to perform this duty, morning and evening, and at other occasions; but also it is incumbent to the head of every family, to have a care that both themselves, and all within their charge, be daily diligent herein.

·II.· The ordinary duties comprehended under the exercise of piety, which should be in families, when they are convened to that effect,·are these, First, Prayer, and praises performed, with a special reference, as well to the public condition of the kirk of God, and this kingdom, as to the present·case of the family, and every member thereof. Next, Reading of the Scriptures, with catechising in a plain way, that the understandings of the simpler may be the better enabled to profit under the public ordinances, and they made more capable to understand the Scriptures when they are read: together with godly conferences, tending to the edification of·all the members in the most holy faith : as also, admonition and rebuke, upon just reasons, from those who have authority in the family.

' III. As the charge and office of interpreting the Holy Scriptures is a part of the ministerial calling, which none (howsoever otherwise qualified) should take upon him in any place, but he that is duly called thereunto by·God, and his kirk ; so in every family,· where there is any that can read, the Holy Scriptures should be read ordinarily to the family ; and it is commendable, that thereafter they confer, and by way of conference make some good use of what hath been read and heard; as for example, if any sin be reproved in the word read, use may be made thereof, to make all the family circumspect, and watchful against the same; or if any judgment be threatened, or mentioned to have been inflicted in that portion of Scripture which is read, use may be made to make all' the family fear, lest the same or a worse judgment befal them, unless they beware of the sin that procured it. And finally, if any duty be required, or comfort held forth in a promise, use may be made to stir up themselves to employ Christ for strength to enable them for doing the commanded duty, and to apply the offered comfort; in all which, the master of the family is to have the chief hand; and any member of the family may propone a question or doubt for resolution.

IV. The head of the family is to take care that none of the family. withdraw himself from any part of family worship : and, seeing the ordinary performance of all the parts of family worship belongeth properly to the head of the family, the minister is to stir up such as are lazy, and train up such as are weak, to a fitness for these exercises : it being always free to persons of quality, to entertain one approved by the Presbytery for performing family exercise ; and in other families, where the head of the family is unfit, that another constantly residing in the family, approved by the minister and session, may be employed in that service ; wherein the minister and session are to be countable to the presbytery. And if a minister, by Divine Providence, be brought to any family, it is requisite, that at no time he convene a part of the family for worship, secluding the rest, except in singular cases, especially concerning these parties, which (in Christian prudence) need not, or ought not, to be imparted to others.

V. Let no idler who hath no particular calling, or vagrant person under pretence of a calling, be suffered to perform worship in families, to or for the same ; seeing persons tainted with errors, or aiming at division, may be ready (after that manner) to creep into houses, and lead captive silly and unstable souls.

VI. At family worship, a special care is to be had that each family keep by themselves; neither requiring, inviting, nor admitting persons from divers families : unless it be those who are lodged with them, or at meal, or otherwise with them upon some lawful occasion.

VII. Whatsoever hath been the effects and fruits of meetings of persons of divers families, in the times of corruption or trouble (in which cases many things are commendable, which otherwise are not tolerable) ; yet, when God hath blessed us with peace and purity of the Gospel, such meetings of persons of divers families (except in cases mentioned in these directions) are to be disapproved, as tending to the hindrance of the religious exercise of each family by itself, to the prejudice of the public ministry, to the renting of the families of particular congregations, and (in progress of time) of the whole kirk; besides many offences which may come thereby, to the hardening of the hearts of carnal men, and grief of the godly.

VIII. On the Lord's day, after every one of the family apart, and the whole family together, have sought the Lord (in whose hands the preparation of men's hearts are) to fit them for the public worship, and to bless to them the public ordinances, the master of the family ought to take care that all within his charge repair to the public worship, that he and they may join with the rest of the congregation: and the public worship being finished, after prayer, he should take an account what they have heard; and thereafter, to spend the rest of the time, which they may spare, in catechising, and in spiritual conferences upon the word of God: or else, (going apart) they ought to apply themselves to reading, meditation, and secret prayer, that they may confirm and increase their communion with God; that so the profit which they found in the public ordinances may be cherished and promoved, and they more edified unto eternal life.

IX. So many as can conceive prayer, ought to make use of that gift of God; albeit, those who are rude and weaker may begin at a set form of prayer, but so as they be not sluggish in stirring up in themselves (according to their daily necessities) the Spirit of prayer, which is given to all the children of God in some measure: to which effect, they ought to be more fervent and frequent in secret prayer to God, for enabling of their hearts to conceive, and their tongues to express convenient desires to God, for their family. And in the mean time, for their greater encouragement, let these materials of prayer be meditated upon, and made use of, as followeth.

' Let them confess to God, how unworthy they are
' to come in his presence, and how unfit to worship his

' majesty; and therefore earnestly ask of God the Spirit
' of prayer.

' They are to confess their sins and the sins of the
' family, accusing, judging, and condemning themselves
' for them, till they bring their souls to some measure
' of true humiliation.

' They are to pour out their souls to God, in the
' name of Christ, by the Spirit, for forgiveness of sins;
' for grace to repent, to believe, and to live soberly,
' righteously, and godly; and that they may serve God
' with joy and delight, walking before him.

' They are to give thanks to God for his many mer-
' cies to his people, and to themselves, and especially
' for his love in Christ, and for the light of the
' Gospel.

' They are to pray for such particular benefits, spi-
' ritual and temporal, as they stand in need of for the
' time (whether it be morning or evening) as anent
' health or sickness, prosperity or adversity.

' They ought to pray for the kirk of Christ in ge-
' neral, for all the reformed kirks, and for this kirk in
' particular, and for all that suffer for the name of Christ;
' for all our superiors, the king's majesty, the queen,
' and their children; for the magistrates, ministers,
' and whole body of the congregation, whereof they are
' members, as well for their neighbours absent in their
' lawful affairs, as for those that are at home.

' The prayer may be closed with an earnest desire
' that God may be glorified in the coming of the king-
' dom of his Son, and in the doing of his will; and
' with assurance that themselves are accepted, and
' what they have asked according to his will shall be
' done.'

X. These exercises ought to be performed in great
sincerity, without delay, laying aside all exercises of
worldly business or hindrances, notwithstanding the
mockings of Atheists and profane men; in respect of the
great mercies of God to this land, and of his severe

corrections wherewith lately he hath exercised us. And to this effect, persons of eminency (and all elders of the kirk) not only ought to stir up themselves and families to diligence herein; but also to concur effectually, that in all other families; where they have power and charge, the said exercises be conscionably performed.

XI. Besides the ordinary duties in families, which are above mentioned, extraordinary duties, both of humiliation and thanksgiving, are to be carefully performed in families, when the Lord by extraordinary occasions (private or public) calleth for them.

XII. Seeing the word of God requireth, that we should consider one another to provoke unto love and good works; therefore, at all times, and especially in this time, wherein profanity abounds, and mockers, walking after their own lusts, think it strange that others run not with them to the same excess of riot; every member of this kirk ought to stir up themselves, and one another, to the duties of mutual edification, by instruction, admonition, rebuke; exhorting one another to manifest the grace of God, in denying ungodliness and worldly lusts, and in living godly, soberly, and righteously in this present world, by comforting the feeble minded, and praying with or for one another; which duties respectively are to be performed upon special occasions offered by Divine Providence; as, namely, when under any calamity, cross, or great difficulty, counsel or comfort is sought, or when an offender is to be reclaimed by private admonition; and if that be not effectual, by joining one or two more in the admonition, according to the rule of Christ; that in the mouth of two or three witnesses every word may be established.

XIII. And because it is not given to every one to speak a word in season to a wearied or distressed conscience, it is expedient, that a person (in that case) finding no ease after the use of all ordinary means, pri-

vate and public, have their address to their own pastor,
or some experienced Christian : but if the person, troubled in conscience, be of that condition, or of that sex,
that discretion, modesty, or fear of scandal, requireth
a godly, grave, and secret friend to be present with
them in their said address, it is expedient that such a
friend be present.

XIV. When persons of diverse families are brought
together by Divine Providence, being abroad upon their
particular vocations, or any necessary occasions; as they
would have the Lord their God with them whithersoever
they go, they ought to walk with God, and not neglect
the duties of prayer and thanksgiving, but take care that
the same be performed by such as the company shall
judge fittest. And that they likewise take heed that no
corrupt communication proceed out of their mouths,
but that which is good, to the use of edifying, that it
may minister grace to the hearers.

The drift and scope of all these directions is no other,
but that, upon the one part, the power and practice of
godliness amongst all the ministers and members of this
kirk, according to their several places and vocations,
may be cherished and advanced, and all impiety and
mocking of religious exercises suppressed : and, upon
the other part, that under the name and pretext of religious exercises, no such meetings or practices be allowed,
as are apt to breed error, scandal, schism, contempt, or
misregard of the public ordinances and ministers, or
neglect of the duties of particular callings, or such other
evils as are the works, not of the Spirit, but of the flesh,
and are contrary to truth and peace.

OVERTURES *of* GENERAL ASSEMBLY

A. D. 1705,

CONCERNING THE DISCIPLINE AND METHOD
OF PROCEEDING IN

KIRK SESSIONS AND PRESBYTERIES.

I. *Of the Constitution of this Judicatory.*

1. THIS judicatory, being the lowest, and which is in every parish, consists of one minister or two, and a competent number of ruling elders, and the deacons of that parish and church are to be present, and have a decisive vote only in matters belonging to their own office, having attending them a clerk and a beadle.

2. All the elders of that church or parish are members of the session, and ought to attend all the meetings thereof, it not being a judicatory made up of delegates.

3. If there be but one minister there, he is moderator *ex officio*, and constant out of necessity.

4. Though an elder, being once so ordained, makes him to be so during life, unless he be censured with deposition or demit his office, and the demission accepted by a judicatory, yet where there are plenty of persons fit to be elders, and plenty of elders, the actual exercise of the office as to constant attendance on the session, &c., may be limited for a time, and others take their turn. When an elder changes his residence, he may officiate as an elder in that parish where he comes to, if duly called thereto by the kirk session, who are to

intimate his name to the people, and have their tacit consent thereto, but no otherwise. Annual elections ought to be rectified, and that new elections of elders, expressed in cases of great necessity, should only be within the compass of four years, and that especially in burghs where there are plenty of persons to choose upon.

II. Of the Election and Constituting of Elders and Deacons.

1. In case there be no eldership in the parish, the election is to be managed by the presbytery, by a list given in to them made up by the heads of families, out of which the presbytery (if the church be vacant) is to try and elect, and, if planted, the minister with the presbytery's assistance.

2. Even where there is a minister and elders in a congregation constituting a session, there may be need of more elders to supply the places of some who may be removed by death or otherwise.

3. It doth most particularly belong to the session, to look among the masters and heads of families, and others (they not being menial servants), for some persons fit to be elders, being such as are of greatest prudence, gravity, and interest in the parish.

4. These ordinarily may be expected to be best had from amongst the deacons of the parish, the qualifications of that office not only fitting much for this, but the experience deacons have by being present at the session, being a further fitting of them for the office of an elder.

5. It will fall out, that sometimes it will be fit and necessary that the minister and present elders do, in a prudent and private way, try the inclination of the judicious of the people, especially the heads of families, and of these quarters of the congregation to which the elders wanting belonged, thereby to prevent the elders naming and bringing to public these persons, who may

be unacceptable where others can be had, and the edification of the congregation would therein be studied.

6. When the kirk sessions have agreed on the nomination, wherein they should endeavour to be unanimous, the persons nominated are to be spoken to, and dealt with to accept of the office, before their names be brought in public, wherein great tenderness and earnestness should be used, it being frequent with many modest and most fit persons to be most hardly and difficultly prevailed with.

7. Though it may be supposed that none will be named to this purpose but such who will be of competent knowledge, yet examination and trial should be taken of his knowledge in the grounds and principles of religion, in cases of conscience, and about the government, discipline of the church, and duties of elders, and that before the session, or two or three elders.

8. When there is hope of success therein, if the session judge it fit, the minister, on the Lord's day after forenoon sermon, is to intimate to the congregation, the necessity of more elders, and the session's nomination, and may desire any person that hath any objections against any of the persons named, to make the same either to the session or any member thereof, betwixt and such a day.

9. When the day cometh wherein the objections are to be brought in, the session must meet, and have the elect elders' edict returned (for which there is to be an interval of nine free days, as in other edicts), and the beadle is to intimate at the door: if there be any objectors, they may appear; if none, then the day is appointed to admit these elders, and the minister is to be condescended upon who is to admit them.

10. When the day is come, it were very fit the minister choosed to preach on such a subject as might relate to the work, shewing the duties of elders and people to them.

11. After sermon is ended in the forenoon, the minister is to show the people, that he is going about to

admit some more elders, and to tell them of all the orderly steps which they have taken preparatory, and that now nothing impedeth his going on.

12. Then the minister calling up the persons chosen to be elders, by name, and they standing together in some conspicuous place, as conveniency will allow, are to be interrogate concerning their orthodoxy, and to be taken solemnly engaged, to adhere to and maintain the doctrine, discipline, worship, and government of the church, and to lay themselves out, both by their example and in the office of elders, to suppress vice, cherish piety, and exercise discipline faithfully and diligently.

13. Then (the elders chosen still standing up) the minister is next by solemn prayer to set them apart *in verbis de presenti.*

14. After prayer the minister is to speak to them now as elders, encouraging them to faithfulness, and threatening, if negligent. 2dly, He is to direct a word of exhortation to the people, shewing them their duty to the elders, and exhorting them to obedience in the Lord, and to strengthen their elders' hands.

15. The same method should be followed in the election and ordination of deacons, that is in elders, *mutatis mutandis.*

III. *Anent Marriage.*

Due caution should be used to observe the acts of the General Assembly anent proclamation of Banns *, and inquiry anent forbidden degrees, the persons desiring marriage being single and free persons, and anent the consent of all concerned.

IV. *Of the Admission of Infants to Baptism.*

1. Children born within the verge of the visible church, of parents one or both professing the Christian religion, have a right to baptism.

---

* See Act 5th of General Assembly, anno 1699, &c.

2. It being the duty of Christian parents to devote their children to God by baptism, and to covenant for their education in the faith of Christ; no other sponsor is to be taken, unless the parents be dead or absent, or grossly ignorant, or under scandal not removed, such being unfit to stand as sponsors, in transacting a solemn covenant with God : in which cases the parent is to be required to provide some fit person, and if it can be one related as a parent to the child should be sponsor.

3. In case of children exposed, whose baptism, after inquiry, cannot be known, the session is to order the presenting of the child to baptism, and the session itself is to see to the Christian education of the child.

4. It were fit that the parent speak to the minister of the parish the day before the child be offered to baptism.

V. *Of Admission to the Lord's Table, and Debarring from it.*

1. Seeing none should be admitted to the Lord's table, who are ignorant or scandalous, therefore they are to be prepared for it by catechising, and instruction in the principles of religion in their younger years. Before the first admission of any to partake thereof, ministers should inquire into, and take trial of, their knowledge of the principles of the Christian religion, and particularly of the nature, uses, and ends of this ordinance of the Supper.

2. Due care also ought to be used, that none be admitted to partake of the Lord's Supper, who are of a scandalous life; and for this end the minister is to inquire at, and consult with the elders, especially these of the bounds, whether they know that person be guilty of any scandal, and that they own and submit to, and ordinarily attend the ordinances of Christ, public and private worship of God, and use the other means of knowledge.

3. At the first admission of any to the Lord's Supper, ministers should put the person to be admitted in mind

of their parents' engagements for them in baptism, and put them explicitly and personally to renew their baptismal covenant, to be the Lord's, and to live unto him, and to serve him all the days of their lives.

4. When any who liveth in one congregation desireth to partake of the Lord's Supper, in a neighbour congregation, they may and ought to be allowed the same, by reason of the communion of saints, if they bring sufficient testimonials of their knowledge and conversation from the minister of their own parish, or from two elders in the absence of the minister.

5. It were fit when any one removeth from one parish to another, that their testimonials bear account, whether they have partaked of the Lord's Supper; and it were fit for this, that there were a record keeped of these who are admitted to the Lord's Supper.

6. With respect to scandals, whose grossness makes it necessary to bring the persons guilty oftener than once before the congregation,—it is overtured, that after they are convict before the session, that it be judicially declared to them, that they have rendered themselves uncapable of communion with the people of God in the Supper of the Lord, and that they are not to be allowed to be sponsors themselves in the baptism of their children till the scandal be removed; and that they be appointed to appear in public to be rebuked for their sin, whether they appear penitent or not, conform to the institution, 1 Tim. v. 20.

7. After a public rebuke, the ministers and elders be at further pains in instructing the minds of scandalous persons if ignorant, in endeavouring to convince their conscience, and to bring them to a due sense of their sin, and to an engagement and serious resolution against all known sin, and to the performance of all known duty.

8. That the session, upon satisfaction with their knowledge and sense of their sin, do admit them to the public profession of their repentance, in order to absolution.

9. If after taking pains on them for some competent

time, for their instruction and conviction, they still remain grossly ignorant, insensible and unreformed ; the sentence of lesser excommunication is to be publicly pronounced against them, from which they are not to be relaxed, nor admitted to make public profession of their repentance in order thereto, till the session be satisfied with their knowledge, seriousness, and reformation.

VI. *Of the Privy Censures in the Sessions.*

1. In every kirk session, there ought to be twice in the year privy censures (as they are called) of the members of the session.

2. At the meeting preceding the same, all the members should be warned to be punctually present that day.

3. Seeing the ministers undergo their privy censures in the presbytery, and that generally there is but one minister in the session, who must be moderator, therefore the ministers are not to undergo this privy censure before the session, but only the elders, deacons, clerk, and beadles.

4. The moderator of the session is to cause the clerk read the roll of the members ; and beginning at the beginning of the roll, they are one by one after another to be removed, and then the rest of the members are by the moderator to be inquired, concerning the walk and conversation of the person removed, concerning his diligence and prudence in his station, and whatever any have observed, and informed worth the noticing, is freely, and with love and tenderness, to be communicated. Privy censures of the members of a session, as also of a presbytery, if rightly managed, may be of great use : but we think our Lord's rule in Matt. xviii. is strictly to be observed in this matter, so that no member or members of a session or presbytery, should inform these judicatories of any thing against another member, until they have first given him private admonition or reproof, of a competent time before, and that has proven ineffectual.

5. The session is to judge of all informations concerning the member removed; and as they judge him deserving, either only the private admonition or reproof of the minister his alone, or any of the elders their alone, or of the moderator, in name of the session *coram*, as the weight of the matter, the edification of the party, and comfort of the session or congregation requireth, is to be done with all love, tenderness, and freedom.

6. If nothing be observed needful to be amended, but an account from all hands of the faithfulness, prudence, and diligence of the member removed, then he is to be exhorted to go on, and encouraged, and God to be blessed on his account; and the moderator, when he is called in, to express the session's satisfaction and comfort therein.

7. After all the elders have thus been removed one after another, and each one after he hath been called in, and got the mind of the session concerning him, and set in his place, the deacons one after another are to undergo their censures.

8. Next after the deacons, the clerk of the session is to be removed, and the members inquired concerning his carriage, and the session books, and other registers of births, baptisms, and burials, should be seen to be exactly kept and put in readiness for the presbytery when called for by them.

9. The beadle or officer should likewise in the same manner be inquired after, and either admonished or encouraged as need requireth.

10. Here also the kirk treasurer's accounts may be taken in, and the whole session put in mind (if need be) of all the duties of their charge, and of the rules of order, when met in judicatories.

VII. *The Method of proceeding in Presbyteries.*

1. This judicatory consists of all the pastors within the bounds, and one ruling elder from each parish therein, who receives a commission from the eldership

M

to be a member of the presbytery, and represent them there till the next synod be over: thus twice a year there are new elections of the ruling elders. The number of parishes associated in presbyteries for their mutual help, is determined by authority of the National Synod, Dec. 17, 18, Art. 8, as the adjacency of the congregations and the easiness of travelling doth best allow. Where there are collegiate ministers, that session may send as many ruling elders. The directory for government saith, that to perform any classical act of government or ordination, there shall be present, at least, a major part of the ministers of the whole classes. Presbyteries should meet every third week, and oftener if business require it.

2. Every meeting of a presbytery is to begin with a sermon by one of the brethren appointed formerly for that effect, upon a text assigned him by them, except when probationers or intrants supply the pulpit in their public trials. The half of the time allowed for this presbyterial exercise is to be taken up in the explicatory and analytic part of the text, and in answering textual and critical questions and difficulties; this part of the work is called *making*, and requires more especially the gift of the doctor: the other half of the time allowed is to be taken up in raising of doctrines and observations from the text, and applying them in their several uses; which last part is called *adding*, and it requires more especially the gift and necessarily the authority of the pastor. After the exercise is over, and the presbytery constitute, the censure of the exercise they have heard useth always to be their first work, which may be done before them who had the exercise: besides this, the brethren of the presbytery, by the Act of Assembly, Dec. 17, 18, 1631, are to have some common head of doctrine publicly disputed in the presbytery among the brethren, every first presbytery of the month, according to the Act of Assembly holden at Dundee. 1598, sess. 12.

3. By the foresaid act 1638, presbyterial meetings are to be weekly, except in places far distant, who between

the first of October and first of April are dispensèd with for meeting once in the fourteen days. Likewise that act appoints all absents to be censured, especially those that should exercise and add, according to the Act of Assembly 1582, April 24.

4. The presbytery treats of such matters as concern the particular churches within their bounds, as the examination, admission, ordination, and censuring of ministers; the licensing of probationers, rebuking of gross or contumacious sinners; the directing of the censure of excommunication; the cognoscing upon references and appeals from kirk-sessions; the revising and rectifying what hath been ill done or negligently omitted by them, at their approving of the kirk-session books and records; the answering of questions, cases of conscience, and solving of difficulties in doctrine or discipline, with petitions from their own or those in other presbyteries; the examining and censuring according to the word of God, any erroneous doctrine, which hath been publicly or more privately vented within their bounds, and the endeavouring the reducing and conversion of any that remain in error and schism, the appointing of visitation of churches by themselves as occasion offers, or the perambulation of parishes in order to their uniting or disjoining; all which are either concluded or continued to further consideration, or referred to the Synod.

5. By 6th chap. 11. Act of Assembly 1707, there are some processes which natively begin at the kirk session, which for the atrocity of the scandal, or difficulty in the affair, or general concern; the session having frequent meetings of the presbytery to have recourse unto, do not determine of themselves, such as scandals of incest, adultery, trilapse in fornication, murder, atheism, idolatry, witchcraft, charming, heresy, and error vented and made public by any in the congregation, schism and separation from the public ordinances, processes in order to the highest censure and continued contumacy. But processes for all such crimes and scandals are to be re-

ferred to the presbytery by an extract of their procedure thereanent; and when there is no confession of the scandals above mentioned, the session is not so much as to proceed to lead probation by witnesses or presumptions, till they be authorized thereto by the presbytery's answer to the reference foresaid.

6. When the process is so clear, as in the case of a judicial confession, then the kirk-session may summon the delinquent when before them *apud acta*, to compear before the presbytery: but where there is any difficulty, they should first inform the presbytery, and get their allowance before the party be summoned before them.

7. When persons censured for these grosser scandals do apply to the kirk-session for relaxation, they may both be privately conferred with, and likewise their acknowledgments heard before the session; but they ought not to be brought before the congregation, in order to their absolution, nor absolved but by direction and order of the presbytery.

8. Presbyteries in some cases may send commissioners to other presbyteries, either to advise them or to seek advice from them. By Act of Assemby, June 18, 1646, it is recommended, that a correspondence be kept among presbyteries constantly by letters, whereby they may be mutually assisting to each other.

9. In every presbytery, at least twice a year, on days for prayer, as should be done in sessions likewise, before each synod there ought to be privy censures, whereby each minister is removed by course, and then inquiry is made at the pastors and elders, if there be any known scandal, fault, or negligence in him, that it may be in a brotherly manner censured; after the ministers, the presbytery clerk is to pass these censures likewise. By the 6th article of the 7th chapter of the French Church, brotherly censures shall be made, as well by the pastors as by the elders which shall be there present, of all things which shall be thought fit to represent unto them.

VIII. *Of Parochial Visitations by the Presbytery.*

1. Parishes are visited by presbyteries, either occasionally, *pro re nata*, according to the weight of the emergent which doth require the visitation, or ordinarily and in course, whereby every congregational church is visited once a year, Assembly 1638, Sess. 23, 24, Art. 3: at least this ordinary visitation should be going round all the parishes in order till they be visited, before others be revisited in ordinary; for by the 16th Act of Assem. 1706, presbyterial visitations of parishes are to be frequent.

2. The presbytery is to cause intimation to be made of their appointed day for the visitation of that parish, by a brother of another congregation, from the pulpit, immediately after the forenoon's sermon, on the Sabbath, ten days preceding the day for the visitation, requiring the minister of the parish to preach at that time and place on his ordinary text, and summoning the heritors, elders, and whole congregation, to be present that day to hear sermon; and thereafter, that the minister, heritors, elders, and heads of families, do attend the presbytery, to acquaint them with the state of that kirk and congregation in every point; and if any of them have certain knowledge of any thing amiss in the minister, elders, deacons, precentor, session-clerk, schoolmaster, or beadle, that they do then acquaint the presbytery therewith.

3. The session registers, together with a catalogue of the minister's books, are to be produced to the presbytery, before the visitation, and given to two of the fittest brethren, and best acquainted with that minister and people, to be seen and revised, and they to report at the visitation.

4. Sermon being ended, and the presbytery constituted, the minister's doctrine he had in his sermon, is first to be considered, as in the presbyterial exercise. Then the Church Bible, Confession of Faith, Acts of the General Assemblies, Acts and Proclamations against,

profaneness, and other acts and papers relative to the church, are all to be called for and produced before the presbytery. The visitors of the sessions registers and minister's library are to make their report. The presbytery at the entry on the visitation having removed the minister, are to cause read over their actings at the last visitation, and see if what was then recommended or ordered hath been made effectual, and take the excuses of absent elders and deacons therefrom; and, if need be, to call in any party for information. If nothing arise from that, to divert the presbytery from the orderly method, all parties being removed, the presbytery is to call in the session *vicissim*, and to inquire them concerning their minister; yea further, by the Act of Assembly, June 13, 1646, at visitation of kirks, the elders, one by one, the rest being removed, are to be called in and examined upon oath concerning the minister's behaviour.

5. By the Act of Assembly 1596, ratified December 17, 18, 1638, at visitation of kirks, the families of ministers are to give an account, and to be tried concerning the good order and behaviour that they observe within their families; and such as are found neglecters of family worship, or instructing of all in their families, or such as remove not those who are offensive therefrom, shall, after due admonition, be judged unfit to rule the house of God: for he ought to be one that ruleth well his own house, 1 Tim. iii. 4.

6. The questions to be inquired by a presbytery at the eldership concerning a minister may be these and such like :—1. Hath your minister a Gospel walk and conversation before the people? And doth he keep family worship? And is he one who rules well his own house? Is he a haunter of ale-houses and taverns? Is he a dancer, carder, or dicer? Is he proud or vainglorious? Is he greedy, or worldly, or an usurer? Is he contentious, a brawler, fighter, or striker? Is he a swearer of small or minced oaths? Useth he to say, *Before God it is so;* or in his common conference, *I protest,* or, *I protest before God?* Or says he, *Lord,*

what is that? all which are more than *Yea* and *Nay*. Is he a filthy speaker or jester? Bears he familiar company with disaffected, profane, or scandalous persons? Is he dissolute, prodigal, light or loose in his carriage, apparel, or words? How spends he the Sabbath after sermon? Saw ye him ever drink healths? Is he at variance with any? Is there any that reproaches him? Or is he well beloved of all? And upon what ground is it that the variance or good liking of the people is?—2. Keeps he much at home at his ministerial work? Or doth he occasion to himself distractions, and unnecessary diversion therefrom? Is he constant at his calling and studies, or takes he but pains, at fits and starts, such as at fasts, communions, visitations, &c.? Is Saturday only his book-day; or is he constant at his calling?—3. Doth he countenance or discourage any that is seeking Christ? Doth he preach sound doctrine, so far as ye can understand? Doth he preach plainly; or is he hard to be understood for his scholastic terms, matter, or manner of preaching? Doth he faithfully reprove sin, especially such as most prevail in the parish? What time of day doth he ordinarily begin sermon on the Sabbath? And when doth he dismiss the people? Spends he too much time in his sermon in repetition of what he said before? Doth he lecture and preach in the forenoon, and preach again in the afternoon on the Lord's day, and that both summer and winter? Doth he read a large portion of Scripture in public, and expound the same? Doth he preach catechetic doctrine ordinarily in the afternoon? Hath he a week day's sermon, and collections on these days? When the Lord, in his providence, is speaking extraordinary things, doth he tie himself to his ordinary text; or makes he choice of one more apposite and suitable to the dispensation? Seeks he to preach Christ, his beauty and excellency, and to open up the power and life of godliness? Endeavours he to discuss cases of conscience, to let you know your spiritual state what it is?—4. Doth he, according to the Act of Assembly 1708, visit the people and families, at least once a year, in a ministerial way, teaching. and. admonishing from house to house? And doth he visit the sick when needful, and pray over them? Doth he visit them who, through age or sickness, cannot come to the public worship? Doth he labour to speak to the sick suitably to their various inward conditions? Doth he not especially visit such as be exercised in conscience? Doth he visit such as are afflicted by death of children or other relations? Visits he the wisdows, orphans, and poor? If he be minister of a burgh, visits he the prisoners? Is he not careful when he visits families to confer with them in private, and pray with them, thereby learning the case of their souls, that so the doctrine in public may the better meet with their condition?—5. Doth he administer the sacrament of baptism in an orderly way, when the congregation is convened, or doth he it at any time privately? Doth he add any word to, or alter the words of institution?— 6. Doth he frequently catechise his parishioners, and administer the sacrament of the Lord's Supper to them? And is he careful in keeping from that holy ordinance, all who are known to be scandalous, grossly ignorant, or erroneous? How often have ye the communion every year? Doth not he begin to catechise young ones about nine or ten years of age, and how censures he contemners of catechizing? What course is taken with contemners of the Lord's Supper upon frivolous pretences? At the Lord's Supper, doth he not cause cut the bread in large and fair shaves, fit for mutual fraction and distribution, that as they give the cup to the nearest assident, so having broken off a part of the bread with their hand for themselves, they give the rest to the person sitting nearest them? Do your people all sit at the Lord's table? In the time of distribution, eating, and drinking, is there any reading or singing of psalms, or is there silence, and so time for meditation, except it be a short, pertinent, and awakening word dropped by the pastor?—7. Hath he a competent number of elders? And hath he deacons in the parish distinct from elders? Doth he keep sessional meetings frequently? And is he impartial in the exercise of discipline against all offenders? Is there frequent meetings of the members of session, for fasting and prayer, according to the Act of Assembly 1699? Doth he travail with public penitents in private to make them sensible of their sin, according to its circumstances, and sensible of mercy, that the love of Christ may overcome the love of sin? And then doth he absolve them, when brought up to some ingenuous confession and resolution for the future? Doth he ever censure persons for living idle, breaking of promise, or for backbiting? Doth he censure keepers of superstitious days? How doth he restrain abuses at penny bridals? Doth your session meet weekly? Doth your minister coolzie any whom another brother hath in process? Or doth he carry any away partially, so that he may become popular? Doth he in session assume to himself a negative voice? When he is necessitated to leave his flock, doth he not acquaint the session with it?—8. Is he careful to take away variances that fall out among families, and compose differences among particular persons in the congregation?

7. After that the elders have answered to these or the like questions, then the heads of families are to be interrogate in general concerning the lives and manners of the members of the session. And the pastor is to answer more particularly to these or the like questions:—1. Is your session rightly constitute, and all the elders and deacons duly admitted according to the Acts of Assembly?—2. Do they all attend Gospel ordinances and the diets of the session?—3. Are they grave, pious, and exemplary in their lives and conversations? Do they worship God in their families? Is any of your elders an ignorant man, a drinker of healths, a tipler, a drinker excessively to drunkenness, a swearer, an observer of yule days, &c.? Is he one that observes not the Sabbath? Is he careful to keep his oath of admission taken before God in face of the congregation, not to delate or censure, but as edification requires?

Do any of them work on solemn fast or thanksgiving days? Is any of them a mocker of piety?—4. Are they diligent, careful, and impartial in the exercise of their offices? Do the elders visit the families within the quarter and bounds assigned to each of them? Are they careful to have the worship of God set up in the families of their bounds? Are they careful in calling for testimonials from persons who come to reside in the parish? Do the elders take all discipline upon themselves without the minister? Or do they labour to carry things factiously, or by plurality of voices, contrary to God's word, and the laudable acts of the presbytery, provincial, or general assemblies?—5. Have the elders subscribed the Confession of Faith? And are they well affected to the government, worship, and discipline of this church?—6. Have the elders and deacons their distinct bounds assigned them for their particular inspection?—7. Does your session always appoint ruling elders to attend presbyteries and synods?—8. Are the deacons faithful in their office, in collecting and distributing all the kirk-goods, and in having a care of the sick poor?—After all these queries are over, the minister and elders are to be severally encouraged or admonished as the presbytery sees need.

8. Then the precentor, schoolmaster, and clerk of the session, who in country congregations are ordinarily one and the same, and after them the beadles, bellman, and church servants being removed, the presbytery is to inquire at the minister, session, and heads of families, concerning their conversation, fidelity, and diligence in their offices, and the presbytery is thereupon to proceed as the matter requires.

9. After all these inquiries, the presbytery removing the heads of families, the minister and elders are to be inquired concerning the congregation :—1. Doth the body of the people attend ordinances duly and timeously and stay till the blessing be pronounced? Are they diligent in improving the means of knowledge, and are they growing therein?—2. Are they submissive to public

and private exhortations, and to the discipline and censure of the church, by admonitions and reproof, as need requires? And do they by their words and actions manifest a suitable respect to their minister and respective elders?—3. Are they careful to educate their children and servants in the knowledge of God? What success hath the Gospel and labours of ministers and elders among them? What scandals, schisms, heresies, or divisions are among them, and if on the growing hand? How do they observe the Lord's day?

10. Then the minister, heritors, session, and heads of families being present, the presbytery is to inquire after the state of the church, as to its fabric, the seats therein and division of the same, the church-yard, dykes, the utensils of the church, communion-cups, clothes, the minister's manse if it be in repair, the glebe and stipend, the salary of the schoolmaster, precentor, session-clerk, and beadles, and how the communion elements are provided; whether they be paid for out of the poor's money, and that when the communion is but celebrated once a year? Inquiry is to be made how much the stipend is, of what nature, how paid, and if there be a decree of locality for it? As also, about the state of the poor, whether there be any mortifications and legacies for them, or other pious uses? And how these are secured, and their interests paid and applied, and how thay have been managed and employed from time to time. Sess. 18, Assem. 1700.

After the visitation is over, all parties are to be called in, and the moderator is to conclude all with prayer.

IX. *Of Ministerial Visitation of Families.*

1. It hath been the laudable practice of this church, at least once a year (if the largeness of the parish, or bodily inability, or other such like do not hinder), for ministers to visit all the families in their parish, and oftener if the bounds be small, and they able to perform it. Among other reasons for these annual visitations of families, this may be one,—that because by the order

prescribed by our Lord, Matt. xviii., there may be several offences known to ministers, elders, or neighbours, which may justly keep back offenders from partaking of the Lord's Supper, and yet it were disorderly and unedifying to remove these offences in a public way, these visitations may serve to purge a congregation of such private scandals.

2. Although in regard of the different circumstances of some parishes, families, and persons, much of the management of the work must be left to the prudence and discretion of ministers, in their respective oversights, yet these following directions are offered by Assembly, 1708, April 27, as helps for the more uniform and successful management thereof, that it be not done in a slight and overly manner, which supposeth the universal practice thereof through this church, and that the total neglecters may be censured therefore as supinely negligent.

3. Such a time of year is to be chosen for ministerial visitation, as the families which he visits may be best at leisure to meet with him; and if that time should happen immediately after the communion, then it is seasonable, as it were, to beat the iron while it is hot. Timeous intimation is to be made to them of the visitation; and the elder of that bounds of the parish which is to be visited, is to accompany the minister; and they should previously confer together concerning the condition and state of the persons and families of those bounds.

4. When they enter a house, they are to express their wishes and desires for the blessing of God upon it, and that, above all, their souls may prosper; then let them take an account of the names of the family, inquire for testimonials from them who are lately come to the parish, and mark them in the roll for catechising, and let them take notice who can read, and of the age of children capable to be catechised; then the minister is to speak to them all in general, of the necessity and advantage of godliness, of justice and charity towards man.

5. He is next more particularly to speak to servants

of their duty, to serve and fear God, to be dutiful, faithful, and obedient servants, and of the promises made to such, commending to them the reading of the Scriptures, secret worship, and love and concord among themselves; and, in particular, a holy care in sanctifying the Lord's day.

6. The minister is to show the children and young servants the advantage of knowing, seeking, and loving God, and remembering their Creator and Redeemer in the days of their youth, and to mind them how they are dedicated to God in baptism : and when of age, and after due instruction in the nature of the covenant of grace, to excite them to engage themselves personally to the Lord, and to design and prepare for the first opportunity they can have of partaking of the Lord's Supper, to be especially careful how they at first communicate.

7. Then he is to speak privately to the heads of the family about their personal duties towards God, and the care of their own souls, and their obligation to promote religion and the worship of God in their family, and to restrain and get vice punished, and piety encouraged, and to be careful that they and all in their house serve the Lord, and sanctify his day. He is more particularly to inquire,—1. Whether God be worshipped in the family, by prayers, praises, and reading of the Scripture?—2. Concerning the behaviour of servants towards God and towards man, if they attend family and public worship? How they sanctify the Lord's Day? and if they be given to secret prayer and reading the Scriptures?—3. If there be catechising in the family? If their children be trained up in reading, according to the Act of Assembly, Aug. 10, 1648 : in all which the minister may intermix suitable directions, encouragements, and admonitions, as may be most edifying.

8. The minister is to inquire who want Bibles; and if they be not able to buy them, let the poor's box be at the expenses; and recommend to the heads of the family to get the Confession of Faith, Catechisms, and other good books, for instructing in life and faith; according to their ability.—2. Those who are tainted

with error or vice are to be admonished secretly, or in the family, as may most edify; and all are to be exhorted to carry toward such as walk orderly according to the rule, Matt. xviii. 15.—3. The minister is to endeavour to remove divisions in the family, or with their neighbours, and exhort them to follow peace with all men as far as is possible.—4. Let it be inquired who have communicated, that they may be called to an account privately how they have profited, and put in mind to pay their vows to the Lord. Confer also with others about the causes of their not communicating.

9. As for those who pretend conscience for not keeping communion with us, or whatever their motives be, ministers ought to deal with God for them, and with themselves in such a way as may be most proper to gain them, and exoner their consciences, waiting if peradventure God will prevail with him. Who can tell if their making them sensible of their tender love and affection to their persons, especially to their souls, giving them all due respect, and doing them all the good they can, yet still discountenancing their sin, may in the end be blessed of God for their good? Judg. v. 22, 23; 2 Tim. ii. 24, 25.

10. Seeing in the whole of this work, there is great need of much prudence, zeal for God, and love to souls, visitation of families should be carried on with dependance on God, and fervent prayer to him, both before a minister set forth to such a work, and with the visited, as there can be access to, and opportunity for it.

X. Of Sanctification of the Lord's Day; and observing Fast and Thanksgiving Days.

1. The Sabbath is to be sanctified by an holy resting all that day, even from such worldly employments and recreations as are lawful on other days, and spending the whole time in the public and private exercises of God's worship, except so much as is to be taken up in the works of necessity and mercy, as our Shorter Catechism beareth, authorised by Assembly, Aug. 28, 1648.

From which we may gather what the church understands
by sanctifying or profaning of the Lord's day, and so
will either approve or censure.

2. By the Act of Assembly 1647, concerning Family
Worship, Dir. 8, the master of the family ought to take
care, that all within his charge repair to the public worship; which being finished, he is to see the rest of that day
spent in the private and secret exercises of piety. Care is
also to be taken that the diet on that day be so ordered,
that neither servants be unnecessarily detained from the
public worship of God, nor any other persons hindered
from sanctifying that day. Private preparation is likewise to be made for the Sabbath by prayer and such holy
exercises, as may dispose to a more comfortable communion with God in his public ordinances. See the
Directory.

3. When some great and notable judgments are either
inflicted or imminent, or by some extraordinary provocation notoriously deserved; as also when some special
blessing is to be sought or obtained, when great duties
are called for, or when sins are extraordinary for their
number or nature; then it is that a church may enjoin
fasting, which is observed by a total abstinence, not only
from all food (unless bodily weakness do manifestly
disable from holding out till the fast be ended, in which
case somewhat may be taken, yet very sparingly, to support nature when ready to faint), but also from all worldly
labour, discourses, and thoughts, and from all bodily
delights, though at other times lawful, rich apparel, or-
naments, and such like, during the fast; and much more
from whatever is in its nature or use scandalous or offensive, as gaudish attire, lascivious habits and gestures,
and other vanities of either sex; which the composers
of the Directory recommend to all ministers in their
places diligently and zealously to reprove, as at other
times, so especially at a fast.

4. The Sabbath before the fast, the causes thereof are
publicly read from the pulpit, and the day of the week
intimated upon which it is to be kept. The people are
then to be earnestly exhorted to prepare themselves for

afflicting . their souls upon that day of extraordinary
humiliation. So large a portion of that day, as conveniently may be, is to be spent in public reading and
preaching of the word, with singing of Psalms, fit to
quicken affections suitable to such a duty, but especially
in prayer to this or the like effect; giving glory to the
great majesty of God the Creator, Preserver, and supreme
Ruler of all the world, acknowledging his manifold
great and tender mercies, especially to the church and
nation, humbly confessing sins of all sorts, with their
several aggravations, justifying God's righteous judgments, as being far less than our sins do deserve, yet
humbly and earnestly imploring his mercy and grace for
ourselves, the church, and nation, the king, and all in
authority, and for all others for whom we are bound to
pray (according as the present exigent requireth), with
more special importunity and enlargement than at other
times; applying by faith the promises and goodness of
God for pardon, help, and deliverance from the evils
felt, feared, or deserved; and for obtaining the blessings
which we need and expect, together with a giving up
of ourselves wholly, and for ever unto the Lord.

5. Beside solemn and general fasts appointed by the
assemblies or their commissions, or by civil authority,
upon application from some church judicatory unto them;
provincial synods, presbyteries, and church sessions may
appoint fast days to be kept within their respective bounds,
as Divine Providence shall administer unto them special
occasions. Likewise families and particular persons may
do the same, providing their fasts be not on those days
on which the congregation is to meet for public worship.
. Our fasting days must be indicted for such causes as
are both clear and just, and when it will be most for
edification ; . for that, as other positive duties doth not
always bind, therefore the church is to take heed of
appointing fasts through insinuations or solicitations
from statesmen, lest they be branded as tools to some
who would fast from strife and debate, that others who
differ from them about state matters may be exposed to
the odium of the people, as ill countrymen.

7. The causes of the fast enumerate in the Act of Assembly 1690, November 12, were these and the like. 1. Perjury, dealing treacherously with the Lord, and being unstedfast in his covenant. 2. Unfruitfulness under the purity of doctrine, worship, and government; "having a form of godliness, but denying the power thereof." 3. Abuse of God's great goodness and deliverance, evidenced by a course of manifest wickedness and shameful debauchery; such as drunkenness, cursing, swearing, adultery, and uncleanness of all sorts. 4. The supremacy; which was advanced in such a way, and to such a height, as never any Christian church acknowledged, and whereby the interest of our Lord Jesus Christ was entirely sacrificed to the lawless wills and lusts of men. 5. Abjured prelacy was introduced, and the government of the church was overturned, without the church's consent, and contrary to the standing acts of our national assemblies. 6. Compliance with that defection both in ministers and others, some from a principle of pride and covetousness, or man-pleasing; and others through infirmity and weakness, or fear of man, and want of courage and zeal for God. 7. Persecution of the godly for non-compliance with that sinful course: many faithful ministers were cast out, and many insufficient and scandalous men thrust in on their charges, and many families ruined because they would not own them as their pastors. 8. Decay of piety under the late prelacy, so that it was enough to make a man be nick-named a fanatic, if he did not run to the same excess of riot with others. 9. Atheism; which discovered itself in some by their dreadful boldness against God, in disputing his Being and Providence, the Divine authority of the Scriptures; the life to come; and immortality of the soul; yea, and scoffed at those things. 10. Imposing and taking unlawful oaths and bonds: lawful oaths have been broken, and ungodly and conscience-polluting oaths have been imposed and taken, whereby the consciences of many, through the land, are become so debauched, that they scruple at no oath, though many

N

have been oppressed and ruined for refusing them. 11. Neglect of the worship of God, both in public, in private families, and in secret. 12. Profanation of the Lord's day succeeded in place of that wonted care of strict and religious sanctifying of it. 13. The shedding of innocent blood. 14. Pride and vanity: yea, Sodom's sins have abounded among us; idleness, fulness of bread, vanity of apparel, and shameful sensuality filled the land. 15. As also, great perverting of justice, by making and executing unrighteous statutes. 16. Silence of ministers at the time of such a great defection, as well as too general a fainting among professors: and as some shewed no zeal in giving seasonable and necessary testimony against the defections and evils of the time, nor keeped a due distance from them; so, on the other hand, some managed their zeal with too little discretion and meekness. 17. The abominable idolatry of the mass was set up in many places, and popish schools erected, whereby shameful advances were made towards Popery. 18. Great ignorance of the way of salvation through the Lord Jesus Christ. Though we profess to acknowledge there can be no pardon of sins, no peace and reconciliation with God but by his blood, yet few know him, or see the necessity and excellency of him; and few esteem, desire, or receive him as he is offered in the Gospel; and as few are acquainted with faith in him, and living by faith on him, so few walk as becometh the Gospel, and imitate our Lord in humility, meekness, self-denial, heavenly-mindedness, zeal for God, and charity towards men. 19. Great contempt of the Gospel, barrenness under it, and a deep security under our sin and danger. 20. Though the Lord, by casting us into the furnace of affliction, hath been giving us a sight of the vanity of all things beside himself; yet to this day there is a woeful selfishness among us, every one seeking his own things, few or none the things of Jesus Christ, the public good, or one another's welfare. 21. A bitter spirit of censoriousness, whereby the most part are more ready to carp at the sins and defections of others, than to repent and mourn for their own. These and the like were the causes of the fast in the year 1690, and to them the fasts appointed since do ordinarily refer. See also how the land expressed the sense it had of the guilt of all ranks in the solemn acknowledgment of public sins, and breaches of the covenant, and a solemn engagement to all the duties contained therein; namely, those which did in a more especial way relate unto the dangers of that time. Act of the Commission of Assembly, October 6, 1648, for renewing of the Solemn League and Covenant ratified by Assembly thereafter.

8. Albeit by the treatise of fasting emitted by the Assembly, Dec. 25, 1565, the Sundays were appointed for some fasts, as being for the greater ease of the people; and since, by the last Act of Assembly, 1646, a fast is appointed on the Sabbath next except one, preceding the then following General Assembly; yet seeing the work to be performed on the first day of the week is by Divine institution already determined, we ought to set about it exactly, which we all acknowledge to be a thanksgiving, and not a fast. Extraordinary duties are not to interfere with the ordinary, nor is one duty to shuffle out another. If either should be allowed, it would look somewhat like the reverse of redeeming the time, for thereby diligence is rather diminished than doubled in the service of God.

9. Days of thanksgiving being intimate on the preceding Sabbath, for some deliverance obtained, or mercy received, are wholly to be spent in the public and private exercise of Divine worship and praises; the people are to rejoice with trembling, and to beware of all excess in eating or drinking. And demonstrations of civil mirth, such as ringing of bells, firing of guns, bonefires, and illuminating of windows, should not be intermixed with the religious duties of that day: but as upon fasts, so upon these days, there should be liberal collections for the poor, that their bowels may bless us, and rejoice the more with us. In the 6th Article the Church

was cautioned against appointing fasts for strife and debate, so I hope they shall be directed to avoid enjoining of thanksgiving days from any false or unjust ends.

Act anent the Administration of the Sacraments. Edinburgh, 31st Oct. 1690, *ante meridiem,* Sess. 15.

The General Assembly considering, that the two sacraments that Christ hath appointed under the New Testament—viz. Baptism and the Lord's Supper—are his solemn ordinances, and seals of the covenant of grace, which is held forth in the preaching of the Gospel ; and that in the use of them, the parties receiving them are solemnly devoted and engaged to God before angels and men, and are solemnly received as members of the church, and do entertain communion with her ; and that by the authority of this church, in her former assemblies, the private use of them hath been condemned, as also, that by allowing the private use of the same in pretended cases of necessity, the superstitious opinion is nourished, that they are necessary to salvation, not only as commanded duties, but as means, without which salvation cannot be attained. Therefore the Assembly hereby discharges the administration of the Lord's Supper to sick persons in their houses, and all other use of the same, except in the public assemblies of the church. And also do discharge the administration of baptism in private ; that is, in any place, or at any time, when the congregation is not orderly called together, to wait on the dispensing of the word ; and appoints that this be carefully observed, when and wherever the Lord giveth his people peace, liberty, and opportunity for their public assemblies, and ordains this present act to be publicly intimate in all the churches.

END OF ACTS.

THE LARGER CATECHISM,

AGREED UPON

BY THE ASSEMBLY OF DIVINES AT WESTMINSTER.

Examined and approved, Anno 1648, by the General Assembly of the Church of Scotland; and ratified by Act of Parliament, 1649.

———

Q. 1. What is the chief and highest end of man?—
A. Man's chief and highest end is to glorify God (*a*), and fully to enjoy him for ever (*b*).

(*a*) Rom. xi. 36; 1 Cor. x. 31;　(*b*) Psal. lxxiii. 24, *to the end;* John xvii. 21—23.

Q. 2. How doth it appear that there is a God?—
A. The very light of nature in man, and the works of God, declare plainly that there is a God (*c*); but his word and Spirit only do sufficiently and effectually reveal him unto men for their salvation (*d*).

(*c*) Rom. i. 19, 20; Psal. xix. 1—3; Acts xvii. 28.
(*d*) 1 Cor. ii. 9, 10; 2 Tim. iii. 15—17; Isai. lix. 21.

Q. 3. What is the word of God?—A. The Holy Scriptures of the Old and New Testament are the word of God (*e*), the only rule of faith and obedience (*f*).

(*e*) 2 Tim. iii. 16; 2 Pet. i. 19—21.　(*f*) Eph. ii. 20; Rev. xxii. 18, 19; Isai. viii. 20; Luke xvi. 29, 31; Gal. i. 8, 9; 2 Tim. iii. 15, 16.

Q. 4. How doth it appear that the Scriptures are the word of God?—A. The Scriptures manifest themselves to be the word of God by their majesty (*g*) and purity (*h*); by the consent of all the parts (*i*), and the scope of the whole, which is to give all glory to God (*k*); by their light and power to convince and convert sinners, to comfort and build up believers unto salvation (*l*) : but the Spirit of God bearing witness by and with the Scriptures in the heart of man, is alone able fully to persuade it that they are the very word of God (*m*).

(*g*) Hos. viii. 12; 1 Cor. ii. 6, 7, 13; Psal. cxix. 18, 129.   (*h*) Psal. xii. 6, and cxix. 140.   (*i*) Acts x. 43, and xxvi. 22.   (*k*) Rom. iii. 19, 27. (*l*) Acts xviii. 28; Heb. iv. 12; Jas. i. 18; Psal. xix. 7—9; Rom. xv. 4; Acts xx. 32.   (*m*) John xvi. 13, 14; 1 John ii. 20, 27; John xx. 31.

Q. 5. What do the Scriptures principally teach?— A. The Scriptures principally teach, what man is to believe concerning God, and what duty God requires of man (*n*).

(*n*) 2 Tim. i. 13.

Q. 6. What do the Scriptures make known of God?— A. The Scriptures make known what God is (*o*), the persons in the Godhead (*p*), his decrees (*q*), and the execution of his decrees (*r*).

(*o*) Heb. xi. 6.   (*p*) 1 John v. 7.   (*q*) Acts xv. 14, 15, 18.   (*r*) Acts iv. 27, 28.

Q. 7. What is God?—A. God is a Spirit (*s*), in and of himself infinite in being (*t*), glory (*u*), blessedness (*w*), and perfection (*x*); all-sufficient (*y*), eternal (*z*), unchangable (*a*), incomprehensible (*b*), every where present (*c*), almighty (*d*), knowing all things (*e*), most wise (*f*), most holy (*g*), most just (*h*), most merciful and gracious, long-suffering, and abundant in godness and truth (*i*).

(*s*) John iv. 24.   (*t*) Exod. iii. 14; Job. xi. 7—9. (*u*) Acts vii. 2.   (*w*) 1 Tim. vi. 15.   (*x*) Matt. v. 48.   (*y*) Gen. xvii. 1.   (*z*) Psal. xc. 2. (*a*) Mal. iii. 6; James i. 17.   (*b*) 1 Kings viii. 27. (*c*) Psal. cxxxix. 1—13.   (*d*) Rev. iv. 8.   (*e*) Heb. iv. 13; Psal. cxlvii. 5.   (*f*) Rom. xvi. 27.

(g) Isai. vi. 3; Rev. xv. 4.   (h) Deut. xxxii. 4. (i) Exod. xxxiv. 6.

Q. 8. Are there more gods than one?—A. There is but one only, the living and true God (k).

(k) Deut. vi. 4; 1 Cor. viii. 4, 6; Jer. x. 10.

Q. 9. How many persons are there in the Godhead? —A. There be three persons in the Godhead, the Father, the Son, and the Holy Ghost; and these three are one, true, eternal God, the same in substance, equal in power and glory, although distinguished by their personal properties (l).

(l) 1 John v. 7; Matt. iii. 16, 17, and xxviii. 19; 2 Cor. xiii. 14; John x. 30.

Q. 10. What are the personal properties of the three persons in the Godhead?—A. It is proper to the Father to beget the Son (m), and to the Son to be begotten of the Father (n), and to the Holy Ghost to proceed from the Father and the Son from all eternity (o).

(m) Heb. i. 5, 6, 8.   (n) John i. 14, 18.   (o) John xv. 26; Gal. iv. 6.

Q. 11. How doth it appear that the Son and the Holy Ghost are God equal with the Father?—A. The Scriptures manifest that the Son and the Holy Ghost are God equal with the Father, ascribing unto them such names (p), attributes (q), works (r), and worship as are proper to God only (s).

(p) Isai. vi. 3, 5, 8, with John xii. 41, and Acts xxviii. 25; 1 John v. 20; Acts v. 3, 4.   (q) John i. 1; Isai. ix. 6; John ii. 24, 25; 1 Cor. ii. 10, 11. (r) Col. i. 16; Gen. i. 2.   (s) Matt. xxviii. 19; 2 Cor. xiii. 14.

Q. 12. What are the decrees of God?—A. God's decrees are the wise, free, and holy acts of the counsel of his will (t), whereby, from all eternity, he hath, for his own glory, unchangeably fore-ordained whatsoever comes to pass in time (u), especially concerning angels and men.

(t) Eph. i. 11; Rom. xi. 33, and ix. 14, 15, 18. (u) Eph. i. 4, 11; Rom. ix. 22, 23; Psal. xxxiii. 11.

Q. 13. What hath God especially decreed concerning angels and men?—A. God, by an eternal and immutable decree, out of his mere love, for the praise of his glorious grace, to be manifested in due time, hath elected some angels to glory (*w*); and, in Christ, hath chosen some men to eternal life, and the means thereof (*x*): and also, according to his sovereign power, and the unsearchable counsel of his own will (whereby he extendeth or withholdeth favour as he pleaseth), hath passed by and fore-ordained the rest to dishonour and wrath, to be for their sin inflicted, to the praise of the glory of his justice (*y*).

(*w*) 1 Tim. v. 21. (*x*) Eph. i. 4—6; 2 Thess. ii. 13, 14. (*y*) Rom. ix. 17, 18, 21, 22; Matt. xi. 25, 26; 2 Tim. ii. 20; Jude 4; 1 Pet. ii. 8.

Q. 14. How doth God execute his decrees?—A. God executeth his decrees in the works of creation and providence, according to his infallible foreknowledge, and the free and immutable counsel of his own will (*z*).

(*z*) Eph. i. 11.

Q. 15. What is the work of creation?—A. The work of creation is that wherein God did in the beginning, by the word of his power, make of nothing the world, and all things therein, for himself, within the space of six days, and all very good (*a*).

(*a*) Gen. i.; Heb. xi. 3; Prov. xvi. 4.

Q. 16. How did God create the angels?—A. God created all the angels (*b*), spirits (*c*), immortal (*d*), holy (*e*), excelling in knowledge (*f*), mighty in power (*g*), to execute his commandments, and to praise his name (*h*), yet subject to change (*i*).

(*b*) Col. i. 16. (*c*) Psal. civ. 4. (*d*) Matt. xxii. 30. (*e*) Matt. xxv. 31. (*f*) 2 Sam. xiv. 17; Matt. xxiv. 36. (*g*) 2 Thess. i. 7. (*h*) Psal. ciii. 20, 21. (*i*) 2 Pet. ii. 4.

Q. 17. How did God create man?—A. After God had made all other creatures, he created man, male and female (*k*); formed the body of the man of the dust of the ground (*l*), and the woman of the rib of the man (*m*); endued them with living, reasonable, and immortal souls (*n*); made them after his own image (*o*), in knowledge (*p*), righteousness, and holiness (*q*): having the law of God written in their hearts (*r*), and power to fulfil it (*s*), with dominion over the creatures (*t*); yet subject to fall (*u*).

  (*k*) Gen. i. 27.   (*l*) Gen. ii. 7.   (*m*) Gen. ii. 22.   (*n*) Gen. ii. 7, with Job xxxv. 11, and Eccles. xii. 7, and Matt. x. 28, and Luke xxiii. 43.   (*o*) Gen. i. 27.   (*p*) Col. iii. 10.   (*q*) Ephes. iv. 24.   (*r*) Rom. ii. 14, 15.   (*s*) Eccles. vii. 29.   (*t*) Gen. i. 28.   (*u*) Gen. iii. 6; Eccles. vii. 29.

Q. 18. What are God's works of providence?—A. God's works of providence are the most holy (*w*), wise (*x*), and powerful preserving (*y*) and governing (*z*) all his creatures; ordering them, and all their actions (*a*), to his own glory (*b*).

  (*w*) Psal. cxlv. 17.   (*x*) Psal. civ. 24; Isa. xxviii. 29.   (*y*) Heb. i. 3.   (*z*) Psal. ciii. 19.   (*a*) Matt. x. 29—31; Gen. xlv. 7.   (*b*) Rom. xi. 36; Isai. lxiii. 14.

Q. 19. What is God's providence towards the angels?—A. God by his providence permitted some of the angels, wilfully and irrecoverably, to fall into sin and and damnation (*c*), limiting and ordering that, and all their sins, to his own glory (*d*); aud established the rest in holiness and happiness (*e*); employing them all (*f*), at his pleasure, in the administrations of his power, mercy, and justice (*g*).

  (*c*) Jude 6; 2 Pet. ii. 4; Heb. ii. 16; John viii. 44.   (*d*) Job i. 12; Matt. viii. 31.   (*e*) 1 Tim. v. 21 ; Mark viii. 38; Heb. xii. 22.   (*f*) Psal. civ. 4.   (*g*) 2 Kings xix. 35; Heb. i. 14.

Q. 20. What was the providence of God toward man in the estate in which he was created?—A. The providence of God toward man in the estate in which he was created, was the placing him in paradise, appoint-

ing him to dress it, giving him liberty to eat of the fruit
of the earth (*h*); putting the creatures under his dominion (*i*), and ordaining marriage for his help (*k*); afford-
ing him communion with himself (*l*); instituting the
Sabbath (*m*); entering into a covenant of life with him,
upon condition of personal, perfect, and perpetual obedience (*n*), of which the tree of life was a pledge (*o*);
and forbidding to eat of the tree of the knowledge of
good and evil upon pain of death (*p*).

    (*h*) Gen. ii. 8, 15, 16.   (*i*) Gen. i. 28.   (*k*) Gen.
    ii. 18.   (*l*) Gen. i. 26—29, and iii. 8.   (*m*) Gen.
    ii. 3.   (*u*) Gal. iii. 12; Rom. x. 5.   (*o*) Gen.
    ii. 9.   (*p*) Gen. ii. 17.

Q. 21. Did man continue in that estate wherein God
at first created him?—A. Our first parents, being left
to the freedom of their own will, through the temptation
of Satan, transgressed the commandment of God in
eating the forbidden fruit; and thereby fell from the
state of innocency wherein they were created (*q*).

    (*q*) Gen. iii. 6—8, 13; Eccles. vii. 29; 2 Cor. xi. 3.

Q. 22. Did all mankind fall in that first transgression?—A. The covenant being made with Adam, as a
public person, not for himself only, but for his posterity, all mankind, descending from him by ordinary
generation (*r*), sinned in him, and fell with him, in that
first transgression (*s*).

    (*r*) Acts xvii. 26.   (*s*) Gen. ii 16, 17, with Rom. v.
    12—20, and 1 Cor. xv. 21, 22.

Q. 23. Into what estate did the Fall bring mankind?
—A. The Fall brought mankind into an estate of sin
and misery (*t*).

    (*t*) Rom. v. 12, and iii. 23.

Q. 24. What is sin?—A. Sin is any want of conformity unto, or transgression of, any law of God given
as a rule to the reasonable creature (*u*).

    (*u*) 1 John iii. 4; Gal. iii. 10, 12.

Q. 25. Wherein consisteth the sinfulness of that estate
whereinto man fell?—A. The sinfulness of that estate

whereinto man fell, consisteth in the guilt of Adam's first sin (*w*), the want of that righteousness wherein he was created, and the corruption of his nature, whereby he is utterly indisposed, disabled, and made opposite unto all that is spiritually good, and wholly inclined to all evil, and that continually (*x*); which is commonly called original sin, and from which do proceed all actual transgressions (*y*).

(*w*) Rom. v. 12, 19.   (*x*) Rom. iii. 10—20; Eph. ii. 1—3; Rom. v. 6, and viii. 7, 8; Gen. vi. 5. (*y*) James i. 14, 15; Matt. xv. 19.

Q. 26. How is original sin conveyed from our first parents unto their posterity?—A. Original sin is conveyed from our first parents unto their posterity by natural generation, so as all that proceed from them in that way are conceived and born in sin (*z*).

(*z*) Psal. li. 5; Job xiv. 4, and xv. 14; John iii. 6.

Q. 27. What misery did the Fall bring upon mankind?—A. The Fall brought upon mankind the loss of communion with God (*a*), his displeasure and curse, so as we are by nature children of wrath (*b*), bond-slaves to Satan (*c*), and justly liable to all punishments in this world and that which is to come (*d*).

(*a*) Gen. iii. 8, 10, 24.   (*b*) Eph. ii. 2, 3.   (*c*) 2 Tim. ii. 26.   (*d*) Gen. ii. 17; Lam. iii. 39; Rom. vi. 23; Matt. xxv. 41, 46; Jude 7.

Q. 28. What are the punishments of sin in this world?—A. The punishments of sin in this world are either inward, as blindness of mind (*e*), a reprobate sense (*f*), strong delusions (*g*), hardness of heart (*h*), horror of conscience (*i*), and vile affections (*k*); or outward, as the curse of God upon the creatures for our sakes (*l*), and all other evils that befal us in our bodies, names, estates, relations, and employments (*m*), together with death itself (*n*).

(*e*) Eph. iv. 18.   (*f*) Rom. i. 28.   (*g*) 2 Thess. ii. 11.   (*h*) Rom. ii. 5.   (*i*) Isai. xxxiii. 14; Gen. iv. 13; Matt. xxvii. 4.   (*k*) Rom. i. 26.

(*l*) Gen. iii. 17. (*m*) Deut. xxviii. 15, *to the end.* (*n*) Rom. vi. 21, 23.

Q. 29. What are the punishments of sin in the world to come?—A. The punishments of sin in the world to come, are everlasting separation from the comfortable presence of God, and most grievous torments in soul and body, without intermission, in hell-fire for ever (*o*).

(*o*) 2 Thess. i. 9; Mark ix. 44, 46, 48; Luke xvi. 24.

Q. 30. Doth God leave all mankind to perish in the estate of sin and misery?— A. God doth not leave all mankind to perish in the estate of sin and misery (*p*), into which they fell by the breach of the first covenant, commonly called the covenant of works (*q*); but, of his mere love and mercy, delivereth his elect out of it, and bringeth them into an estate of salvation by the second covenant, commonly called the Covenant of Grace (*r*).

(*p*) 1 Thess. v. 9: (*q*) Gal. iii. 10, 12. (*r*) Titus iii. 4—7; Gal. iii. 21; Rom. iii. 20—22.

Q. 31. With whom was the covenant of grace made? —A. The covenant of grace was made with Christ, as the second Adam, and in him with all the elect as his seed (*s*).

(*s*) Gal. iii. 16; Rom. v. 15, *to the end*; Isai. liii. 10, 11.

Q. 32. How is the grace of God manifested in the second covenant?—A. The grace of God is manifested in the second covenant, in that he freely provideth and offereth to sinners a Mediator (*t*), and life and salvation by him (*u*): and, requiring faith as the condition to interest them in him (*w*), promiseth and giveth his Holy Spirit (*x*) to all his elect, to work in them that faith (*y*), with all other saving graces (*z*); and to enable them unto all holy obedience (*a*), as the evidence of the truth of their faith (*b*), and thankfulness to God (*c*), and as the way which he hath appointed them to salvation (*d*).

(*t*) Gen. iii. 15; Isai. xlii. 6; John vi. 27. (*u*) 1 John v. 11, 12. (*w*) John iii. 16, and i. 12. (*x*) Prov. i. 23.

(*y*) 2 Cor. iv. 13.   (*z*) Gal. v. 22, 23.   (*a*) Ezek.
xxxvi. 27.   (*b*) James ii. 18, 22.   (*c*) 2 Cor.
v. 14, 15.   (*d*) Eph. ii. 10.

Q. 33. Was the covenant of grace always administered after one and the same manner?—A. The covenant of grace was not always administered after the
same manner, but the administrations of it under the
Old Testament were different from those under the
New (*e*).

(e) 2 Cor. iii. 6—9.

Q. 34. How was the covenant of grace administered
under the Old Testament?—A. The covenant of grace
was administered under the Old Testament by pro-
mises (*f*), prophecies (*g*), sacrifices (*h*), circumcision (*i*),
the passover (*k*), and other types and ordinances; which
did all fore-signify Christ then to come, and were for
that time sufficient to build up the elect in faith in the
promised Messiah (*l*), by whom they then had full remission of sin and eternal salvation (*m*).

(*f*) Rom. xv. 8.   (*g*) Acts iii. 20, 24.   (*h*) Heb.
x. 1.   (*i*) Rom. iv. 11.   (*k*) 1 Cor. v. 7.
(*l*) Heb. viii. ix. x.; xi. 13.   (*m*) Gal. iii. 7—9, 14.

Q. 35. How is the covenant of grace administered
under the New Testament?—A. Under the New Testament, when Christ the substance was exhibited, the
same covenant of grace was, and still is, to be administered in the preaching of the word (*n*), and the administration of the sacraments of Baptism (*o*) and the
Lord's Supper (*p*); in which grace and salvation is held
forth in more fulness, evidence, and efficacy, to all
nations (*q*).

(*n*) Mark xvi. 15.   (*o*) Matt. xxviii. 19, 20.
(*p*) 1 Cor. xi. 23—25.   (*q*) 2 Cor. iii. 6; *to the
end;* Heb. viii. 6, 10, 11; Matt. xxviii. 19.

Q. 36. Who is the Mediator of the covenant of
grace?—A. The only Mediator of the covenant of grace
is the Lord Jesus Christ (*r*), who, being the eternal Son
of God, of one substance, and equal with the Father (*s*),

in the fulness of time became man (*t*), and so was, and
continues to be, God and man, in two entire distinct
natures, and one person, for ever (*u*).

   (*r*) 1 Tim. ii. 5.   (*s*) John i. 14, and x. 30 ;
     Phil. ii. 6.   (*t*) Gal. iv. 4.   (*u*) Luke i. 35 ;
     Rom. ix. 5 ; Col. ii. 9 ; Heb. vii. 24, 25.

   Q. 37. How did Christ, being the Son of God, become man ?—A. Christ, the Son of God, became man, by
taking to himself a true body and a reasonable soul (*w*) ;
being conceived by the power of the Holy Ghost, in the
womb of the Virgin Mary, of her substance, and born
of her (*x*), yet without sin (*y*).

   (*w*) John i. 14 ; Matt. xxvi. 38.   (*x*) Luke i. 27,
     31, 35, 42 ; Gal. iv. 4.   (*y*) Heb. iv. 15, and
     vii. 26.

   Q. 38. Why was it requisite that the Mediator should
be God ?—A. It was requisite that the Mediator should
be God, that he might sustain and keep the human
nature from sinking under the infinite wrath of God,
and the power of death (*z*) ; give worth and efficacy to
his sufferings, obedience, and intercession (*a*) ; and to
satisfy God's justice (*b*), procure his favour (*c*), purchase
a peculiar people (*d*), give his Spirit to them (*e*), con-
quer all their enemies (*f*), and bring them to everlasting salvation (*g*).

   (*z*) Acts ii. 24, 25 ; Rom. i. 4, with Rom. iv. 25 ;
     Heb. ix. 14.   (*a*) Acts xx. 28 ; Heb. ix. 13 ;
     Heb. vii. 25—28.   (*b*) Rom. iii. 24—26.
     (*c*) Eph. i. 6 ; Matt. iii. 17.   (*d*) Titus ii. 13, 14.
     (*e*) Gal. iv. 6.   (*f*) Luke i. 68, 69, 71, 74.
     (*g*) Heb. v. 8, 9 ; Heb. ix. 11—16.

   Q. 39. Why was it requisite that the Mediator should
be man ?—A. It was requisite that the Mediator should
be man, that he might advance our nature (*h*), perform
obedience to the law (*i*), suffer and make intercession
for us in our nature (*k*), and have a fellow-feeling of our
infirmities (*l*), that we might receive the adoption of
sons (*m*), and have comfort and access with boldness
unto the Throne of Grace (*n*).

(*h*) Heb. ii. 16. (*i*) Gal. iv. 4. (*k*) Heb. ii. 14; vii. 24, 25. (*l*) Heb. iv. 15. (*m*) Gal. iv. 5: (*n*) Heb. iv. 16.

Q. 40. Why was it requisite that the Mediator should be God and man in one person ?—A. It was requisite that the Mediator, who was to reconcile God and man, should himself be both God and man; and this in one person, that the proper works of each nature might be accepted of God for us (*o*), and relied on by us as the works of the whole Person (*p*).

(*o*) Matt. i. 21, 23; iii. 17; Heb. ix. 14. (*p*) 1 Pet. ii. 6.

Q. 41. Why was our Mediator called Jesus ?—A. Our Mediator was called Jesus, because he saveth his people from their sins (*q*).

(*q*) Matt. i. 21.

Q. 42. Why was our Mediator called Christ?—A. Our Mediator was called Christ, because he was anointed with the Holy Ghost above measure (*r*), and so set apart, and fully furnished with all authority and ability (*s*), to execute the offices of Prophet (*t*), Priest (*u*), and King of his church (*w*), in the estate both of his humiliation and exaltation.

(*r*) John iii. 34; Psal. xlv. 7. (*s*) John vi. 27; Matt. xxviii. 18—20. (*t*) Acts iii. 21, 22; Luke iv. 18, 21. (*u*) Heb. v. 5—7, and iv. 14, 15. (*w*) Psal. ii. 6; Matt. xxi. 5; Isai. ix. 6, 7; Phil. ii. 8—11.

Q. 43. How doth Christ execute the office of a Prophet?—A. Christ executeth the office of a Prophet, in his revealing to the church (*x*), in all ages, by his Spirit and word (*y*), in divers ways of administration (*z*), the whole will of God (*a*), in all things concerning their edification and salvation (*b*).

(*x*) John i. 18. (*y*) 1 Pet. i. 10—12. (*z*) Heb. i. 1, 3. (*a*) John xv. 15. (*b*) Acts xx. 32; Eph. iv. 11—13; John xx. 31.

Q. 44. How doth Christ execute the office of a Priest?

—A. Christ executeth the office of a Priest, in his once offering himself a sacrifice without spot to God (c), to be a reconciliation for the sins of his people (d), and in making continual intercession for them (e).

(c) Heb. ix. 14, 28.   (d) Heb. ii. 17.   (e) Heb. vii. 25.

Q. 45. How doth Christ execute the office of a King —A. Christ executeth the office of a King, in calling out of the world a people to himself (f), and giving them officers (g), laws (h), and censures, by which he visibly governs them (i), in bestowing saving grace upon his elect (k), rewarding their obedience (l), and correcting them for their sins (m); preserving and supporting them under all their temptations and sufferings (n), restraining and overcoming all their enemies (o) and powerfully ordering all things for his own glory (p), and their good (q); and also in taking vengeance on the rest, who know not God, and obey not the Gospel (r).

(f) Acts xv. 14—16; Isai. lv. 4, 5; Gen. xlix. 10; Psal. cx. 3.   (g) Eph. iv. 11, 12; 1 Cor. xii. 28. (h) Isai. xxxiii. 22.   (i) Matt. xviii. 17, 18; 1 Cor. y. 4, 5.   (k) Acts v. 31.   (l) Rev. xxii. 12; Rev. ii. 10.   (m) Rev. iii. 19.   (n) Isai. lxiii. 9.   (o) 1 Cor. xv. 25; Psal. cx. *throughout*. (p) Rom. xiv. 10, 11.   (q) Rom. viii. 28. (r) 2 Thess. i. 8, 9; Psal. ii. 8, 9.

Q. 46. What was the estate of Christ's humiliation ?— A. The estate of Christ's humiliation was, that low condition, wherein he, for our sakes, emptying himself of his glory, took upon him the form of a servant, in his conception and birth, life, death, and after his death, until his resurrection (s).

(s) Phil. ii. 6—8; Luke i. 31; 2 Cor. viii. 9; Acts ii. 24.

Q. 47. How did Christ humble himself in his conception and birth ?—A. Christ humbled himself in his conception and birth, in that, being from all eternity the Son of God in the bosom of the Father, he was pleased, in the fulness of time, to become the Son of man, made of a woman of low estate, and to be born of her, with divers circumstances of more than ordinary abasement (*t*).

(*t*) John i. 14, 18; Gal. iv. 4; Luke ii. 7.

Q. 48. How did Christ humble himself in his life?—A. Christ humbled himself in his life, by subjecting himself to the Law (*u*), which he perfectly fulfilled (*w*); and by conflicting with the indignities of the world (*x*), temptations of Satan (*y*), and infirmities in his flesh, whether common to the nature of man, or particularly accompanying that his low condition (*z*).

(*u*) Gal. iv. 4.　　(*w*) Matt. v. 17; Rom. v. 19.
(*x*) Psal. xxii. 6; Heb. xii. 2, 3.　(*y*) Matt. iv.
1—12; Luke iv. 13.　　(*z*) Heb. ii. 17, 18, and
iv. 15; Isai. lii. 13, 14.

Q. 49. How did Christ humble himself in his death? —A. Christ humbled himself in his death, in that, having been betrayed by Judas (*a*), forsaken by his disciples (*b*), scorned and rejected by the world (*c*), condemned by Pilate, and tormented by his persecutors (*d*); having also conflicted with the terrors of death, and the powers of darkness, felt and borne the weight of God's wrath (*e*), he laid down his life an offering for sin (*f*), enduring the painful, shameful, and cursed death of the cross (*g*).

(*a*) Matt. xxvii. 4.　(*b*) Matt. xxvi. 56.　(*c*) Isai.
liii. 2, 3.　(*d*) Matt. xxvii. 26—50; John xix. 34.
(*e*) Luke xxii. 44; Matt. xxvii. 46.　　(*f*) Isai.
liii. 10.　(*g*) Phil. ii. 8; Heb. xii. 2; Gal. iii. 13.

Q. 50. Wherein consisted Christ's humiliation after his death?—A. Christ's humiliation after his death consisted in his being buried (*h*), and continuing in the state of the dead, and under the power of death, till the third day (*i*); which hath been otherwise expressed in these words, *He descended into hell.*

(*h*) 1 Cor. xv. 34.　　(*i*) Psal. xvi. 10, with Acts ii.
24—27, 31; Rom. vi. 9; Matt. xii. 40.

O

Q. 51. What was the estate of Christ's exaltation?—
A. The estate of Christ's exaltation comprehendeth his
resurrection (*k*), ascension (*l*), sitting at the right hand
of the Father (*m*), and his coming again to judge the
world (*n*).

(*k*) 1 Cor. xv. 4.   (*l*) Mark xvi. 19.   (*m*) Eph.
i. 20.   (*n*) Acts i. 11, and xvii. 31.

Q. 52. How was Christ exalted in his resurrection?
—A. Christ was exalted in his resurrection, in that,
not having seen corruption in death, of which it was
not possible for him to be held (*o*), and having the very
same body in which he suffered, with the essential properties thereof (*p*), but without mortality, and other
common infirmities belonging to this life, really united
to his soul (*q*), he rose again from the dead the third
day, by his own power (*r*); whereby he declared himself to be the Son of God (*s*), to have satisfied Divine
justice (*t*), to have vanquished death, and him that had
the power of it (*u*), and to be Lord of quick and
dead (*w*); all which he did as a public Person (*x*), the
Head of his church (*y*), for their justification (*x*),
quickening in grace (*a*), support against enemies (*b*, and
to assure them of their resurrection from the dead at the
last day (*c*).

(*o*) Acts ii. 24, 27.   (*p*) Luke xxiv. 39.   (*q*) Rom.
vi. 9; Rev. i. 18.   (*r*) John x. 18.   (*s*) Rom.
i. 4.   (*t*) Rom. viii. 34.   (*u*) Heb. ii. 14.
(*w*) Rom. xiv. 9.   (*x*) 1 Cor. xv. 21, 22.   (*y*) Eph.
i. 20, 22, 23; Col. i. 18.   (*z*) Rom. iv. 25.
(*a*) Eph. ii. 1, 5, 6; Col. ii. 12.   (*b*) 1 Cor. xv.
25—27.   (*c*) 1 Cor. xv. 20.

Q. 53. How was Christ exalted in his ascension?—
A. Christ was exalted in his ascension, in that, having
after his resurrection often appeared unto and conversed
with his Apostles, speaking to them of the things pertaining to the kingdom of God (*d*), and giving them
commission to preach the Gospel to all nations (*e*), forty
days after his resurrection, he, in our nature, and as

our Head (*f*), triumphing over enemies (*g*), visibly went up into the highest heavens, there to receive gifts for men (*h*), to raise up our affections thither (*i*), and to prepare a place for us (*k*), where himself is, and shall continue till his second coming at the end of the world (*l*).

(*d*) Acts i. 2, 3. (*e*) Matt. xxviii. 19, 20. (*f*) Heb. vi. 20. (*g*) Eph. iv. 8. (*h*) Acts i. 9—11; Eph. iv. 10; Psal. lxviii. 18. (*i*) Col. iii. 1, 2. (*k*) John xiv. 3. (*l*) Acts iii. 21.

Q. 54. How is Christ exalted in his sitting at the right hand of God?—A. Christ is exalted in his sitting at the right hand of God, in that, as God-Man, he is advanced to highest favour with God the Father (*m*), with all fulness of joy (*n*), glory (*o*), and power over all things in heaven and earth (*p*), and doth gather and defend his church, and subdue their enemies, furnisheth his ministers and people with gifts and graces (*q*), and maketh intercession for them (*r*).

(*m*) Phil. ii. 9. (*n*) Acts ii. 28, with Psal. xvi. 11. (*o*) John xvii. 5. (*p*) Eph. i. 22; 1 Pet. iii. 22. (*q*) Eph. iv. 10—12; Psal. cx. *throughout*. (*r*) Rom. viii. 34.

Q. 55. How doth Christ make intercession?—A. Christ maketh intercession, by his appearing in our nature continually before the Father in heaven (*s*), in the merit of his obedience and sacrifice on earth (*t*), declaring his will to have it applied to all believers (*u*), answering all accusations against them (*w*), procuring for them quiet of conscience, notwithstanding daily failing (*x*), access with boldness to the Throne of Grace (*y*), and acceptance of their persons (*z*) and services (*a*).

(*s*) Heb. ix. 12, 24. (*t*) Heb. i. 3. (*u*) John iii. 16; John xvii. 9, 20, 24. (*w*) Rom. viii. 33, 34. (*x*) Rom. v. 1, 2; 1 John ii. 1, 2. (*y*) Heb. iv. 16. (*z*) Eph. i. 6. (*a*) 1 Pet. ii. 5.

Q. 56. How is Christ to be exalted in his coming

again to judge the world ?—A. Christ is to be exalted in his coming again to judge the world, in that he, who was unjustly judged and condemned by wicked men (b), shall come again at the last day in great power (c), and in the full manifestation of his own glory, and of his Father's, with all his holy angels (d), with a shout, with the voice of the archangel, and with the trumpet of God (e), to judge the world in righteousness (f).

(b) Acts iii. 14, 15.　(c) Matt. xxiv. 30.　(d) Luke ix. 26; Matt. xxv. 31.　(e) 1 Thess. iv. 16.　(f) Acts xvii. 31.

Q. 57. What benefits hath Christ procured by his mediation?—A. Christ by his mediation hath procured redemption (g), with all other benefits of the covenant of grace (h).

(g) Heb. ix. 12.　(h) 2 Cor. i. 20.

Q. 58. How do we come to be made partakers of the benefits which Christ hath procured?—A. We are made partakers of the benefits which Christ hath procured, by the application of them unto us (i), which is the work especially of God the Holy Ghost (k).

(i) John i. 11, 12.　(k) Titus iii. 5, 6.

Q. 59. Who are made partakers of redemption through Christ?—A. Redemption is certainly applied and effectually communicated to all those for whom Christ hath purchased it (l), who are in time, by the Holy Ghost, enabled to believe in Christ, according to the Gospel (m).

(l) Eph. i. 13, 14; John vi. 37, 39, and x. 15, 16.　(m) Eph. ii. 8; 2 Cor. iv. 13.

Q. 60. Can they who have never heard the Gospel, and so know not Jesus Christ, nor believe in him, be saved by their living according to the light of nature?—A. They who, having never heard the Gospel (n), know not Jesus Christ (o), and believe not in him, cannot be saved (p), be they never so diligent to frame their lives according to the light of nature (q), or the law of that religion which they profess (r); neither is there salvation in any other, but in Christ alone (*s*), who is the Saviour only of his body the church (*t*).

(*n*) Rom. x. 14. (*o*) 2 Thess. i. 8, 9 ; Eph. ii. 12 ; John i. 10—12. (*p*) John viii. 24 ; Mark xvi. 16. (*q*) 1 Cor. i. 20—24. (*r*) John iv. 22 ; Rom. ix. 31, 32 ; Phil. iii. 4—9. (*s*) Acts iv. 12. (*t*) Eph. v. 23.

Q. 61. Are all they saved who hear the Gospel, and live in the church ?—A. All that hear the Gospel, and live in the visible church, are not saved ; but they only who are true members of the church invisible (*u*).

(*u*) John xii. 38—40 ; Rom. ix. 6 ; Matt. xxii. 14, and vii. 21 ; Rom. xi. 7.

Q. 62. What is the visible church ?—A. The visible church is a society made up of all such, as in all ages and places of the world do profess the true religion (*w*), and of their children (*x*).

(*w*) 1 Cor. i. 2, and xii. 13 ; Rom. xv. 9—12 ; Rev. vii. 9 ; Psal. ii. 8, xxii. 27—31, and xlv. 17 ; Matt. xxviii. 19, 20 ; Isai. lix. 21. (*x*) 1 Cor. vii. 14 ; Acts ii. 39 ; Rom. xi. 16 ; Gen. xvii. 7.

Q. 63. What are the special privileges of the visible church ?—A. The visible church hath the privilege of being under God's special care and government (*y*), of being protected and preserved in all ages, notwithstanding the opposition of all enemies (*z*), and of enjoying the communion of saints, the ordinary means of salvation (*u*) ; offers of grace by Christ to all the members of it in the ministry of the Gospel, testifying, that whosoever believes in him shall be saved (*b*), and excluding none that will come unto him (*c*).

(*y*) Isai. iv. 5, 6 ; 1 Tim. iv. 10. (*z*) Psal. cxv. *throughout* ; Isai. xxxi. 4, 5 ; Zech. xii. 2—4, 8, 9. (*a*) Acts ii. 39, 42. (*b*) Psal. cxlvii. 19, 20 ; Rom. ix. 4 ; Eph. iv. 11, 12 ; Mark xvi. 15, 16. (*c*) John vi. 37.

Q. 64. What is the invisible church ?—A. The invisible church is the whole number of the elect that have been, are, or shall be gathered into one, under Christ the Head (*d*).

(*d*) Eph. i. 10, 22, 23 ; John x. 16, and xi. 52.

Q. 65. What special benefits do the members of the invisible church enjoy by Christ?—A. The members of the invisible church, by Christ, enjoy union and communion with him, in grace and glory (*e*).

(*e*) John xvii. 21 ; Eph. ii. 5, 6 ; John xvii. 24.

Q. 66. What is that union which the elect have with Christ?—A. The union which the elect have with Christ, is the work of God's grace (*f*), whereby they are spiritually and mystically, yet really and inseparably, joined to Christ, as their Head and Husband (*g*), which is done in their effectual calling (*h*).

(*f*) Eph. i. 22, and ii. 6—8.   (*g*) 1 Cor. vi. 17 ;
John x. 28 ; Eph. v. 23, 30.   (*h*) 1 Pet. v. 10 ;
1 Cor. i. 9.

Q. 67. What is effectual calling?—A. Effectual calling is the work of God's almighty power and grace (*i*), whereby, out of his free and especial love to his elect, and from nothing in them moving him thereunto (*k*), he doth in his accepted time invite and draw them to Jesus Christ by his word and Spirit (*l*), savingly enlightening their minds (*m*), renewing and powerfully determining their wills (*n*), so as they, although in themselves dead in sin, are hereby made willing and able freely to answer his call, and to accept and embrace the grace offered and conveyed therein (*o*).

(*i*) John v. 25 ; Eph. i. 18—20 ; 2 Tim. i. 8, 9.
(*k*) Titus iii. 4, 5 ; Eph. ii. 4, 5, 7—9; Rom. ix. 11.
(*l*) 2 Cor. v. 20, with vi. 1, 2 ; John vi. 44 ;
2 Thess. ii. 13, 14.   . (*m*) Acts xxvi. 18 ; 1 Cor.
ii. 10, 12.   (*n*) Ezek. xi. 19, and xxxvi. 26, 27 ;
John vi. 45.   (*o*) Eph. ii. 5 ; Phil ii. 13 ;
Deut. xxx. 6.

Q. 68. Are the elect only effectually called?—A. All the elect, and they only, are effectually called (*p*), although others may be, and often are, outwardly called by the ministry of the word (*q*), and have some common operations of the Spirit (*r*), who, for their wilful neglect and contempt of the grace offered to them, being justly left in their unbelief, do never truly come to Jesus Christ (*s*).

(*p*) Acts xiii. 48.   (*q*) Matt. xxii. 14.   (*r*) Matt. vii. 22, and xiii. 20, 21 ; Heb. vi. 4, 5.   (*s*) John xii. 38—40; Acts xxviii. 25—27; John vi. 64, 65; Psal. lxxxi. 11, 12.

Q. 69. What is the communion in grace which the members of the invisible church have with Christ?— A. The communion in grace, which the 'members of the invisible church have with Christ, is their partaking of the virtue of his mediation, in their justification (*t*), adoption (*u*), sanctification, and whatever else in this life manifests their union with him (*w*).

(*t*) Rom. viii. 30.   (*u*) Eph. i. 5.   (*w*) 1 Cor. i. 30.

Q. 70. What is justification?—A. Justification is an act of God's free grace unto sinners (*x*), in which he pardoneth all their sins, accepteth and accounteth their persons righteous in his sight (*y*), not for any thing wrought in them, or done by them (*z*), but only for the perfect obedience and full satisfaction of Christ, by God imputed to them (*a*), and received by faith alone (*b*).

(*x*) Rom. iii. 22, 24, 25; Rom. iv. 5.   (*y*) 2 Cor. v. 19, 21 ; Rom. iii. 22, 24, 25, 27, 28.   (*z*) Tit. iii. 5, 7; Eph. i. 7.   (*a*) Rom. v. 17—19; Rom. iv. 6—8.   (*b*) Acts x. 43; Gal. ii. 16; Phil. iii. 9.

Q. 71. How is justification an act of God's free grace?—A. Although Christ, by his obedience and death, did make a proper, real, and full satisfaction to God's justice, in the behalf of them that are justified (*c*); yet, inasmuch as God accepteth the satisfaction from a Surety, which he might have demanded of them, and did provide this Surety, his own only Son (*d*), imputing his righteousness to them (*e*), and requiring nothing of them for their justification, but faith (*f*), which also is his gift (*g*), their justification is to them of free grace (*h*). · · · ·

(*c*) Rom. v. 8—10, 19.   (*d*) 1 Tim. ii. 5, 6; Heb.
· x. 10; Matt. xx. 28; Dan. ix. 24, 26; Isai. liii.
4—6, 10—12; Heb. vii. 22; Rom. viii. 32; 1 Pet.
i. 18, 19.   (*e*) 2 Cor. v. 21.   (*f*) Rom. iii.
24, 25.   (*g*) Eph. ii. 8.   (*h*) Eph. i. 7.

Q. 72. What is justifying faith?—A. Justifying faith is a saving grace (*i*), wrought in the heart of a sinner by the Spirit (*k*) and word of God (*l*); whereby he, being convinced of his sin and misery, and of the disability in himself, and all other creatures, to recover him out of his lost condition (*m*), not only assenteth to the truth of the promise of the Gospel (*n*), but receiveth and resteth upon Christ, and his righteousness, therein held forth for pardon of sin (*o*), and for the accepting and accounting of his person righteous in the sight of God for salvation (*p*).

(*i*) Heb. x. 39.   (*k*) 2 Cor. iv. 13; Eph. i. 17—19.
(*l*) Rom. x. 14, 17.   (*m*) Acts ii. 37, and xvi. 30;
John xvi. 8, 9; Rom. v. 6; Eph. ii. 1; Acts iv. 12.
(*n*) Eph. i. 13.   (*o*) John i. 12; Acts xvi. 31,
and x. 43.   (*p*) Phil. iii. 9; Acts xv. 11.

Q. 73. How doth faith justify a sinner in the sight of God?—A. Faith justifies a sinner in the sight of God, not because of those other graces which do always accompany it, or of good works that are the fruits of it (*q*), nor as if the grace of faith, or any act thereof, were imputed to him for his justification (*r*); but only as it is an instrument, by which he receiveth and applieth Christ and his righteousness (*s*).

(*q*) Gal. iii. 11; Rom. iii. 28.   (*r*) Rom. iv. 5,
· with Rom. x. 10.   (*s*) John i. 12; Phil. iii 9;
Gal. ii. 16.

Q. 74. What is adoption?—A. Adoption is an act of the free grace of God (*t*), in and for his only Son Jesus Christ (*u*), whereby all those that are justified, are received into the number of his children (*w*), have his name put upon them (*x*), the Spirit of his Son given to them (*y*), are under his fatherly care and dispensations (*z*), admitted to all the liberties and privileges of the sons of God, made heirs of all the promises, and fellow-heirs with Christ in glory (*a*).

(*t*) 1 John iii. 1.   (*u*) Eph. i. 5; Gal. iv. 4, 5.
(*w*) John i. 12.   (*x*) 2 Cor. vi. 18; Rev. iii. 12.
(*y*) Gal. iv. 6.   (*z*) Psal. ciii. 13 ; Prov. xiv. 26 ;
Matt. vi. 32.   (*a*) Heb. vi. 12 ; Rom. viii. 17.

Q. 75. What is sanctification?—A. Sanctification is a work of God's grace, whereby they, whom God hath, before the foundation of the world, chosen to be holy, are in time, through the powerful operation of his Spirit (*b*), applying the death and resurrection of Christ unto them (*c*), renewed in their whole man after the image of God (*d*), having the seeds of repentance unto life, and of all other saving graces, put into their hearts (*e*), and those graces so stirred up, increased, and strengthened (*f*), as that they more and more die unto sin, and rise unto newness of life (*g*).

(*b*) Eph. i. 4; 1 Cor. vi. 11; 2 Thess. ii. 13. (*c*) Rom.
vi. 4—6.   (*d*) Eph. iv. 23, 24.   (*e*) Acts
xi. 18; 1 John iii. 9.   (*f*) Jude 20; Heb. vi.
11, 12; Eph. iii. 16—19; Col. i. 10, 11. (*g*) Rom.
vi. 4, 6, 14; Gal. v. 24.

Q. 76. What is repentance unto life?—A. Repentance unto life is a saving grace (*h*), wrought in the heart of a sinner by the Spirit (*i*) and Word of God (*k*), whereby out of the sight and sense, not only of the danger (*l*), but also of the filthiness and odiousness of his sins (*m*), and upon the apprehension of God's mercy in Christ to such as are penitent (*n*), he so grieves for (*o*), and hates his sins (*p*), as that he turns from them all to God (*q*), purposing and endeavouring constantly to walk with him in all the ways of new obedience (*r*).

(*h*) 2 Tim. ii. 25.   (*i*) Zech. xii. 10.   (*k*) Acts
xi. 18, 20, 21.   (*l*) Ezek. xviii. 28, 30, 32;
.. Luke xv. 17, 18: Hos. ii. 6, 7.   (*m*) Ezek. xxxvi.

31; Isai. xxx. 22. (*n*) Joel ii. 12, 13. (*o*) Jer. xxxi. 18, 19. (*p*) 2 Cor. vii. 11. (*q*) Acts xxvi. 18; Ezek. xiv. 6; 1 Kings viii. 47, 48. (*r*) Psal. cxix. 6, 59, 128; Luke i. 6; 2 Kings xxiii. 25.

Q. 77. Wherein doth justification and sanctification differ?—A. Although sanctification be inseparably joined with justification (*s*), yet they differ, in that, God, in justification imputeth the righteousness of Christ (*t*); in sanctification, his Spirit infuseth grace, and enableth to the exercise thereof (*u*): in the former, sin is pardoned (*w*); in the other, it is subdued (*x*): the one doth equally free all believers from the revenging wrath of God, and that perfectly in this life, that they never fall into condemnation (*y*); the other is neither equal in all (*z*), nor in this life perfect in any (*a*), but growing up to perfection (*b*).

(*s*) 1 Cor. vi. 11, and i. 30. (*t*) Rom. iv. 6, 8.
(*u*) Ezek. xxxvi. 27. (*w*) Rom. iii. 24, 25.
(*x*) Rom. vi. 6, 14. (*y*) Rom. viii. 33, 34.
(*z*) 1 John ii. 12—14; Heb. v. 12—14. (*a*) 1 John i. 8, 10. (*b*) 2 Cor. vii. 1; Phil. iii. 12—14.

Q. 78. Whence ariseth the imperfection of sanctification in believers?—A. The imperfection of sanctification in believers ariseth from the remnants of sin abiding in every part of them, and the perpetual lustings of the flesh against the Spirit, whereby they are often foiled with temptations, and fall into many sins (*c*), are hindered in all their spiritual services (*d*), and their best works are imperfect and defiled in the sight of God (*e*).

(*c*) Rom. vii. 18, 23; Mark xiv. 66 *to the end;* Gal. ii. 11, 12. (*d*) Heb. xii. 1. (*e*) Isai. lxiv. 6; Exod. xxviii. 38.

Q. 79. May not true believers, by reason of their imperfections, and the many temptations and sins they are overtaken with, fall away from the state of grace?—A. True believers, by reason of the unchangeable love of God (*f*), and his decree and covenant, to give them perseverance(*g*), their inseparable union with Christ(*h*), his continual intercession for them (*i*), and the Spirit and seed of God abiding in them (*k*); can neither totally nor finally fall away from the state of grace (*l*), but are kept by the power of God through faith unto salvation (*m*).

 (*f*) Jer. xxxi. 3.   (*g*) 2 Tim. ii. 19; Heb. xiii. 20, 21; 2 Sam. xxiii. 5.   (*h*) 1 Cor. i. 8, 9; (*i*) Heb. vii. 25; Luke xxii. 32.   (*k*) 1 John iii. 9, and ii. 27.   (*l*) Jer. xxxii. 40; John x. 28. (*m*) 1 Pet. i. 5.

Q. 80. Can true believers be infallibly assured that they are in the estate of grace, and that they shall persevere therein unto salvation?—A. Such as truly believe in Christ, and endeavour to walk in all good conscience before him (*n*), may, without extraordinary revelation, by faith grounded upon the truth of God's promises, and by the Spirit enabling them to discern in themselves those graces to which the promises of life are made (*o*), and bearing witness with their spirits that they are the children of God (*p*), be infallibly assured that they are in the estate of grace, and shall persevere therein unto salvation (*q*).

 (*n*) 1 John ii. 3.   (*o*) 1 Cor. ii. 12; 1 John iii. 14, 18, 19, 21, 24; iv. 13, 16; Heb. vi. 11, 12. (*p*) Rom. viii. 16.   (*q*) 1 John v. 13.

Q. 81. Are all true believers at all times assured of their present being in the estate of grace, and that they shall be saved?—A. Assurance of grace and salvation not being of the essence of faith (*r*), true believers may wait long before they obtain it (*s*); and after the enjoyment thereof, may have it weakened and intermitted through manifold distempers, sins, temptations, and desertions (*t*); yet are they never left without such a presence and support of the Spirit of God, as keeps them from sinking into utter despair (*u*).

 (*r*) Eph. i. 13.   (*s*) Isai. l. 10; Psal. lxxxviii. *throughout.*   (*t*) Psal. lxxvii. 1—12; Cant. v.

2, 3, 6 ; Psal. li. 8, 12, and xxxi. 22, and xxii. 1°
(*u*) 1 John iii. 9 ; Job xiii. 15 ; Psal. lxxiii. 15, 23 ;
Isai. liv. 7—10.

Q. 82. What is the communion in glory which the
members of the invisible church have with Christ?—
A. The communion in glory which the members of the
invisible church have with Christ, is in this life (*w*), immediately after death (*x*), and at last perfected at the
resurrection and day of judgment (*y*).

(*w*) 2 Cor. iii. 18.　(*x*) Luke xxiii. 43.　(*y*) 1 Thess.
iv. 17.

Q. 83. What is the communion in glory with Christ,
which the members of the invisible church enjoy in this
life?—A. The members of the invisible church have
communicated to them, in this life, the first-fruits of
glory with Christ, as they are members of him their Head,
and so in him are interested in that glory which he is fully
possessed of (*z*) ; and as an earnest thereof, enjoy the
sense of God's love (*a*), peace of conscience, joy in the
Holy Ghost, and hope of glory (*b*) ; as, on the contrary,
the sense of God's avenging wrath, horror of conscience,
and a fearful expectation of judgment, are to the wicked
the beginning of their torments, which they shall endure
after death (*c*).

(*z*) Eph. ii. 5, 6.　　　(*a*) Rom. v. 5, with 2 Cor.
i. 22.　(*b*) Rom. v. 1, 2, and xiv. 17.　(*c*) Gen.
iv. 13 ; Matt. xxvii. 4 ; Heb. x. 27 ; Rom. ii. 9 ;
Mark ix. 44.

Q. 84. Shall all men die?—A. Death being threatened, as the wages of sin (*d*), it is appointed unto all
men once to die (*e*), for that all have sinned (*f*).

(*d*) Rom. vi. 23.　(*e*) Heb. ix. 27.　(*f*) Rom. v. 12.

Q. 85. Death being the wages of sin, why are not the
righteous delivered from death, seeing all their sins are
forgiven in Christ?—A. The righteous shall be delivered from death itself at the last day, and even in death
are delivered from the sting and curse of it (*g*) ; so that
although they die, yet it is out of God's love (*h*), to free
them perfectly from sin and misery (*i*), and to make

them capable of further communion with Christ in glory, which they then enter upon (*k*).

(*g*) 1 Cor. xv. 26, 55—57; Heb. ii. 15.   (*h*) Isai. lvii. 1, 2; 2 Kings xxii. 20.   (*i*) Rev. xiv. 13; Eph. v. 27.   (*k*) Luke xxiii. 43; Phil. i. 23.

. Q. 86. What is the communion in glory with Christ, which the members of the invisible church enjoy immediately after death?—A. The communion in glory with Christ, which the members of the invisible church enjoy. immediately after death, is, in that their souls are then made perfect in holiness(*l*), and received into the highest heavens (*m*), where they behold the face of God in light and glory (*n*), waiting for the full redemption of their bodies (*o*), which even in death continue united to Christ (*p*), and rest in their graves as in their beds (*q*), till at the last day they be again united to their souls(*r*): whereas the souls of the wicked are at death cast into hell, where they remain in torments and utter darkness, and their bodies kept in their graves, as in their prisons, till the resurrection and judgment of the great day (*s*).

(*l*) Heb. xii. 23.   (*m*) 2 Cor. v. 1, 6, 8; Phil. i. 23, with Acts iii. 21, and Eph. iv. 10.   (*n*) 1 John iii. 2; 1 Cor. xiii. 12.   (*o*) Rom. viii. 23; Psal. xvi. 9.   (*p*) 1 Thess. iv. 14.   (*q*) Isai. lvii. 2. (*r*) Job xix. 26, 27.   (*s*) Luke xvi. 23, 24; Acts i. 25; Jude 6, 7.

Q. 87. What are we to believe concerning the resurrection?—A. We are to believe, that at the last day there shall be a general resurrection of the dead, both of the just and unjust (*t*), when they that are then found alive shall in a moment be changed, and the self-same bodies of the dead which were laid in the grave, being then again united to their souls for ever, shall be raised up by the power of Christ (*u*); the bodies of the just, by the Spirit of Christ, and by virtue of his resurrection, as their Head, shall be raised in power, spiritual, incorruptible, and made like to his glorious body (*w*); and. the bodies of the wicked shall be raised up in dishonour, by him, as an offended Judge (*x*).

(*t*) Acts xxiv. 15.　　　(*u*) 1 Cor. xv. 51—53;
1 Thess. iv. 15—17; John v. 28, 29.　(*w*) 1 Cor.
xv. 21, 23, 42—44; Phil. iii. 21.　　(*x*) John v.
27—29; Matt. xxv. 23.

Q. 88. What shall immediately follow after the resurrection?—A. Immediately after the resurrection shall
follow the general and final judgment of angels and
men (*y*), the day and hour whereof no man knoweth,
that all may watch and pray, and be ever ready for the
coming of the Lord (*z*).

(*y*) 2 Pet. ii. 4; Jude 6, 7, 14, 15; Matt. xxv. 46.
(*z*) Matt. xxiv. 36, 42, 44; Luke xxi. 35, 36.

Q. 89. What shall be done to the wicked at the day
of judgment?—A. At the day of judgment the wicked
shall be set on Christ's left hand (*a*), and upon clear
evidence, and full conviction of their own consciences (*b*),
shall have the fearful but just sentence of condemnation
pronounced against them (*c*); and thereupon shall be
cast out from the favourable presence of God, and the
glorious fellowship with Christ, his saints, and all his
holy angels, into hell, to be punished with unspeakable
torments, both of body and soul, with the devil and his
angels for ever (*d*).

(*a*) Matt. xxv. 33.　(*b*) Rom. ii. 15, 16.　(*c*) Matt.
xxv. 41—43.　　(*d*) Luke xvi. 26; 2 Thess.
i. 8, 9.

Q. 90. What shall be done to the righteous at the
day of judgment?—A. At the day of judgment, the
righteous, being caught up to Christ in the clouds (*e*),
shall be set on his right hand, and there openly acknowledged and acquitted (*f*); shall join with him in the
judging of reprobate angels and men (*g*), and shall be
received into heaven (*h*), where they shall be fully and
for ever freed from all sin and misery (*i*), filled with in-
conceivable joys (*k*), made perfectly holy and happy,
both in body and soul, in the company of innumerable
saints and holy angels (*l*), but especially in the imme-
diate vision and fruition of God the Father, of our
Lord Jesus Christ, and of the Holy Spirit, to all eter-

nity (*m*); and this is the perfect and full communion which the members of the invisible church shall enjoy with Christ in glory at the resurrection and day of judgment.

(*e*) 1 Thess. iv. 17.   (*f*) Matt. xxv. 33; x. 32.
 (*g*) 1 Cor. vi. 2, 3.   (*h*) Matt. xxv. 34, 46.
 (*i*) Eph. v. 27; Rev. xiv. 13. (*k*) Psal. xvi. 11;
 (*l*) Heb. xii. 22, 23. (*m*) 1 John iii. 2; 1 Cor.
 xiii. 12; 1 Thess. iv. 17, 18.

Having seen what the Scriptures principally teach us to believe concerning God, it follows to consider what they require as the duty of man.

Q. 91. What is the duty which God requireth of man? —A. The duty which God requireth of man, is obedience to his revealed will (*n*).

(*n*) Rom. xii. 1, 2; Micah vi. 8; 1 Sam. xv. 22.

Q. 92. What did God at first reveal unto men as the rule of his obedience?—A. The rule of obedience revealed to Adam in the estate of innocency, and to all mankind in him, beside a special command, not to eat of the fruit of the tree of the knowledge of good and evil, was the moral law (*o*).

(*o*) Gen. i. 26, 27; Rom. ii. 14, 15; Rom. x. 5; Gen. ii. 17.

Q. 93. What is the moral law?—A. The moral law is, the declaration of the will of God to mankind, directing and binding every one to personal, perfect, and perpetual conformity and obedience thereunto, in the frame and disposition of the whole man, soul and body (*p*); and in performance of all those duties of holiness and righteousness which he oweth to God and man (*q*): promising life upon the fulfilling, and threatening death upon the breach of it (*r*).

(*p*) Deut. v. 1—3, 31—33; Luke x. 26, 27; Gal. iii.

10; 1 Thess. v. 23. (*q*) Luke i. 75; Acts
xxiv. 16. (*r*) Rom. x. 5; Gal. iii. 10, 12.

Q. 94. Is there any use of the moral law to man since
the Fall?—A. Although no man, since the Fall, can
attain to righteousness and life by the moral law (*s*), yet
there is great use thereof, as well common to all men,
as peculiar either to the unregenerate or to the regenerate (*t*).

(*s*) Rom. viii. 3; Gal. ii. 16. (*t*) 1 Tim. i. 8.

Q. 95. Of what use is the moral law to all men?—
A. The moral law is of use to all men, to inform them
of the holy nature and will of God (*u*), and of their
duty binding them to walk accordingly (*w*); to convince them of their disability to keep it, and of the sinful pollution of their nature, hearts, and lives (*x*); to
humble them in the sense of their sin and misery (*y*),
aud thereby help them to a clearer sight of the need
they have of Christ (*z*), and of the perfection of his obedience (*a*).

(*u*) Lev. xi 44, 45, and xx. 7, 8; Rom. vii. 12;
(*w*) Mic. vi. 8; James ii. 10, 11. (*x*) Psal. xix
11, 12; Rom. iii. 20; vii. 7. (*y*) Rom. iii
9, 23. (*z*) Gal. iii. 21, 22. (*a*) Rom. x. 4.

Q. 96. What peculiar use is there of the moral law
to unregenerate men?—A. The moial law is of use to
unregenerate men, to awaken their consciences to flee
from the wrath to come (*b*), and to drive them to Christ (*c*);
or, upon their continuance in the estate and way of
sin, to leave them inexcusable (*d*), and under the curse
thereof (*e*).

(*b*) 1 Tim. i. 9, 10. (*c*) Gal. iii. 24. (*d*) Rom.
i. 20, compared with Rom. ii. 15. (*e*) Gal.
iii. 10.

Q. 97. What special use is there of the moral law to
the regenerate?—A. Although they that are regenerate,
and believe in Christ, be delivered from the moral law
as a covenant of works (*f*), so as thereby they are
neither justified (*g*) nor condemned (*h*), yet, beside the

general uses thereof common to them with all men, it is of special use to shew them how much they are bound to Christ for his fulfilling it, and enduring the curse thereof in their stead, and for their good (*i*); and thereby to provoke them to more thankfulness (*k*), and to express the same in their greater care to conform themselves thereunto as the rule of their obedience (*l*).

(*f*) Rom. vi. 14, and vii. 4, 6; Gal. iv. 4, 5.
(*g*) Rom. iii. 20.   (*h*) Gal. v. 23; Rom. viii. 1.
(*i*) Rom. vii. 24, 25; Gal. iii. 13, 14; Rom. viii.
3, 4.   (*k*) Luke i. 68, 69, 74, 75; Col. i. 12—14.
(*l*) Rom. vii. 22, and xii. 2; Titus ii. 11—14.

Q. 98. Wherein is the moral law summarily comprehended?—A. The moral law is summarily comprehended in the Ten Commandments, which were delivered by the voice of God upon mount Sinai, and written by him in two tables of stone (*m*), and are recorded in the xx th chapter of Exodus; the first four commandments containing our duty to God, and the other six our duty to man (*n*).

(*m*) Deut. x. 4; Exod. xxxiv. 1—4.   (*n*) Matt.
xxii. 37—40.

Q. 99. What rules are to be observed for the right understanding of the Ten Commandments?—A. For the right understanding of the Ten Commandments, these rules are to be observed :

i. That the law is perfect, and bindeth every one to full conformity in the whole man unto the righteousness thereof, and unto entire obedience for ever; so as to require the utmost perfection of every duty, and to forbid the least degree of every sin (*o*).

(*o*) Psal. xix. 7; Jas. ii. 10; Matt. v. 21, *to the end.*

ii. That it is spiritual, and so reacheth the understanding, will, affections, and all other powers of the soul, as well as words, works, and gestures (*p*).

(*p*) Rom. vii. 14; Deut. vi. 5, compared with Matt.
xxii. 37—39; Matt. v. 21, 22, 27, 28, 36, *to the end.*

iii. That one and the same thing, in divers respects, is required or forbidden in several commandments (*q*).

(q) Col. iii. 5; Amos viii. 5; Prov. i. 19; 1 Tim. vi. 10.

iv. That as, where a duty is commanded, the contrary sin is forbidden (r); and, where a sin is forbidden, the contrary duty is commanded (s): so, where a promise is annexed, the contrary threatening is included (t); and, where a threatening is annexed, the contrary promise is included (u).

(r) Isai. lviii. 13; Deut. vi. 13, compared with Matt. iv. 9, 10; Matt. xv. 4—6. (s) Matt. v. 21—25; Eph. iv. 28. (t) Exod. xx. 12, with Prov. xxx. 17. (u) Jer. xviii. 7, 8; Exod. xx. 7, compared with Psal. xv. 1, 4, 5, and xxiv. 4, 5.

v. That what God forbids, is at no time to be done (w); what he commands, is always our duty (x); and yet every particular duty is not to be done at all times (y).

(w) Job xiii. 7, 8; Rom. iii. 8; Job xxxvi. 21; Heb. xi. 25. (x) Deut. iv. 8, 9. (y) Matt. xii. 7.

vi. That, under one sin or duty, all of the same kind are forbidden or commanded, together with all the causes, means, occasions, and appearances thereof, and provocations thereunto (z).

(z) Matt. v. 21, 22, 27, 28; xv. 4—6; Heb. x. 24, 25; 1 Thess. v. 22; Jude 23; Gal. v. 26; Col. iii. 21.

vii. That what is forbidden or commanded to ourselves, we are bound, according to our places, to endeavour that it may be avoided or performed by others, according to the duty of their places (a).

(a) Exod. xx. 10; Lev. xix. 17; Gen. xviii. 19; Josh. xxiv. 15; Deut. vi. 6, 7.

viii. That, in what is commanded to others, we are bound according to our places and callings to be helpful to them (b), and to take heed of partaking with others in what is forbidden them (c).

(b) 2 Cor. i. 24. (c) 1 Tim. v. 22; Eph. v. 11.

Q. 100. What special things are we to consider in the Ten Commandments?—A. We are to consider, in the

Ten Commandments, the preface, the substance of the Commandments themselves, and several reasons an-nexed to some of them, the more to enforce them.

Q. 101. What is the preface to the Ten Command-ments?—A. The preface to the Ten Commandments is contained in these words, " I am the Lord thy God, which have brought thee out of the land of Egypt, out of the house of bondage (d)." Wherein God mani-festeth his sovereignty, as being Jehovah, the Eternal, Immutable, and Almighty God (e), having his Being in and of himself (f), and giving being to all his words(g) and works (h); and that he is a God in covenant, as with Israel of old, so with all his people (i), who, as he brought them out of their bondage in Egypt, so he de-livereth us from our spiritual thraldom (k); and that therefore we are bound to take him for our God alone, and to keep all his commandments (l).

(d) Exod. xx. 2.   (e) Isai. xliv. 6.   (f) Exod. iii. 14.   (g) Exod. vi. 3.   (h) Acts xvii. 24, 28.   (i) Gen. xvii. 7, with Rom. iii. 29. (k) Luke i. 74, 75.   (l) 1 Pet. i. 15—18; Levit. xviii. 30, and xix. 37.

Q. 102. What is the sum of the four Commandments which contain our duty to God?—A. The sum of the four Commandments containing our duty to God, is to love the Lord our God with all our heart, and with all our soul, and with all our strength, and with all our mind (m).

(m) Luke x. 27.

Q. 103. Which is the First Commandment?—A. The First Commandment is, " Thou shalt have no other gods before me (n)."

(n) Exod. xx. 3.

Q. 104. What are the duties required in the First Commandment?—A. The duties required in the First Commandment, are the knowing and acknowledging of God to be the only true God, and our God (o), and to worship and glorify him accordingly (p), by thinking (q) meditating (r), remembering (s), highly esteeming (t),

P 2

honouring (*u*), adoring (*w*), choosing (*x*), loving (*y*), desiring (*z*); fearing of him (*a*); believing him (*b*), trusting (*c*), hoping (*d*), delighting (*e*), rejoicing in him (*f*) ;
being zealous for him (*g*), calling upon him, giving all
praise and thanks (*h*), and yielding all obedience and
submission to him, with the whole man (*i*); being careful in all things to please him (*k*), and sorrowful when
in any thing he is offended (*l*); and walking humbly
with him (*m*).

. (*o*) 1 Chron. xxviii. 9; Deut. xxvi. 17; Isai. xliii.
     10; Jer. xiv. 22.   (*p*) Psal. xcv. 6, 7; Matt.
     iv. 10 ; Psal. xxix. 2.   (*q*) Mal. iii. 16.   (*r*) Psal.
     lxiii. 6.   (*s*) Eccles. xii. 1.   (*t*) Psal. lxxi. 19.
     (*u*) Mal. i. 6.   (*w*) Isai. xlv. 23.   (*x*) Josh.
     xxiv. 15, 22.   (*y*) Deut. vi. 5.   (*z*) Psal.
     lxxiii. 25.   (*a*) Isai. viii. 13.   (*b*) Exod.
     xiv. 31.   (*c*) Isai. xxvi. 4.   (*d*) Psal. cxxx. 7.
     (*e*) Psal. xxxvii. 4.   (*f*) Psal. xxxii. 11.
     (*g*) Rom. xii. 11, compared with Numb. xxv. 11.
     (*h*) Phil. iv. 6.   (*i*) Jer. vii. 23; James iv. 7.
     (*k*) 1 John iii. 22.   (*l*) Jer. xxxi. 18; Psal. cxix.
     136.   (*m*) Micah vi. 8.

   Q. 105. What are the sins forbidden in the First
Commandment?—A. The sins forbidden in the First
Commandment, are atheism, in denying, or not having
a God (*n*); idolatry, in having, or worshipping more
gods than one, or any with or instead of the true God (*o*);
the not having and avouching him for God, and our
God (*p*); the omission or neglect of any thing due to
him required in this commandment (*q*); ignorance (*r*),
forgetfulness (*s*), misapprehensions (*t*), false opinions (*u*),
unworthy and wicked thoughts of him (*w*), bold and
curious searching into his secrets (*x*), all profaneness (*y*),
hatred of God (*z*), self-love (*a*), self-seeking (*b*), and all
other inordinate and immoderate setting of our mind,
will, or affections upon other things, and taking them
off from him in whole or in part (*c*); vain credulity (*d*),
unbelief (*e*), heresy (*f*), misbelief (*g*), distrust (*h*), despair (*i*), incorrigibleness (*k*), and insensibleness under

judgments (*l*), hardness of heart (*m*), pride (*n*), presumption (*o*), carnal security (*p*), tempting of God (*q*), using unlawful means (*r*), and trusting in lawful means (*s*), carnal delights, and joys (*t*); corrupt, blind, and indiscreet zeal (*u*); lukewarmness (*w*), and deadness in the things of God (*x*), estranging ourselves, and apostatizing from God (*y*); praying, or giving any religious worship to saints, angels, or any other creatures (*z*); all compacts, and consulting with the devil (*a*), and hearkening to his suggestions (*b*); making men the lords of our faith and conscience (*c*); slighting and despising God and his commands (*d*), resisting and grieving of his Spirit (*e*), discontent and impatience at his dispensasations, charging him foolishly for the evils he inflicts on us (*f*), and ascribing the praise of any good we either are, have, or can do, to fortune (*g*), idols (*h*), ourselves (*i*), or any other creature (*k*).

(*n*) Psal. xiv. 1 ; Eph. ii. 12.   (*o*) Jer. ii. 27, 28, compared with 1 Thess. i. 9.   (*p*) Psal. lxxxi. 11. (*q*) Isai. xliii. 22—24.   (*r*) Jer. iv. 22 ; Hosea iv. 1, 6.   (*s*) Jer. ii. 32.   (*t*) Acts xvii. 23, 29. (*u*) Isai. xl. 18.   (*w*) Psal. l. 21.   (*x*) Deut. xxix. 29.   (*y*) Titus i. 16 ; Heb. xii. 16. (*z*) Rom. i. 30.   (*a*) 2 Tim. iii. 2.   (*b*) Phil. ii. 21.   (*c*) 1 John ii. 15, 16 ; 1 Sam. ii. 29 ; Col. iii. 2, 5.   (*d*) 1 John iv. 1.   (*e*) Heb. iii. 12.   (*f*) Gal. v. 20 ; Tit. iii. 10.   (*g*) Acts xxvi. 9.   (*h*) Psal. lxxviii. 22.   (*i*) Gen. iv. 13.   (*k*) Jer. v. 3.   (*l*) Isai. xlii. 25. (*m*) Rom. ii. 5.   (*n*) Jer. xiii. 15.   (*o*) Psal. xix. 13.   (*p*) Zeph. i. 12.   (*q*) Matt. iv. 7. (*r*) Rom. iii. 8.   (*s*) Jer. xvii. 5.   (*t*) 2 Tim. iii. 4.   (*u*) Gal. iv. 17 ; John xvi. 2 ; Rom. x. 2 ; Luke ix. 54, 55.   (*w*) Rev. iii. 16. (*x*) Rev. iii. 1.   (*y*) Ezek. xiv. 5 ; Isai. i. 4.   (*z*) Rom. x. 13, 14 ; Hosea iv. 12 ; Acts x. 25, 26 ; Rev. xix. 10 ; Matt. iv. 10 ; Col. ii. 18 ; Rom. i. 25. (*a*) Lev. xx. 6 ; 1 Sam. xxviii. 7, 11, compared with 1 Chron. x. 13, 14.   (*b*) Acts v. 3.   (*c*) 2 Cor.

i. 24 ; Matt. xxiii. 9.　　　(d) Deut. xxxii 15 ;
2 Sam. xii. 9 ; Prov. xiii. 13.　　(e) Acts vii. 51 ;
Eph. iv. 30.　　(f) Psal. lxxiii. 2, 3, 13—15, 22 ;
Job i. 22.　　(g) 1 Sam. vi. 7—9.　　(h) Dan.
v. 23.　(i) Deut. viii. 17 ; Dan. iv. 30.　(k) Hab.
i. 16.

Q. 106. What are we especially taught by these words,
" before Me," in the First Commandment?—A. These
words, " before Me," or before my face, in the First
Commandment, teach us, that God, who seeth all things,
takes special notice of, and is much displeased with, the
sin of having any other god ; that so it may be an argu-
ment to dissuade from it, and to aggravate it, as a most
impudent provocation (l) ; as also to persuade us to do,
as in his sight, whatever we do in his service (m).

(l) Ezek. viii. 5, to the end ; Psal. xliv. 20, 21.
(m) 1 Chron. xxviii. 9.

Q. 107. Which is the Second Commandment?—
A. The Second Commandment is, " Thou shalt not
make unto thee any graven image, or any likeness of
any thing that is in heaven above, or that is in the earth
beneath, or that is in the water under the earth ; thou
shalt not bow down thyself to them, nor serve them :
for I the Lord thy God am a jealous God, visiting the
iniquities of the fathers upon the children, unto the
third and fourth generation of them that hate me ; and
shewing mercy unto thousands of them that love me
and keep my commandments (n).

(n) Exod. xx. 4—6.

Q. 108. What are the duties required in the Second
Commandment?—A. The duties required in the Second
Commandment are, the receiving, observing, and keeping pure and entire all such religious worship and ordinances as God hath instituted in his word (o) ; particularly prayer and thanksgiving in the name of Christ (p) ;
the reading, preaching, and hearing of the word (q), the
administration and receiving of the sacraments (r),
church government and discipline (s), the ministry and
maintenance thereof (t), religious fasting (u), swearing

by the name of God (*w*), and vowing unto him (*x*): as also the disapproving, detesting, opposing all false worship (*y*); and, according to each one's place and calling, removing it, and all monuments of idolatry (*z*).

(*o*) Deut. xxxii. 46, 47; Matt. xxviii. 20; Acts ii. 42; 1 Tim. vi. 13, 14.   (*p*) Phil. iv. 6; Eph. v. 20. (*q*) Deut. xvii. 18, 19; Acts xv. 21; 2 Tim. iv. 2; James i. 21, 22; Acts x. 33.   (*r*) Matt. xxviii. 19; 1 Cor. xi. 23—30.   (*s*) Matt. xviii. 15—17; xvi. 19; 1 Cor. v., and xii. 28.   (*t*) Eph. iv. 11, 12; 1 Tim. v. 17, 18; 1 Cor. ix. 7—15. (*u*) Joel ii. 12, 13; 1 Cor. vii. 5.   (*w*) Deut. vi. 13.   (*x*) Isai. xix. 21; Psal. lxxvi. 11. (*y*) Acts xvii. 16, 17; Psal. xvi. 4.   (*z*) Deut. vii. 5; Isai. xxx. 22.

Q. 109. What are the sins forbidden in the Second Commandment?—A. The sins forbidden in the Second Commandment, are, all devising (*a*), counselling (*b*), commanding (*c*), using (*d*), and any ways approving any religious worship, not instituted by God himself(*e*); tolerating a false religion (*f*); the making any repre-sentation of God, of all, or any of the Three Persons, either inwardly in our mind, or outwardly in any kind of image, or likeness of any creature whatsoever (*g*); all worshipping of it (*h*), or God in it, or by it (*i*); the making of any representation of feigned deities (*k*), and all worship of them, or service belonging to them (*l*); all supersitious devices (*m*), corrupting the worship of God (*n*), adding to it, or taking from it (*o*), whether in-vented and taken up of ourselves (*p*), or received by tradition from others (*q*), though under the title of antiquity (*r*), custom (*s*), devotion (*t*), good intent, or any other pretence whatsoever (*u*); simony(*w*), sacrilege(*x*); all neglect (*y*), contempt(*z*), hindering (*a*), and opposing the worship and ordinances which God hath appointed (*b*).

(*a*) Num. xv. 39.   (*b*) Deut. xiii. 6—8.   (*c*) Hos. v. 11; Mic. vi. 16.   (*d*) 1.Kings xi. 33, and xii. 33.   (*e*) Deut. xii. 30—32.   (*f*) Deut.

xiii. 6—12; Zech. xiii. 2, 3; Rev. ii. 2, 14, 15, 20, and xvii. 12, 16, 17. (g) Deut. iv. 15—19; Acts xvii. 29; Rom. i. 21—23, 25. (h) Dan. iii. 18; Gal. iv. 8. (i) Exod. xxxii. 5. (k) Exod. xxxii. 8. (l) 1 Kings xviii. 26, 28; Isai. lxv. 11. (m) Acts xvii. 22; Col. ii. 21—23. (n) Mal. i. 7, 8, 14. (o) Deut. iv. 2. (p) Psal. cvi. 39. (q) Matt. xv. 9. (r) 1 Pet. i. 18. (s) Jer. xliv. 17. (t) Isai. lxv. 3—5; Gal. i. 13, 14. (u) 1 Sam. xiii. 11, 12, 15, 21. (w) Acts viii. 18. (x) Rom. ii. 22; Mal. iii. 8. (y) Exod. iv. 24—26. (z) Matt. xxii. 5; Mal. i. 7, 13. (a) Matt. xxiii. 13. (b) Acts. xiii. 44, 45; 1 Thess. ii. 15, 16.

Q. 110. What are the reasons annexed to the Second Commandment, the more to enforce it?—A. The reasons annexed to the Second Commandment, the more to enforce it, contained in these words, "For I the Lord thy God am a jealous God, visiting the iniquity of the fathers upon the children, unto the third and fourth generation of them that hate me; and shewing mercy unto thousands of them that love me, and keep my commandments (c)," are, beside God's sovereignty over us, and propriety in us (d), his fervent zeal for his own worship (e), and his revengeful indignation against all false worship, as being a spiritual whoredom (f); accounting the breakers of this commandment, such as hate him, and threatening to punish them unto divers generations (g); and esteeming the observers of it, such as love him, and keep his commandments, and promising mercy to them unto many generations (h).

(c) Exod. xx. 5, 6. (d) Psal. xlv. 11; Rev. xv. 3, 4. (e) Exod. xxxiv. 13, 14. (f) 1 Cor. x. 20—22; Jer. vii. 18—20; Ezek. xvi. 26, 27; Deut. xxxii. 16—20. (g) Hosea ii. 2—4. (h) Deut. v. 29.

Q. 111. Which is the Third Commandment?— A. The Third Commandment is, "Thou shalt not take the name of the Lord thy God in vain; for the Lord will not hold him guiltless, that taketh his Name in vain (*i*).

(*i*) Exod. xx. 7.

Q. 112. What is required in the Third Commandment?—A. The Third Commandment requires, that the Name of God, his titles, attributes (*k*), ordinances(*l*), the word (*m*), sacraments (*n*), prayer (*o*), oaths (*p*), vows (*q*), lots (*r*), his works (*s*), and whatsoever else there is whereby he makes himself known, be holily and reverently used, in thought (*t*), meditation (*u*), word (*w*), writing (*x*), by an holy profession (*y*), and answerable conversation(*z*), to the glory of God (*a*), and the good of ourselves (*b*), and others (*c*).

(*k*) Matt. vi. 9; Deut. xxviii. 58; Psal. xxix. 2, and lxviii. 4; Rev. xv. 3, 4. (*l*) Mal. i. 14; Eccles. v. 1. (*m*) Psal. cxxxviii. 2. (*n*) 1 Cor. xi. 24, 25, 28, 29. (*o*) 1 Tim. ii. 8. (*p*) Jer. iv. 2. (*q*) Eccles. v. 2, 4—6. (*r*) Acts i. 24, 26. (*s*) Job xxxvi. 24. (*t*) Mal. iii. 16. (*u*) Psal. viii. *throughout.* (*w*) Col. iii. 17; Psal. cv. 2, 5. (*x*) Psal. cii. 18. (*y*) 1 Pet. iii. 15; Micah iv. 5. (*z*) Phil. i. 27. (*a*) 1 Cor. x. 31. (*b*) Jer. xxxii. 39. (*c*) 1 Pet. ii. 12.

Q. 113. What are the sins forbidden in the Third Commandment?—A. The sins forbidden in the Third Commandment are, the not using of God's name as is required(*d*); and the abuse of it in an ignorant(*e*),vain(*f*), irreverent, profane(*g*), superstitious(*h*), or wicked mentioning, or otherwise using his titles, attributes (*i*), ordinances (*k*), or works (*l*), by blasphemy (*m*), perjury (*n*), all sinful cursings (*o*), oaths (*p*), vows (*q*), and lots (*r*); violating of our oaths and vows, if lawful (*s*); and fulfilling them, if of things unlawful (*t*); murmuring and quarrelling at (*u*), curious prying into (*w*), and misapplying of God's decrees (*x*) and providences (*y*); misinterpreting (*z*), misapplying (*a*), or any way perverting the word, or any part of it (*b*), to profane jests (*c*), curious or unprofitable questions, vain-janglings, or the

maintaining of false doctrines (*d*); abusing it, the creatures, or any thing contained under the name of God,
to charms (*e*), or sinful lusts and practices (*f*); the
maligning (*g*), scorning (*h*), reviling (*i*), or any ways
opposing of God's truth, grace, and ways (*k*); making
profession of religion in hypocrisy, or for sinister
ends (*l*); being ashamed of it (*m*), or a shame to it, by
uncomfortable (*n*), unwise (*o*), unfruitful (*p*), and offensive walking (*q*), or backsliding from it (*r*).

(*d*) Mal. ii. 2. (*e*) Acts xvii. 23. (*f*) Prov.
xxx. 9. (*g*) Mal. i. 6, 7, 12, and iii. 14.
(*h*) 1 Sam. iv. 3—5; Jer. vii. 4, 9, 10, 14, 31;
Col. ii. 20—22. (*i*) 2 Kings xviii. 30, 35;
Exod. v. 2; Psal. cxxxix. 20. (*k*) Psal. l. 16, 17.
(*l*) Isai. v. 12. (*m*) 2 Kings xix. 22; Lev.
xxiv. 11. (*n*) Zech. v. 4, and viii. 17. (*o*) 1 Sam.
xvii. 43; 2 Sam. xvi. 5. (*p*) Jer. v. 7, and
xxiii. 10. (*q*) Deut. xxiii. 18; Acts xxiii.
12, 14. (*r*) Esther iii. 7, and ix. 24; Psal.
xxii. 18. (*s*) Psal. xxiv. 4; Ezek. xvii. 16,
18, 19. (*t*) Mark vi. 26; 1 Sam. xxv. 22,
32—34. (*u*) Rom. ix. 14, 19, 20. (*w*) Deut.
xxix. 29. (*x*) Rom. iii. 5, 7, and vi. 1.
(*y*) Eccles. viii. 11, and ix. 3; Psal. xxxix. *throughout*.
(*z*) Matt. v. 21, *to the end*. (*a*) Ezek. xiii. 22.
(*b*) 2 Pet. iii. 16; Matt. xxii. 24—31. (*c*) Isai.
xxii. 13; Jer. xxiii. 34, 36, 38. (*d*) 1 Tim. i.
4, 6, 7, and vi. 4, 5, 20; 2 Tim. ii. 14; Tit. iii. 9.
(*e*) Deut. xviii. 10—14; Acts xix. 13. (*f*) 2 Tim.
iv. 3, 4; Rom. xiii. 13, 14; 1 Kings xxi. 9, 10;
Jude 4. (*g*) Acts xiii. 45; 1 John iii. 12.
(*h*) Psal. i. 1; 2 Pet. iii. 3. (*i*) 1 Pet. iv. 4.
(*k*) Acts xiii. 45, 46, 50, iv. 18, and xix. 9; 1 Thess.
ii. 16; Heb. x. 29. (*l*) 2 Tim. iii. 5; Matt.
xxiii. 14, and vi. 1, 2, 5, 16. (*m*) Mark viii. 38.
(*n*) Psal. lxxiii. 14, 15. (*o*) 1 Cor. vi. 5, 6;
Eph. v. 15—17. (*p*) Isai. v. 4; 2 Pet. i.
8, 9. (*q*) Rom. ii. 23, 24. (*r*) Gal. iii.
1, 3; Heb. vi. 6.

Q. 114. What reasons are annexed to the Third Commandment?—A. The reasons annexed to the Third Commandment in these words, " the Lord thy God," and " for the Lord will not hold him guiltless that taketh his name in vain(s)," are, because he is the Lord and our God : and therefore his name is not to be profaned, or any way abused by us (t); especially, because he will be so far from acquitting and sparing the transgressors of this commandment, as that he will not suffer them to escape his righteous judgment (u), albeit many such escape the censures and punishments of men (w).

(s) Exod. xx. 7.   (t) Levit. xix. 12.   (u) Ezek. xxxvi. 21—23; Deut. xxviii. 58, 59; Zech. v. 2—4:   (w) 1 Sam. ii. 12, 17, 22, 24, compared with iii. 13.

Q. 115. Which is the Fourth Commandment?—A. The Fourth Commandment is, " Remember the Sabbath-day to keep it holy : six days shalt thou labour, and do all thy work; but the seventh day is the Sabbath of the Lord thy God : in it thou shalt not do any work, thou, nor thy son, nor thy daughter, thy man-servant, nor thy maid-servant, nor thy cattle, nor thy stranger that is within thy gates : for in six days the Lord made heaven and earth, the sea, and all that in them is; and rested the Seventh-day; wherefore the Lord blessed the Sabbath-day, and hallowed it (x)."

(x) Exod. xx. 8—11.

Q. 116. What is required in the Fourth Commandment?—A. The Fourth Commandment requireth of all men, the sanctifying, or keeping holy to God, such set times as he hath appointed in his word; expressly one whole day in seven, which was the seventh from the beginning of the world to the resurrection of Christ, and the first day of the week ever since; and so to continue to the end of the world, which is the Christian Sabbath (y), and in the New Testament called the Lord's-day (z).

(y) Deut. v. 12—14; Gen. ii. 2, 3; 1 Cor. xvi. 1, 2;

Acts xx. 7; Matt. v. 17, 18; Isai. lvi 2, 4, 6, 7.
(z) Rev. i. 10.

Q. 117. How is the Sabbath, or Lord's-day, to be
sanctified?—A. The Sabbath, or Lord's-day, is to be
sanctified by an holy resting all the day (a), not only
from such works as are at all times sinful, but even from
such worldly employments and recreations as are on
other days lawful (b), and making it our delight to
spend the whole time (except so much of it as is to be
taken up in works of necessity and mercy (c) in the
public and private exercises of God's worship (d); and
to that end we are to prepare our hearts, and with
such foresight, diligence, and moderation, to dispose,
and seasonably to dispatch our worldly business, that
we may be the more free and fit for the duties of that
day (e).

(a) Exod. xx. 8, 10.   (b) Exod xvi. 25—28;
Neh. xiii. 15—22; Jer. xvii. 21, 22.   (c) Matt.
xii. 1—13.   (d) Isai. lviii. 13; Luke iv. 16;
Acts xx. 7; 1 Cor. xvi. 1, 2; Psal. xcii. *title;*
Isai. lxvi. 23; Lev. xxiii. 3.   (e) Exod. xx. 8;
Luke xxiii. 54, 56; Exod. xvi. 22, 25, 26, 29;
Neh. xiii. 19.

Q. 118. Why is the charge of keeping the Sabbath
more especially directed to governors of families and
other superiors?—A. The charge of keeping the Sabbath is more specially directed to governors of families
and other superiors, because they are bound not only
to keep it themselves, but to see that it be observed by
all those that are under their charge; and because they
are prone oft-times to hinder them by employments of
their own (f).

(f) Exod. xx. 10; Josh. xxiv. 15; Neh. xiii. 15, 17;
Jer. xvii. 20—22; Exod. xxiii. 12.

Q. 119. What are the sins forbidden in the Fourth
Commandment?—A. The sins forbidden in the Fourth
Commandment are, all omissions of the duties re-
quired (g); all careless, negligent, and unprofitable

performing of them, and being weary of them (h); all profaning the day by idleness, and doing that which is in itself sinful (i); and by all needless works, words, and thoughts, about our worldly employments and re-creations (k).

(g) Ezek. xxii. 26.　　　　(h) Acts xx. 7, 9; Ezek. xxxiii. 30—32; Amos viii. 5; Mal. i. 13.　(i) Ezek. xxiii. 38.　　(k) Jer. xvii. 24, 27; Isai. lviii. 13.

Q. 120. What are the reasons annexed to the Fourth Commandment, the more to enforce it?—A. The reasons annexed to the Fourth Commandment, the more to enforce it, are taken from the equity of it, God allow-ing us six days of seven for our own affairs, and reserv-ing but one for himself, in these words, " Six days shalt thou labour and do all thy works " (l): from God's challenging a special propriety in that day; " the seventh day is the Sabbath of the Lord thy God " (m): from the example of God, who " in six days made heaven and earth, the sea and all that in them is, and rested the seventh day ;" and from that blessing which God put upon that day, not only in sanctifying it to be a day for his service, but in ordaining it to be a means of blessing to us in our sanctifying it: " where-fore the Lord blessed the Sabbath-day, and hallowed it " (n).

(l) Exod. xx. 9.　　(m) Exod. xx. 10.　　(n) Exod. xx. 11.

Q. 121. Why is the word " remember" set in the beginning of the Fourth Commandment?—A. The word " remember" is set in the beginning of the Fourth Commandment (o), partly because of the great benefit of remembering it; we being thereby helped in our preparation to keep it (p); and, in keeping it, better to keep all the rest of the Commandments (q), and to continue a thankful remembrance of the two great benefits of creation and redemption, which con-tain a short abridgment of religion (r); and partly because we are very ready to forget it (s), for that there is less light of nature for it (*t*), and yet it restraineth our natural liberty in things at other times lawful (*u*); that it cometh but once in seven days, and many worldly businesses come between, and too often take off our minds from thinking of it, either to prepare for it, or to sanctify it (*w*); and that Satan with his instruments much labour to blot out the glory, and even the memory of it, to bring in all irreligion and impiety (*x*).

(*o*) Exod. xx. 8.   (*p*) Exod. xvi. 23; Luke xxiii. 54, 56, with Mark xv. 42; Neh. xiii. 19.   (*q*) Psal. xcii. *title*, with ver. 13, 14; Ezek. xx. 12, 19, 20. (*r*) Gen. ii. 2, 3; Psal. cxviii. 22, 24, with Acts iv. 10, 11; Rev. i. 10.   (*s*) Ezek. xxii. 26. (*t*) Neh. ix. 14.   (*u*) Exod. xxxiv. 21.   (*w*) Deut. v. 14, 15; Amos viii. 5.   (*x*) Lam. i. 7; Jer. xvii. 21—23; Neh. xiii. 15—23.

Q. 122. What is the sum of the six Commandments which contain our duty to man?—A. The sum of the six Commandments which contain our duty to man is, to love our neighbour as ourselves (*y*), and to do to others what we would have them to do to us (*z*).

   (*y*) Matt. xxii. 39.   (*z*) Matt. vii. 12.

Q. 123. Which is the Fifth Commandment?—A. The Fifth Commandment is, " Honour thy father and thy mother: that thy days may be long upon the land, which the Lord thy God giveth thee" (*a*).

     (*a*) Exod. xx. 12.

Q. 124. Who are meant by father and mother in the Fifth Commandment?—A. By father and mother, in the Fifth Commandment, are meant, not only natural parents (*b*), but all superiors in age (*c*) and gifts (*d*); and especially such, as by God's ordinance are over us in place of authority, whether in family (*e*), church (*f*), r commonwealth (*g*).

   (*b*) Prov. xxiii. 22, 25; Eph. vi. 1, 2.   (*c*) 1 Tim. v. 1, 2.   (*d*) Gen. iv. 21, 22, and xlv. 8.

(e) 2 Kings v. 13.　　　　(f) 2 Kings ii. 12, and
xiii. 14; Gal. iv. 19.　　　(g) Isai. xlix. 23.

Q. 125. Why are superiors styled father and mother?
—A. Superiors are styled father and mother, both to
teach them in all duties towards their inferiors, like
natural parents, to express love and tenderness to them
according to their several relations (h), and to work
inferiors to a greater willingness and cheerfulness in
performing their duties to their superiors, as to their
parents (i).

(h) Eph. vi. 4; 2 Cor. xii. 14; 1 Thess. ii. 7, 8, 11;
Num. xi. 11, 12.　　　　(i) 1 Cor. iv. 14—16;
2 Kings v. 13.

Q. 126. What is the general scope of the Fifth Commandment?—A. The general scope of the Fifth Commandment is, the performance of those duties which
we mutually owe in our several relations, as inferiors,
superiors, equals (k).

(k) Eph. v. 21; 1 Pet. ii. 17; Rom. xii. 10.

Q. 127. What is the honour that inferiors owe to their
superiors?—A. The honour which inferiors owe to their
superiors, is all due reverence in heart (l), word (m),
and behaviour (n); prayer and thanksgiving for them (o);
imitation of their virtues and graces (p); willing obedience to their lawful commands and counsels (q); due
submission to their corrections (r); fidelity to (s), defence (t), and maintenance of, their person and authority
according to their several ranks, and the nature of their
places (u); bearing with their infirmities and covering
them in love (w), that so they may be an honour to
them and to their government (x).

(l) Mal. i. 6; Lev. xix. 3.　　　(m) Prov. xxxi. 28;
1 Pet. iii. 6.　　(n) Lev. xix. 32; 1 Kings ii. 19.
(o) 1 Tim. ii. 1, 2.　　　(p) Heb. xiii. 7; Phil.
iii. 17.　　(q) Eph. vi. 1—7; 1 Pet. ii. 13, 14;
Rom. xiii. 1—5; Heb. xiii. 17; Prov. iv. 3, 4,
and xxiii. 22; Exod. xviii. 19, 24.　　(r) Heb.
xii. 9; 1 Pet. ii. 18—20.　　　(s) Titus ii. 9, 10.

(*t*) 1 Sam. xxvi. 15, 16; 2 Sam. xviii. 3; Esther vi. 2. (*u*) Matt. xxii. 21; Rom. xiii. 6, 7; 1 Tim. v. 17, 18; Gal. vi. 6; Gen. xlv. 11, and xlvii. 12. (*w*) 1 Pet. ii. 18; Prov. xxiii. 22; Gen. ix. 23. (*x*) Psal. cxxvii. 3—5; Prov. xxxi. 23.

Q. 128. What are the sins of inferiors against their superiors?—A. The sins of inferiors against their superiors are, all neglect of the duties required toward them (*y*), envying at (*z*), contempt of (*a*), and rebellion (*b*) against their persons (*c*) and places (*d*), in their lawful counsels (*e*), commands, and corrections (*f*); cursing, mocking (*g*), and all such refractory and scandalous carriage, as proves a shame and dishonour to them and their government (*h*).

(*y*) Matt. xv. 4—6. (*z*) Num. xi. 28, 29. (*a*) 1 Sam. viii. 7; Isai. iii. 5. (*b*) 2 Sam. xv. 1—12. (*c*) Exod. xxi. 15. (*d*) 1 Sam. x. 27. (*e*) 1 Sam. ii. 25. (*f*) Deut. xxi. 18—21. (*g*) Prov. xxx. 11. 17. (*h*) Prov. xix. 26.

Q. 129. What is required of superiors towards their inferiors?—A. It is required of superiors, according to that power they receive from God, and that relation wherein they stand, to love (*i*), pray for (*k*), and bless their inferiors (*l*); to instruct (*m*), counsel, and admonish them (*n*); countenancing (*o*), commending (*p*), and rewarding such as do well (*q*); discountenancing (*r*), reproving, and chastising such as do ill (*s*); protecting (*t*) and providing for them all things necessary for soul (*u*) and body (*w*); and, by grave, wise, holy, and exemplary carriage, to procure glory to God (*x*), honour to themselves (*y*), and so preserve that authority which God hath put upon them (*z*).

(*i*) Col. iii. 19; Titus ii. 4. (*k*) 1 Sam. xii. 23; Job i. 5. (*l*) 1 Kings viii. 55, 56; Heb. vii. 7; Gen. xlix. 28. (*m*) Deut. vi. 6, 7. (*n*) Eph. vi. 4. (*o*) 1 Pet. iii. 7. (*p*) 1 Pet. ii. 14; Rom. xiii. 3. (*q*) Esther vi. 3. (*r*) Rom.

· xiii. 3, 4. (s) Prov. xxix. 15 ; 1 Pet. ii. 14.
(t) Job xxix. 12—17 ; Isai. i. 10, 17. (u) Eph.
vi. 4. (w) 1 Tim. v. 8. (x) 1 Tim. iv.
12 ; Titus ii. 3—5. (y) 1 Kings iii. 28.
(z) Titus ii. 15.

Q. 130. What are the sins of superiors?—A. The
sins of superiors are, beside the neglect of the duties
required of them (a), an inordinate seeking of them-
selves(b), their own glory(c), ease, profit, or pleasure(d);
commanding things unlawful (e), or not in the power of
inferiors to perform(f); counselling(g), encouraging(h),
or favouring them in that which is evil (i); dissuading,
discouraging, or discountenancing them in that which
is good (k); correcting them unduly (l); careless ex-
posing, or leaving them to wrong, temptation, and
danger (m); provoking them to wrath (n), or any way
dishonouring themselves, or lessening their authority,
by an unjust, indiscreet, rigorous, or remiss behaviour (o).

(a) Ezek. xxxiv. 2—4. (b) Phil. ii. 21. (c) John
v. 44, and vii. 18. (d) Isai. lvi. 10, 11 ; Deut.
xvii. 17. (e) Dan. iii. 4—6 ; Acts iv. 17, 18.
(f) Exod. v. 10—18 ; Matt. xxiii. 2, 4. (g) Matt.
xiv. 8, compared with Mark vi. 24. (h) 2 Sam.
xiii. 28. (i) 1 Sam. iii. 13. (k) John vii.
46—49 ; Col. iii. 21 ; Exod. v. 17. (l) 1 Pet.
ii. 18—20 ; Heb. xii. 10 ; Deut. xxv. 3. (m) Gen.
xxxviii. 11, 26 ; Acts xviii. 17. (n) Eph. vi. 4.
(o) Gen. ix. 21 ; 1 Kings xii. 13—19 ; 1 Kings i. 6 ;
1 Sam. ii. 29—31.

Q. 131. What are the duties of equals?—A. The
duties of equals are, to regard the dignity and worth of
each other (p), in giving honour to go one before ano-
ther(q), and to rejoice in each other's gifts and advancement, as in their own (r).

(p) 1 Pet. ii. 17. (q) Rom. xii. 10. (r) Rom.
xii. 15, 16 ; Phil. ii. 3, 4.

Q. 132. What are the sins of equals?—A. The sins
of equals are, beside the neglect of the duties required(s),

Q

the undervaluing of the worth (*t*), envying the gifts (*u*), grieving at the advancement or prosperity one of another (*w*), and usurping pre-eminence one over another (*x*).

(*s*) Rom. xiii. 8.   (*t*) 2 Tim. iii. 3.   (*u*) Acts vii. 9 ; Gal. v. 26.   (*w*) Num. xii. 2 ; Esther vi. 12, 13.   (*x*) 3 John 9 ; Luke xxii. 24.

Q. 133. What is the reason annexed to the Fifth Commandment, the more to enforce it?—A. The reason annexed to the Fifth Commandment, in these words, " That thy days may be long upon the land, which the Lord thy God giveth thee (*y*)," is an express promise of long life and prosperity, as far as it shall serve for God's glory and their own good, to all such as keep this commandment (*z*).

(*y*) Exod. xx. 12.   (*z*) Deut. v. 16 ; 1 Kings viii. 25 ; Eph. vi. 2, 3.

Q. 134. Which is the Sixth Commandment?—A. The Sixth Commandment is, " Thou shalt not kill (*a*)."

(*a*) Exod. xx. 13.

Q. 135. What are the duties required in the Sixth Commandment?—A. The duties required in the Sixth Commandment are, all careful studies and lawful endeavours to preserve the life of ourselves (*b*) and others (*c*) ; by resisting all thoughts and purposes (*d*), subduing all passions (*e*), and avoiding all occasions (*f*), temptations (*g*), and practices which tend to the unjust taking away the life of any (*h*); by just defence thereof against violence (*i*), patient bearing of the hand of God (*k*), quietness of mind (*l*), cheerfulness of spirit (*m*), a sober use of meat (*n*), drink (*o*), physic (*p*), sleep (*q*), labour (*r*), and recreations (*s*); by charitable thoughts (*t*), love (*u*), compassion (*w*), meekness, gentleness, kindness (*x*); peaceable (*y*), mild, and courteous speeches and behaviour (*z*); forbearance, readiness to be reconciled, patient bearing and forgiving of injuries, and requiting good for evil (*a*), comforting and succouring the distressed, and protecting and defending the innocent (*b*).

(*b*) Eph. v. 28, 29,   (*c*) 1 Kings xviii. 4.   (*d*) Jer.
xxvi. 15, 16; Acts xxiii. 12,15,17, 21, 27.   (*e*) Eph.
iv. 26, 27.   (*f*) 2 Sam. ii. 22; Deut. xxii. 8.
(*g*) Matt. iv. 6, 7; Prov. i.10,11,15,16.   (*h*) 1 Sam.
xxiv. 12, and xxvi. 9—11; Gen. xxxvii. 21, 22.
(*i*) Psal. lxxxii. 4; Prov. xxiv. 11, 12; 1 Sam.
xiv. 45.   (*k*) Jas. v. 7—11; Heb. xii. 9.
(*l*) 1 Thess. iv. 11; 1 Pet. iii. 4; Psal. xxxvii.
8—11.   (*m*) Prov. xvii. 22.   (*n*) Prov.
xxv. 16, 27.   (*o*) 1 Tim. v. 23.   (*p*) Isai.
xxxviii 21.   (*q*) Psal. cxxvii. 7.   (*r*) Eccles.
v. 12; 2 Thess. iii. 10, 12; Prov. xvi. 26.
(*s*) Eccles. iii. 4, 11.   (*t*) 1 Sam. xix. 4, 5.
and xxii. 13, 14.   (*u*) Rom. xiii. 10.   (*w*) Luke
x. 33—35   (*x*) Col. iii. 12, 13.   (*y*) Jas.
iii. 17.   (*z*) 1 Pet. iii. 8—11; Prov. xv. 1;
Judg. viii. 1—3.   (*a*) Matt. v. 24; Eph. iv.
2, 32; Rom. xii. 17, 20, 21.   (*b*) 1 Thess. v.
14; Job xxxi. 19, 20; Matt. xxv. 35, 36; Prov.
xxxi. 8, 9.

Q. 136. What are the sins forbidden in the Sixth
Commandment?—A. The sins forbidden in the Sixth
Commandment are, all taking away the life of ourselves (*c*), or of others (*d*), except in case of public justice (*e*), lawful war (*f*), or necessary defence (*g*); the
neglecting or withdrawing the lawful and necessary
means of preservation of life (*h*), sinful anger (*i*), hatred (*k*), envy (*l*), desire of revenge (*m*); all excessive
passions (*n*), distracting cares (*o*), immoderate use of
meat, drink (*p*), labour (*q*), and recreations (*r*); provoking words (*s*), oppression (*t*), quarrelling (*u*), striking,
wounding (*w*), and whatsoever else tends to the destruction of the life of any (*x*).

(*c*) Acts xvi. 28.   (*d*) Gen. ix. 6.   (*e*) Num.
xxxv. 31, 33.   (*f*) Jer. xlviii. 10; Deut. xx.
(*g*) Exod. xxii. 2, 3.   (*h*) Matt. xxv. 42, 43;
Jas. ii. 15, 16; Eccles. vi. 1, 2.   (*i*) Matt. v. 22.
(*k*) 1 John iii. 15; Lev. xix. 17.   (*l*) Prov.
xiv. 30.   (*m*) Rom. xii. 19.   (*n*) Eph. iv. 31.

228 . APPENDIX.

(*o*) Matt. vi. 31, 34.　　(*p*) Luke xxi. 34; Rom.
xiii. 13.　　(*q*) Eccles. xii. 12, and ii. 22, 23.
(*r*) Isai. v. 12.　　(*s*) Prov. xv. 1, and xii. 18.
(*t*) Ezek. xviii. 18; Exod. i. 14.　　(*u*) Gal.
v. 15; Prov. xxiii. 29.　　(*w*) Num. xxxv.
16—18, 21.　　(*x*) Exod. xxi. 18, *to the end.*

Q. 137. Which is the Seventh Commandment?—
A. The Seventh Commandment is, "Thou shalt not
commit adultery (*y*)."

(*y*) Exod. xx. 14.

Q. 138. What are the duties required in the Seventh
Commandment?—A. The duties required in the Seventh Commandment are, chastity in body, mind, affections (*z*), words (*a*), and behaviour (*b*); and the preservation of it in ourselves and others (*c*); watchfulness
over the eyes, and all the senses (*d*); temperance (*e*),
keeping of chaste company (*f*), modesty in apparel (*g*),
marriage by those that have not the gift of continency (*h*),
conjugal love (*i*) and cohabitation (*k*), diligent labour in
our callings (*l*), shunning all occasions of uncleanness,
and resisting temptations thereunto (*m*).

(*z*) 1 Thess. iv. 4; Job xxxi. 1; 1 Cor. vii. 34.
(*a*) Col. iv. 6.　　(*b*) 1 Pet. iii. 2.　　(*c*) 1 Cor.
vii. 2, 35, 36.　　(*d*) Job xxxi. 1.　　(*e*) Acts
xxiv. 24, 25.　(*f*) Prov. ii. 16—20.　(*g*) 1 Tim.
ii. 9　　(*h*) 1 Cor. vii. 2, 9.　　(*i*) Prov. v.
19, 20.　　(*k*) 1 Pet. iii. 7.　　(*l*) Prov. xxxi.
11, 27, 28.　　(*m*) Prov. v. 8; Gen. xxxix.
8—10.

Q. 139. What are the sins forbidden in the Seventh
Commandment?—A. The sins forbidden in the Seventh
Commandment, besides the neglect of the duties required (*n*), are adultery, fornication (*o*), rape, incest (*p*),
sodomy, and all unnatural lusts (*q*); all unclean imaginations, thoughts, purposes, and affections (*r*), all corrupt or filthy communications, or listening thereunto (*s*);
wanton looks (*t*); impudent, or light behaviour; immo-
dest apparel (*u*); prohibiting of lawful (*w*), and dispensing with unlawful marriages (*x*); allowing, tole-

rating, keeping of stews, and resorting to them (*y*); intangling vows of single life (*z*); undue delay of marriage (*a*); having more wives and husbands than one, at the same time (*b*); unjust divorce (*c*), or desertion (*d*); idleness, gluttony, drunkenness (*e*), unchaste company (*f*), lascivious songs, books, pictures, dancings, stage plays (*g*), and all other provocations to, or acts of uncleanness, either in ourselves or others (*h*).

(*n*) Prov. v. 7.   (*o*) Heb. xiii. 4; Gal. v. 19. (*p*) 2 Sam. xiii. 14; 1 Cor. v. 1.   (*q*) Rom. i. 24, 26, 27; Lev. xx. 15, 16.   (*r*) Matt. v. 28, and xv. 19; Col. iii. 5.   (*s*) Eph. v. 3, 4; Prov. vii. 5, 21, 22.   (*t*) Isai. iii. 16; 2 Pet. ii. 14.   (*u*) Prov. vii. 10, 13.   (*w*) 1 Tim. iv. 3.   (*x*) Lev. xviii. 1—21; Mark vi. 18; Mal. ii. 11, 12.   (*y*) 1 Kings xv. 12; 2 Kings xxiii. 7; Deut. xxiii. 17, 18; Lev. xix. 29; Jer. v. 7; Prov. vii. 24—27.   (*z*) Matt. xix. 10, 11. (*a*) 1 Cor. vii. 7—9; Gen. xxxviii. 26.   (*b*) Mal. ii. 14, 15; Matt. xix. 5.   (*c*) Mal. ii. 16; Matt. v. 32.   (*d*) 1 Cor. vii. 12, 13.   (*e*) Ezek. xvi. 49; Prov. xxiii. 30—33.   (*f*) Gen. xxxix. 10; Prov. v. 8.   (*g*) Eph. v. 4; Ezek. xxiii. 14—16; Isai. xxiii. 15—17, and iii. 16; Mark vi. 22; Rom. xiii. 13; 1 Pet. iv. 3.   (*h*) 2 Kings ix. 30, with Jer. iv. 30, and Ezek. xxiii. 40.

Q. 140. Which is the Eighth Commandment?— A. The Eighth Commandment is, " Thou shalt not steal (*i*)."

(*i*) Exod. xx. 15.

Q. 141. What are the duties required in the Eighth Commandment?—A. The duties required in the Eighth Commandment are, truth, faithfulness, and justice in contracts and commerce between man and man (*k*); rendering to every one his due (*l*); restitution of goods unlawfully detained from the right owners thereof (*m*); giving and lending freely according to our abilities, and the necessities of others (*n*); moderation of our judgments, wills, and affections, concerning worldly goods (*o*);

a provident care and study to get (*p*), keep, use, and dispose those things which are necessary and convenient for the sustentation of our nature, and suitable to our condition (*q*); a lawful calling (*r*), and diligence in it (*s*); frugality (*t*); avoiding unnecessary law-suits (*u*), and suretyship, or other like engagements (*w*); and an endeavour, by all just and lawful means, to procure, preserve, and further the wealth and outward estate of others, as well as our own (*x*).

(*k*) Psal. xv. ii. 4; Zech. vii. 4, 10, and viii. 16, 17. (*l*) Rom. xiii. 7. (*m*) Levit. vi. 2—5, with Luke xix. 8. (*n*) Luke vi. 30, 38; 1 John iii. 17; Eph. iv. 28; Gal. vi. 10. (*o*) 1 Tim. vi. 6—9; Gal. vi. 14. (*p*) 1 Tim. v. 8. (*q*) Prov. xxvii. 23, *to the end;* Eccles. ii. 24, and iii. 12, 13; 1 Tim. vi. 17, 18; Isai. xxxviii. 1; Matt. xi. 8. (*r*) 1 Cor. vii. 20; Gen. ii. 15, and iii. 19. (*s*) Eph. iv. 28; Prov. x. 4. (*t*) John vi. 12; Prov. xxi. 20. (*u*) 1 Cor. vi. 1—9. (*w*) Prov. vi. 1—6, and xi. 15. (*x*) Levit. xxv. 35; Deut. xxii. 1—4; Exod. xxiii. 4, 5; Gen. xlvii. 14, 20; Phil. ii. 4; Matt. xxii. 39.

Q. 142. What are the sins forbidden in the Eighth Commandment?—A. The sins forbidden in the Eighth Commandment, beside the neglect of the duties required (*y*), are theft (*z*), robbery (*a*), man-stealing (*b*), and receiving any thing that is stolen (*c*), fraudulent dealing (*d*), false weights and measures (*e*), removing land-marks (*f*), injustice and unfaithfulness in contracts between man and man (*g*), or in matters of trust (*h*); oppression (*i*), extortion (*k*), usury (*l*), bribery (*m*), vexatious law-suits (*n*), unjust inclosures and depopulations (*o*), engrossing commodities to enhance the price (*p*), unlawful callings (*q*), and all other unjust or sinful ways of taking or withholding from our neighbour what belongs to him, or of enriching ourselves (*r*); covetousness (*s*), inordinate prizing and affecting worldly goods (*t*); distrustful and distracting cares and studies in getting, keeping, and using them (*u*); envying at the

prosperity of others (*w*): as likewise idleness (*x*), pro-
digality, wasteful gaming, and all other ways whereby
we do unduly prejudice our own outward estate (*y*),
and defrauding ourselves of the due use and comfort of
that estate which God hath given us (*z*).

(*y*) Jas. ii. 15, 16; 1 John iii. 17. (*z*) Eph. iv. 28.
(*a*)Psal. lxii. 10. (*b*) 1 Tim. i. 10. (*c*) Prov.
xxix. 24; Psal. l. 18. (*d*) 1 Thess. iv. 6.
(*e*) Prov. xi. 1, and xx. 10. (*f*) Deut. xix. 14;
Prov. xxiii. 10. (*g*) Amos viii. 5; Psal.
xxxvii. 21. (*h*) Luke xvi. 10—12. (*i*) Ezek.
xxii. 28; Lev. xxv. 17. (*k*) Matt. xxiii. 25;
Ezek. xxii. 12. (*l*) Psal. xv. 5. (*m*) Job
xv. 34. (*n*) 1 Cor. vi. 6—8; Prov. iii. 29, 30.
(*o*) Isai. v. 8; Micah ii. 2. (*p*) Prov. xi. 26.
(*q*) Acts xix. 19, 24, 25. : (*r*) Job xx. 19;
Jas. v. 4; Prov. xxi. 6. (*s*) Luke xii. 15.
(*t*) 1 Tim. vi. 5; Col. iii. 2; Prov. xxiii. 5; Psal.
lxii. 10. (*u*) Matt. vi. 25, 31, 34; Eccles. v. 12.
(*w*) Psal. lxxiii. 3, and xxxvii. 1, 7. (*x*) 2 Thess.
iii. 11; Prov. xviii. 9. (*y*) Prov. xxi. 17,
xxiii. 20, 21, and xxviii. 19. (*z*) Eccles. iv. 8,
and vi. 2; 1 Tim. v. 8.

Q. 143. Which is the Ninth Commandment?—A. The
Ninth Commandment is, " Thou shalt not bear false
witness against thy neighbour (*a*)."

(*a*) Exod. xx. 16.

Q. 144. What are the duties required in the Ninth
Commandment?—A. The duties required in the Ninth
Commandment are, the preserving and promoting of
truth between man and man (*b*); and the good name
of our neighbour, as well as our own (*c*), appearing and
standing for the truth (*d*), and from the heart (*e*); sincerely (*f*), freely (*g*), clearly (*h*), and fully (*i*), speaking
the truth, and only the truth; in matters of judgment
and justice (*k*), and in all other things whatsoever (*l*); a
charitable esteem of our neighbours (*m*); loving, desiring, and rejoicing in their good name (*n*); sorrowing
for (*o*); and covering of their infirmities (*p*); freely ac-

knowledging their gifts and graces (q), defending their innocency (r); a ready receiving of a good report (s), and unwillingness to admit of an evil report concerning them (t); discouraging tale-bearers (u), flatterers (w), and slanderers (x); love and care of our own good name, and defending it when need requireth (y); keeping of lawful promises (z); studying and practising of whatsoever things are true, honest, lovely, and of good report (a).

(b) Zech. viii. 16.   (c) 3 John 12.   (d) Prov. xxxi. 8, 9.   (e) Psal. xv. 2.   (f) 2 Chron. xix. 9.   (g) 1 Sam. xix. 4, 5.   (h) Josh. vii. 19.   (i) 2 Sam. xiv. 18—20.   (k) Lev. xix. 15; Prov. xiv. 5, 25.   (l) 2 Cor. i. 17, 18; Eph. iv. 25.   (m) Heb. vi. 9; 1 Cor. xiii. 7. (n) Rom. i. 8; 2 John 4; 3 John 3, 4.   (o) 2 Cor. ii. 4, and xii. 21.   (p) Prov. xvii. 9; 1 Pet. iv. 8.   (q) 1 Cor. i. 4, 5, 7; 2 Tim. i. 4, 5. (r) 1 Sam. xxii. 14.   (s) 1 Cor. xiii. 6, 7. (t) Psal. xv. 3.   (u) Prov. xxv. 23.   (w) Prov. xxvi. 24, 25.   (x) Psal. ci. 5.   (y) Prov. xxii. 1; John viii. 49.   (z) Psal. xv. 4.   (a) Phil. iv. 8.

Q. 145. What are the sins forbidden in the Ninth Commandment?—A. The sins forbidden in the Ninth Commandment are, all prejudicing the truth, and the good name of our neighbours, as well as our own (b), especially in public judicature (c); giving false evidence (d), suborning false witnesses (e), wittingly appearing and pleading for an evil cause, out-facing and overbearing the truth (f), passing unjust sentence (g), calling evil good, and good evil; rewarding the wicked according to the work of the righteous, and the righteous according to the work of the wicked (h); forgery (i), concealing the truth, undue silence in a just cause (k), and holding our peace when iniquity calleth for either a reproof from ourselves (l), or complaint to others (m); speaking the truth unseasonably (n), or maliciously to a wrong end (o), or perverting it to a wrong meaning (*p*), or in doubtful and equivocal expressions, to the prejudice of truth or justice (*q*): speaking untruth (*r*), lying (*s*), slandering (*t*), backbiting (*u*), detracting (*w*), tale-bearing (*x*), whispering (*y*), scoffing (*z*), reviling (*a*), rash (*b*), harsh (*c*), and partial censuring (*d*); miscontructing intentions, words, and actions (*e*); flattering (*f*), vain-glorious boasting (*g*), thinking or speaking too highly or too meanly of ourselves or others (*h*), denying the gifts and graces of God (*i*), aggravating smaller faults (*k*); hiding, excusing, or extenuating of sins, when called to a free confession (*l*); unnecessary discovering of infirmities (*m*); raising false rumours (*n*); receiving and countenancing evil reports (*o*), and stopping our ears against just defence (*p*); evil suspicion (*q*), envying or grieving at the deserved credit of any (*r*), endeavouring or desiring to impair it (*s*), rejoicing in their disgrace and infamy (*t*); scornful contempt (*u*), fond admiration (*w*), breach of lawful promises (*x*), neglecting such things as are of good report (*y*), and practising or not avoiding ourselves, or not hindering what we can in others, such things as procure an ill name (*z*).

(*b*) 1 Sam. xvii. 28; 2 Sam xvi. 3, and i 9, 10, 15, 16. (*c*) Lev. xix. 15; Heb. i. 4. (*d*) Prov. xix. 5, and vi. 16, 19. (*e*) Acts vi 13. (*f*) Jer. ix. 3, 5; Acts xxiv. 2, 5; Psal. xii. 3, 4, and lii. 1—4. (*g*) Prov. xvii. 15; 1 Kings xxi. 9—14. (*h*) Isai. v. 23. (*i*) Psal cxix. 69; Luke xix. 8, and xvi. 5, 7. (*k*) Lev. v. 1; Deut. xiii. 8; Acts v. 3, 8, 9; 2 Tim. iv. 16. (*l*) 1 Kings i. 6; Lev. xix. 17. (*m*) Isai. lix. 4. (*n*) Prov. xxix. 11. (*o*) 1 Sam. xxii. 9, 10, with Psal. lii. 1—4. (*p*) Psal. lvi. 5; John ii. 19, compared with Matt. xxvi. 60, 61. (*q*) Gen. iii. 5, and xxvi. 7, 9. (*r*) Isai. lix. 13. (*s*) Lev. xix. 11; Col. iii. 9. (*t*) Psal. l. 20. (*u*) Psal. xv. 3. (*w*) Jas. iv. 11; Jer. xxxviii. 4. (*x*) Lev. xix. 16. (*y*) Rom. i. 29, 30. (*z*) Gen. xxi. 9, compared with Gal. iv. 29. (*a*) 1 Cor.

vi. 10.   (b) Matt. vii. 1.   ; (c) Acts xxviii. 4.
(d) Gen. xxxviii. 24; Rom. ii. 1.   (e) Neh.
vi. 6—8; Rom. iii. 8; Psal. lxix. 10; 1 Sam. i.
13—15; 2 Sam. x. 3.   (f) Psal. xii. 2, 3.
(g) 2 Tim. iii. 2.   (h) Luke xviii. 9, 11; Rom.
xii. 16; 1 Cor. iv. 6; Acts xii. 22; Exod. iv.
10—14.   (i) Job xxvii. 5, 6, and iv. 6.
(k) Matt. vii. 3—5.   (l) Prov. xxviii. 13, and
xxx. 20; Gen. iii. 12, 13; Jer. ii. 35; 2 Kings v.
25; Gen. iv. 9. .   (m) Gen. ix. 22; Prov. xxv.
9, 10.   (n) Exod. xxiii. 1.   (o) Prov.
xxix. 12.   (p) Acts vii. 56, 57; Job xxxi.
13, 14.   (q) 1 Cor. xiii. 5; 1 Tim. vi. 4.
(r) Num. xi. 29; Matt. xxi. 15.   (s) Ezra iv.
12, 13.   (t) Jer. xlviii. 27.   (u) Psal. xxxv.
15, 16, 21; Matt. xxvii. 28, 29.   (w) Jude 16;
Acts xii. 22.   (x) Rom. i. 31; 2 Tim. iii. 3.
(y) 1 Sam. ii. 24.   (z) 2 Sam. xiii. 12, 13; Prov.
v. 8, 9, and vi. 33. .

Q. 146. Which is the Tenth Commandment?—
A. The Tenth Commandment is, " Thou shalt not covet
thy neighbour's house, thou shalt not covet thy neighbour's wife, nor his man-servant, nor his maid-servant,
nor his ox, nor his ass, nor any thing that is thy neighbour's (a)."

(a) Exod. xx. 17.

Q. 147. What are the duties required in the Tenth
Commandment?—A. The duties required in the Tenth
Commandment are, such a full contentment with our own
condition (b), and such a charitable frame of the whole
soul toward our neighbour, as that all our inward motions and affections touching him tend unto, and further
all that good which is his (c).

(b) Heb. xiii. 5; 1 Tim. vi. 6.   (c) Job xxxi. 29;
   Rom. xii. 15; Psal. cxii. 7—9; 1 Tim. i. 5;
   Esther x. 3; 1 Cor. xiii. 4—7.   . ,

Q. 148. What are the sins forbidden in the Tenth
Commandment?—A. The sins forbidden in the Tenth

Commandment are, discontentment with our own estate (*d*), envying (*e*), and grieving at the good of our neighbour (*f*), together with all inordinate motions and affections to any thing that is his (*g*).

(*d*) 1 Kings xxi. 4; Esther v. 13; 1 Cor. x. 10. (*e*) Gal. v. 26; Jas. iii. 14, 16. (*f*) Psal. cxii. 9, 10; Neh. ii. 10. (*g*) Rom. vii. 7, 8, and xiii. 9; Col. iii. 5; Deut. v. 21.

Q. 149. Is any man able perfectly to keep the Commandments of God?—A. No man is able, either of himself (*h*), or by any grace received in this life, perfectly to keep the commandments of God (*i*), but doth daily break them in thought (*k*), word, and deed (*l*).

(*h*) Jas. iii. 2; John xv. 5; Rom. viii. 3. (*i*) Eccles. vii. 20; 1 John i. 8, 10; Gal. v. 17; Rom. vii. 18, 19. (*k*) Gen. vi. 5, and viii. 21. (*l*) Rom. iii. 9—21; Jas. iii. 2—13.

Q. 150. Are all transgressions of the law of God equally heinous in themselves, and in the sight of God? —A. All transgressions of the law of God are not equally heinous: but some sins in themselves, and by reason of several aggravations, are more heinous in the sight of God than others (*m*).

(*m*) John xix. 11; Ezek. viii 6, 13, 15; John v. 16; Psal. lxxviii. 17, 32, 56.

Q. 251. What are those aggravations which make some sins more heinous than others?—A. Sins receive their aggravations,—1. From the persons offending (*n*), if they be of riper age (*o*), greater experience or grace (*p*), eminent for profession (*q*), gifts (*r*), places (*s*), office (*t*), guides to others (*u*), and whose example is likely to be followed by others (*w*).

(*n*) Jer. ii. 8. (*o*) Job xxxii. 7, 9; Eccles. iv. 13. (*p*) 1 Kings xi. 4, 9. (*q*) 2 Sam xii. 14; 1 Cor. v. 1. (*r*) Jas. iv. 17; Luke xii. 47, 48. (*s*) Jer. v. 4, 5.; (*t*) 2 Sam. xii. 7—9; Ezek. viii. 11, 12. (*u*) Rom. ii. 17—25. (*w*) Gal. ii 11—14.

2. From the parties offended (*x*), if immediately against God (*y*), his attributes (*z*), and worship (*a*); against Christ, and his grace (*b*); the Holy Spirit (*c*), his witness (*d*) and workings (*e*); against superiors, men of eminency (*f*), and such as we stand especially related and engaged unto (*g*); against any of the saints (*h*), particularly weak brethren (*i*), the souls of them or any other (*k*), and the common good of all, or many (*l*).

(*x*) Matt. xxi. 38, 39. (*y*) 1 Sam. ii. 25; Acts v. 4; Psal. li. 4. (*z*) Rom. ii. 4. (*a*) Mal. i. 8, 14. (*b*) Heb. ii. 2, 3, and xii. 25. (*c*) Heb. x. 29; Matt. xii. 31, 32. (*d*) Eph. iv. 30. (*e*) Heb. vi. 4, 5. (*f*) Jude 8; Num. xii. 8, 9; Isai. iii. 5. (*g*) Prov. xxx. 17; 2 Cor. xii. 15; Psal. lv. 12—15. (*h*) Zeph. ii. 8, 10, 11; Matt. xviii. 6; 1 Cor. vi. 8; Rev. xvii. 6. (*i*) 1 Cor. viii. 11, 12; Rom. xiv. 13, 15, 21. (*k*) Ezek. xiii. 19; 1 Cor. viii. 12; Rev. xviii. 13; Matt. xxiii. 15. (*l*) 1 Thess. ii. 15, 16; Josh. xxii. 20.

3. From the nature or quality of the offence (*m*), if it be against the express letter of the law (*n*), break many commandments, contain in it many sins (*o*); if not only conceived in the heart, but breaks forth in words and actions (*p*), scandalize others (*q*), and admit of no reparation (*r*); if against means (*s*), mercies (*t*), judgments (*u*), light of nature (*w*), conviction of conscience (*x*), public or private admonition (*y*), censures of the church (*z*), civil punishments (*a*), and our own prayers, purposes, promises (*b*), vows (*c*), covenants (*d*), and engagements to God or men (*e*), if done deliberately (*f*), wilfully (*g*), presumptuously (*h*), impudently (*i*), boastingly (*k*), maliciously (*l*), frequently (*m*), obstinately (*n*), with delight (*o*), continuance (*p*), or relapsing after repentance (*q*).

(*m*) Prov. vi. 30, *to the end*. (*n*) Ezra ix. 10—12; 1 Kings xi. 9, 10. (*o*) Col. iii. 5; 1 Tim. vi. 10; Prov. v. 8—12, and vi. 32, 33; Josh. vii. 21.

(p) Jas. i. 14, 15; Matt. v. 22; Micah ii. 1.
(q) Matt. xviii. 7.; Rom. ii. 23, 24.　(r) Deut.
xxii. 22, compared with 28, 29; Prov. vi. 32—35.
(s) Matt. xi. 21—24; John xv. 22.　(t) Isai.
i. 3; Deut. xxxii. 6.　(u) Amos iv. 8—11;
Jer. v. 3.　(w) Rom. i. 26, 27.　(x) Rom.
i. 32; Dan. v. 22; Titus iii. 10, 11.　(y) Prov.
xxix. 1.　(z) Titus iii. 10; Matt. xviii. 17.
(a) Prov. xxvii. 22, and xxiii. 35.　(b) Psal.
lxxviii. 34—37; Jer. ii. 20, and xlii. 6, 20, 21.
(c) Eccles. v. 4—6; Prov. xx. 25.　(d) Lev.
xxvi. 25.　(e) Prov. ii. 17; Ezek. xvii. 18, 19.
(f) Psal. xxxvi. 4.　(g) Jer. vi. 16.　(h) Num.
xv. 30; Exod. xxi. 14.　(i) Jer. iii. 3; Prov.
vii. 13.　(k) Psal. lii. 1.　(l) 3 John 10.
(m) Num. xiv. 22.　(n) Zech. vii. 11, 12.
(o) Prov. ii. 14.　(p) Isai. lvii. 17.　(q) Jer.
xxxiv. 8—11; 2 Pet. ii. 20—22.

4. From circumstances of time (r) and place (s); if
on the Lord's-day (t), or other times of Divine worship (u), or immediately before (w), or after these (x),
or other helps to prevent or remedy such miscarriages (y);
if in public, or in the presence of others, who are
thereby likely to be provoked or defiled (z).

(r) 2 Kings v. 26.　(s) Jer. vii. 10; Isai. xxvi. 10.
(t) Ezek. xxiii. 37—39.　(u) Isai. lviii. 3—5;
Num. xxv. 6, 7.　(w) 1 Cor. xi. 20, 21.
(x) Jer. vii. 8—10; Prov. vii. 14, 15; John xiii.
27, 30.　(y) Ezra ix. 13, 14.　(z) 2 Sam.
xvi. 22; 1 Sam. ii. 22—24.

Q. 152. What doth every sin deserve at the hand of
God?—A. Every sin, even the least, being against the
sovereignty (a), goodness (b), and holiness of God (c),
and against his righteous law (d), deserveth his wrath
and curse (e), both in this life (f), and that which is to
come (g); and cannot be expiated but by the blood
of Christ (h).

(a) Jas. ii. 10, 11.　(b) Exod. xx. 1, 2.　(c) Hab.
i. 13; Lev. x. 3, and xi. 44, 45.　(d) 1 John

iii. 4; Rom. vii. 12. . . (e) Eph. v. 6; Gal. iii. 10. (f) Lam. iii. 39; Deut. xxviii. 15, *to the end.* (g) Matt. xxv. 41. ' ' (h) Heb. ix. 22; 1 Pet. i. 18, 19.

Q. 153. What doth God require of us, that we may escape his wrath and curse due to us by reason of the transgression of the law?—A. That we may escape the wrath and curse of God due to us by reason of the transgression of the law, he requireth of us repentance toward God, and faith toward our Lord Jesus Christ(i), and the diligent use of the outward means whereby Christ communicates to us the benefits of his mediation (k).

(i) Acts xx. 21. (k) Prov. ii. 1—6, and viii. 33, *to the end.*

Q. 154. What are the outward means whereby Christ communicates to us the benefits of his mediation?—A. The outward and ordinary means whereby Christ communicates to his church the benefits of his mediation, are, all his ordinances, especially the word, sacraments, and prayer; all which are made effectual to the elect for their salvation (l).

(l) Matt. xxviii. 19, 20; Acts ii. 42, 46, 47.

Q. 155. How is the word made effectual to salvation?—A. The Spirit of God maketh the reading, but especially the preaching of the word, an effectual means of enlightening(m), convincing, and humbling sinners(n); of driving them out of themselves, and drawing them unto Christ (o); of conforming them to his image (p), and subduing them to his will(q); of strengthening them against temptations and corruptions (r); of building them up in grace (s), and establishing their hearts in holiness and comfort through faith unto salvation (t).

(m) Neh. viii. 8; Acts xxvi. 18; Psal. xix. 8. (n) 1 Cor. xiv. 24, 25; 2 Chron. xxxiv. 18, 19, 26—28. (o) Acts ii. 37, 41, and viii. 27—39. (p) 2 Cor. iii. 18. (q) 2 Cor. x. 4—6; Rom. vi. 17. (r) Matt. iv. 4, 7, 10; Eph. vi. 16, 17;

Rom. xvi. 25; 1 Cor. x. 11.   (s) Acts xx. 31;
2 Tim. iii. 15—17.   (t) Rom. xvi. 25; 1 Thess.
iii. 2, 10, 11, 13; Rom. xv. 4, x. 13—17, and
i. 16.

Q. 156. Is the word of God to be read by all?—
A. Although all are not to be permitted to read the
word publicly to the congregation (u), yet all sorts of
people are bound to read it apart by themselves (w),
and with their families (x); to which end, the Holy
Scriptures are to be translated out of the original into
vulgar languages (y).

(u) Deut. xxxi. 9, 11—13; Neh. viii. 2, 3, and ix.
   3—5.   (w) Deut. xvii. 19; Rev. i. 3; John
   v. 39; Isai. xxxiv. 16.   (x) Deut. vi. 6—9; Gen.
   xviii. 17, 19; Psal. lxxviii. 5—7.   (y) 1 Cor.
   xiv. 6, 9, 11, 12, 15, 16, 24, 27, 28.

Q. 157. How is the word of God to be read?—
A. The Holy Scriptures are to be read, with an high
and reverent esteem of them (z), with a firm persuasion
that they are the very word of God (a), and that he
only can enable us to understand them (b); with desire
to know, believe, and obey the will of God revealed
in them (c); with diligence (d), and attention to the
matter and scope of them (e); with meditation (f), application (g), self-denial (h), and prayer (i).

(z) Psal. xix. 10; Neh. viii. 3—10; Exod. xxiv. 7;
   2 Chron. xxxiv. 27; Isa. lxvi. 2.   (a) 2 Pet.
   i. 19—21.   (b) Luke xxiv. 45; 2 Cor. iii.
   13—16.   (c) Deut. xvii. 19, 20.   (d) Acts
   xvii. 11.   (e) Acts viii. 30, 34; Luke x. 26—28.
   (f) Psal. i. 2, and cxix. 97.   (g) 2 Chron.
   xxxiv. 21.   (h) Prov. iii. 5; Deut. xxxiii. 3.
   (i) Prov. ii. 1—7; Psal. cxix. 18; Neh. viii. 6, 8.

Q. 158. By whom is the word of God to be preached?
—A. The word of God is to be preached only by such
as are sufficiently gifted (k), and also duly approved and
called to that office (l).

(k) 1 Tim. iii. 2, 6; Eph. iv. 8—11; Hosea iv. 6;

Mal. ii. 7; 2 Cor iii 6   (*l*) Jer. xiv. 15;
Rom.. x. 15; Heb. v. 4; 1 Cor. xii. 28, 29';
1 Tim. iii. 10, iv. 14, and v. 22.

Q. 159. How is the word of God to be preached by
those that. are called thereunto?—A. They that are
called to labour in the ministry of the word, are to
preach sound doctrine (*m*), diligently (*n*), in season,
and out of season (*o*); plainly (*p*), not in the enticing
words of man's wisdom, but in demonstration of the
Spirit and of power (*q*); faithfully (*r*) making known
the whole counsel of God (*s*); wisely (*t*) applying
themselves to the necessities and capacities of the
hearers (*u*); zealously (*w*), with fervent love to God (*x*),
and the souls of his people (*y*); sincerely (*z*) aiming
at his glory (*a*), and their conversion (*b*), edification (*c*),
and salvation (*d*).

(*m*) Titus ii. 1, 8.   (*n*) Acts xviii. 25.   (*o*) 2 Tim.
iv. 2.   (*p*) 1 Cor. xiv. 19.   (*q*).1 Cor. ii. 4.
(*r*) Jer. xxiii. 28; 1 Cor. iv. 1, 2.   (*s*) Acts
xx. 27. (*t*) Col. i. 28; 2 Tim. ii. 15. (*u*) 1 Cor.
iii. 2; Heb. v. 12—14; Luke xii. 42. (*w*) Acts
xviii. 25.   (*x*) 2 Cor. v. 13, 14; Phil. i. 15—17.
(*y*) Col. iv. 12; 2 Cor. xii. 15.   (*z*) 2 Cor.
ii. 17, and iv. 2.   (*a*) 2 Thess. ii. 4—6; John
vii. 18.   (*b*) 1 Cor. ix. 19—22.   (*c*) 2 Cor.
xii. 19; Eph. iv. 12.   (*d*) 2 Tim. iv. 16; Acts
xxvi. 16—18.

Q. 160. What is required of those that hear the word
preached?—A. It is required of those that hear the
word preached, that they attend upon it with diligence (*e*), preparation (*f*), and prayer (*g*); examine
what they hear by the Scriptures (*h*); receive the truth
with faith (*i*), love (*k*), meekness (*l*), and readiness of
mind (*m*), as the word of God (*n*); meditate (*o*) and
confer of it (*p*); hide it in their hearts (*q*), and bring
forth the fruit of it in their lives (*r*).

(*e*) Prov. viii. 34.   (*f*) 1 Pet. ii. 1, 2; Luke
viii. 18.   (*g*) Psal. cxix. 18; Eph. vi. 18, 19.

(*h*) Acts xvii. 11.   (*i*) Heb. iv. 2.   (*k*) 2 Thess.
ii. 10.·   (*l*) Jas. i. 21.   (*m*) Acts xvii. 11.
(*n*) 1 Thess. ii. 13.   (*o*) Luke ix. 44; Heb. ii. 1.
(*p*) Luke xxiv. 14; Deut. vi. 6, 7.   (*q*) Prov.
ii. 1; Psal. cxix. 11.   ·   (*r*) Lukn viii. 15;
Jas. i 25.

Q. 161. How do the Sacraments become effectual
means of salvation?—A. The Sacraments become effectual means of salvation, not by any power in themselves, or any virtue derived from the piety and intention of him by whom they are administered; but only
by the working of the Holy Ghost, and the blessing of
Christ, by whom they are instituted (*s*).

(*s*) 1 Pet. iii. 21; Acts viii. 13, with 23; 1 Cor. iii.
6, 7, and xii. 13.

Q. 162. What is a sacrament?—A. A sacrament is
an holy ordinance instituted by Christ in his church (*t*),
to signify, seal, and exhibit (*u*), unto those that are
within the covenant of grace (*w*), the benefits of his
mediation (*x*); to strengthen and increase their faith,
and all other graces (*y*); to oblige them to obedience (*z*);
to testify and cherish their love and communion one
with another (*a*), and to distinguish them from those
that are without (*b*)

(*t*) Gen. xvii. 7, 10; Exod. xii.; Matt. xxviii. 19, and
xxvi. 27, 28.   (*u*) Rom. iv. 11; 1 Cor. xi.
·24, 25.   (*w*) Rom. xv. 8; Exod. xii. 48.
(*x*) Acts ii. 38; 1 Cor. x. 16.   (*y*) Rom. iv.
11; Gal. iii. 27.   ·   (*z*) Rom. vi. 3, 4; 1 Cor.
x. 21.   (*a*) Eph. iv. 2—5; 1 Cor. xii. 13.
(*b*) Eph. ii. 11, 12; Gen. xxxiv. 14.

Q. 163. What are the parts of a sacrament?—A. The
parts of a sacrament are two; the one an outward and
sensible sign, used according to Christ's own appointment; the other an inward and spiritual grace thereby
signified (*c*).

(*c*) Matt. iii. 11; 1 Pet. iii. 21; Rom. ii. 28, 29. ·

Q. 164. How many sacraments hath Christ instituted
in his church under the New Testament?—A. Under

. R

the New Testament Christ hath instituted in his church only two sacraments, Baptism and the Lord's Supper(*d*).

(*d*) Matt. xxviii. 19; 1 Cor. xi. 20, 23; Matt. xxvi. 26—28.

Q. 165. What is Baptism?—A. Baptism is a sacrament of the New Testament, wherein Christ hath ordained the washing with water, in the name of the Father, and of the Son, and of the Holy Ghost (*e*), to be a sign and seal of ingrafting into himself (*f*), of remission of sins by his blood (*g*), and regeneration by his Spirit (*h*); of adoption (*i*), and resurrection unto everlasting life (*k*); and whereby the parties baptized are solemnly admitted into the visible church (*l*), and enter into an open and professed engagement to be wholly and only the Lord's (*m*).

(*e*) Matt. xxviii. 19.　　(*f*) Gal. iii. 27.　　(*g*) Mark i. 4; Rev. i. 5.　　(*h*) Titus iii. 5; Eph. v. 26. (*i*) Gal. iii. 26, 27.　　(*k*) 1 Cor. xv. 26; Rom. vi. 5.　　(*l*) 1 Cor. xii. 13.　　(*m*) Rom. vi. 4.

Q 166. Unto whom is Baptism to be administered? —A. Baptism is not to be administered to any that are out of the visible church, and so strangers from the covenant of promise, till they profess their faith in Christ, and obedience to him (*n*): but infants descending from parents, either both, or but one of them, professing faith in Christ, and obedience to him, are, in that respect, within the covenant, and to be baptized (*o*).

(*n*) Acts viii. 36, 37, and ii. 38.　　　　(*o*) Gen. xvii. 7, 9, with Gal. iii. 9, 14, Col. ii. 11, 12, Acts ii. 38, 39, and Rom. iv. 11, 12; 1 Cor. vii. 14; Matt. xxviii. 19; Luke viii. 15, 16; Rom. xi. 16.

Q. 167. How is our Baptism to be improved by us? —A. The needful, but much neglected, duty of improving our Baptism, is to be performed by us all our life long, especially in the time of temptation, and when we are present at the administration of it to others (*p*); by serious and thankful consideration of the nature of it, and of the ends for which Christ instituted it, the privileges and benefits conferred and sealed thereby, and our solemn vow made therein (*q*); by being humbled for our sinful defilement, our falling short of and walking contrary to the grace of baptism and our engagements (*r*); by growing up to assurance of pardon of sin, and of all other blessings sealed to us in that sacrament (*s*); by drawing strength from the death and resurrection of Christ, into whom we are baptized, for the mortifying of sin, and quickening of grace (*t*); and by endeavouring to live by faith (*u*), to have our conversation in holiness and righteousness (*w*), as those that have therein given up their names to Christ (*x*); and to walk in brotherly love, as being baptized by the same Spirit into one body (*y*).

(*p*) Col. ii. 11, 12; Rom. vi. 4, 6, 11.   (*q*) Rom. vi. 3—5.   (*r*) 1 Cor. i. 11—13; Rom. vi. 2, 3. (*s*) Rom. iv. 11, 12; 1 Pet. iii. 21.   (*t*) Rom. vi. 3—5.   (*u*) Gal. iii. 26, 27.   (*w*) Rom. vi. 22.   (*x*) Acts ii. 38.   (*y*) 1 Cor. xii 13, 25—27.

Q. 168. What is the Lord's Supper?—A. The Lord's Supper is a sacrament of the New Testament (*z*), wherein, by giving and receiving bread and wine, according to the appointment of Jesus Christ, his death is shewed forth; and they that worthily communicate, feed upon his body and blood, to their spiritual nourishment and growth in grace (*u*); have their union and communion with him confirmed (*b*); testify and renew their thankfulness (*c*) and engagement to God (*d*), and their mutual love and fellowship each with other, as members of the same mystical body (*e*).

(*z*) Luke xxii. 20.   (*a*) Matt. xxvi. 26—28; 1 Cor. xi. 23—26.   (*b*) 1 Cor. x. 16.   (*c*) 1 Cor. xi. 24—26.   (*d*) 1 Cor. x. 14—16, 21. (*e*) 1 Cor. x 17.

Q. 169. How hath Christ appointed bread and wine to be given and received in the sacrament of the Lord's Supper?—A. Christ hath appointed the ministers of his word, in the administration of this sacrament of the Lord's Supper, to set apart the bread and wine from common use, by the word of institution, thanksgiving and prayer; to take and break the bread, and to give both the bread and wine to the communicants, who are, by the same appointment, to take and eat the bread, and to drink the wine, in thankful remembrance, that the body of Christ was broken and given, and his blood shed for them (*f*).

(*f*) 1 Cor. xi. 23, 24; Matt. xxvi. 26—28; Mark xiv. 22—24; Luke xxii. 19, 20.

Q. 170. How do they that worthily communicate in the Lord's Supper, feed upon the body and blood of Christ therein?—A. As the body and blood of Christ are not corporally or carnally present in, with, under the bread and wine in the Lord's Supper (*g*),; and yet are spiritually present to the faith of the receiver, no less truly and really, than the elements themselves are to their outward senses (*h*); so they that worthily communicate in the sacrament of the Lord's Supper, do therein feed upon the body and blood of Christ, not after a corporal or carnal, but in a spiritual manner, yet truly and really (*i*), while by faith they receive and apply unto themselves Christ crucified, and all the benefits of his death (*k*).

(*g*) Acts iii. 21.   (*h*) Matt. xxvi. 26, 28.   (*i*) 1 Cor. xi. 24—29.   (*k*) 1 Cor. x. 16.

Q. 171. How are they that receive the sacrament of the Lord's Supper, to prepare themselves before they come unto it?—A. They that receive the sacrament of the Lord's Supper, are, before they come, to prepare themselves thereunto by examining themselves (*l*), of their being in Christ (*m*), of their sins and wants (*n*), of the truth and measure of their knowledge (*o*), faith (*p*), repentance (*q*), love to God and the brethren (*r*), charity to all men (*s*); forgiving those that have done them wrong (*t*); of their desires after Christ (*u*), and of their new obedience (*w*); and by renewing the exercise of these graces (*x*), by serious meditation (*y*), and fervent prayer (*z*).

(*l*) 1 Cor. xi. 28.   (*m*) 2 Cor. xiii. 5.   (*n*) 1 Cor.

v. 7, compared with Exod xii. 15.   (*o*) 1 Cor.
xi. 29.   (*p*) 2 Cor. xiii. 5 ; Matt. xxvi. 28.
(*q*) Zech. xii. 10 ; 1 Cor. xi. 31.   (*r*) 1 Cor.
x. 16, 17 ; Acts ii. 46, 47.   (*s*) 1 Cor. v. 8,
and xi. 18, 20.   (*t*) Matt. v. 23, 24.   (*u*) Isai.
lv. 1 ; John vii. 37.   (*w*) 1 Cor. v. 7, 8.
(*x*) 1 Cor. xi. 25, 26, 28 ; Heb. x. 21, 22, 24 ; Psal.
xxvi. 6.   (*y*) 1 Cor. xi. 24, 25.   (*z*) 2 Chron.
xxx. 18, 19 ; Matt. xxvi. 26.

Q. 172. May one who doubteth of his being in Christ,
or of his due preparation, come to the Lord's Supper ?
—A. One who doubteth of his being in Christ, or of
his due preparation to the sacrament of the Lord's
Supper, may have true interest in Christ, though he be
not yet assured thereof (*a*) ; and in God's account hath
it, if he be duly affected with the apprehension of the
want of it (*b*) ; and unfeignedly desires to be found in
Christ (*c*), and to depart from iniquity (*d*) ; in which
case, because promises are made, and this sacrament
is appointed for the relief even of weak and doubting
Christians (*e*), he is to bewail his unbelief (*f*), and labour to have his doubts resolved (*g*) ; and so doing he
may and ought to come to the Lord's Supper, that he
may be further strengthened (*h*).

(*a*) Isai. l. 10 ; 1 John v. 13 ; Psal lxxxviii. *through-*
out, and lxxi. 1—12 ; Jonah ii. iv. 7.   (*b*) Isai.
liv. 7—10 ; Matt. v. 3, 4 ; Psal. xxxi. 22, and lxxiii.
13, 22, 23.   (*c*) Phil. iii. 8, 9 ; Psal. x. 17, and
xlii. 1, 2, 5, 11.   (*d*) 2 Tim. ii. 19 ; Isai. l. 10 ;
Psal. lxvi. 18—20.   (*e*) Isai. xl. 11, 29, 31 ;
Matt. xi. 28, xii. 20, and xxvi. 28.   (*f*) Mark
ix. 24.   (*g*) Acts ii. 37, and xvi. 30.   (*h*) Rom.
xi. ; 1 Cor. xi. 28.

Q. 173. May any, who profess the faith, and desire
to come to the Lord's Supper, be kept from it ?—
A. Such as are found to be ignorant or scandalous, notwithstanding the profession of the faith, and desire to
come to the Lord's Supper, may and ought to be kept
from that sacrament, by the power which Christ hath

left in his church (*i*), until they receive instruction, and manifest their reformation (*k*).

(*i*) 1 Cor. xi. 27, *to the end*, compared with Matt. vii. 6; 1 Cor. v.; Jude 23; 1 Tim. v. 22. (*k*) 2 Cor. ii. 7.

Q. 174. What is required of them that receive the sacrament of the Lord's Supper, in the time of the administration of it?—A. It is required of them that receive the sacrament of the Lord's Supper, that during the time of the administration of it, with all holy reverence and attention they wait upon God in that ordinance (*l*), diligently observe the sacramental elements and actions (*m*), heedfully discern the Lord's body (*n*), and affectionately meditate on his death and sufferings (*o*), and thereby stir up themselves to a vigorous exercise of their graces (*p*), in judging themselves (*q*), and sorrowing for sin (*r*); in earnest hungering and thirsting after Christ (*s*); feeding on him by faith (*t*), receiving of his fulness (*u*), trusting in his merits (*w*), rejoicing in his love (*x*), giving thanks for his grace (*y*); in renewing of their covenant with God (*z*), and love to all the saints (*a*).

(*l*) Lev. x. 3; Heb. xii. 28; Psal. v. 7; 1 Cor. xi. 17, 26, 27.   (*m*) Exod. xxiv. 8, compared with Matt. xxvi. 28.   (*n*) 1 Cor. xi. 29.   (*o*) Luke xxii. 19.   (*p*) 1 Cor. xi. 26, and x. 3—5, 11, 14. (*q*) 1 Cor. xi. 31.   (*r*) Zech. xii. 10. -   (*s*) Rev. xxii. 17.   (*t*) John vi. 35.   (*u*) John i. 16. (*w*) Phil. iii. 9.   (*x*) Psal. lxiii. 4, 5; 2 Chron. xxx. 21.   (*y*) Psal. xxii. 26.   (*z*) Jer. l. 5; Psal. l. 5.   (*a*) Acts ii. 42.

Q. 175. What is the duty of Christians, after they have received the sacrament of the Lord's Supper?— A. The duty of Christians, after they have received the sacrament of the Lord's Supper, is seriously to consider how they have behaved themselves therein, and with what success (*b*); if they find quickening and comfort, to bless God for it (*c*), beg the continuance of it (*d*), watch against relapses (*e*), fulfil their vows (*f*), and encourage themselves to a frequent attendance on that ordinance(*g*); but, if they find no present benefit, more exactly to review their preparation to, and carriage at, the sacrament (*h*): in both which, if they can approve themselves to God and their own consciences, they are to wait for the fruit of it in due time (*i*); but if they see they have failed in either, they are to be humbled (*k*), and to attend upon it afterward with more care and diligence(*l*).

(*b*) Psal. xxviii. 7, and lxxxv. 8 ; 1 Cor. xi. 17, 30, 31. (*c*) 2 Chron xxx. 21—26 ; Acts ii. 42, 46, 47. (*d*) Psal. xxxvi. 10; Cant. iii. 4 ; 1 Chron. xxix. 18. (*e*) 1 Cor. x. 3—5, 12. (*f*) Psal. l. 14. (*g*) 1 Cor. xi. 25, 26; Acts ii. 42, 46. (*h*) Cant. v. 1—6. (*i*) Psal. cxxiii. 1, 2, and xlii. 5, 8 ; Psal. xliii. 3—5. (*k*) 2 Chron. xxx. 18, 19 ; Isai. i. 16, 18. (*l*) 2 Cor. vii. 11 ; 1 Chron. xv. 12—14.

Q. 176. Wherein do the sacraments of Baptism and the Lord's Supper agree ?—A. The sacraments of Baptism and the Lord's Supper agree, in that the author of both is God (*m*), the spiritual part of both is Christ, and his benefits (*n*); both are seals of the same covenant (*o*), are to be dispensed by ministers of the Gospel, and by none other (*p*), and to be continued in the church of Christ until his second coming (*q*).

(*m*) Matt. xxviii. 19 ; 1 Cor. xi. 23. (*n*) Rom. vi. 3, 4; 1 Cor. x. 16. (*o*) Rom. iv. 11, compared with Col. ii. 11, 12 ; Matt. xxvi. 27, 28. (*p*) John i. 33; Matt. xxviii. 19; 1 Cor. xi. 23; and iv. 1; Heb. v. 4. (*q*) Matt. xxviii. 19, 20; 1 Cor. xi. 26.

Q. 177. Wherein do the sacraments of Baptism and the Lord's Supper differ ?—A. The sacraments of Baptism and the Lord's Supper differ, in that Baptism is to be administered but once with water, to be a sign and seal of our regeneration and ingrafting into Christ (*r*), and that even to infants (*s*); whereas the Lord's Supper is to be administered often in the elements of bread and wine, to represent and exhibit Christ as spiritual nourishment to the soul (*t*), and to confirm our continuance and growth in him (*u*), and that only to such as are of years and ability to examine themselves (*w*).

(*r*) Matt. iii. 11; Titus iii. 5; Gal. iii. 27.　(*s*) Gen. xvii. 7, 9; Acts ii. 38, 39; 1 Cor. vii. 14.　(*t*) 1 Cor. xi. 23—26.　　(*u*) 1 Cor. x. 16.　　(*w*) 1 Cor. xi. 28, 29.

Q. 178. What is Prayer?—A. Prayer is an offering up of our desires unto God (*x*), in the name of Christ (*y*), by the help of his Spirit (*z*), with confession of our sins (*a*), and thankful acknowledgment of his mercies (*b*).

(*x*) Psal. lxxxii. 8.　　(*y*) John xvi. 23.　　(*z*) Rom. viii. 26.　　　(*a*) Psal. xxxii. 5, 6; Dan. ix. 4. (*b*) Phil. iv. 6.

Q. 179. Are we to pray unto God only?—A. God only being able to search the hearts (*c*), hear the requests (*d*), pardon the sins (*e*), and fulfil the desires of all (*f*), and only to be believed in (*g*) and worshipped with religious worship (*h*), prayer, which is a special part thereof (*i*), is to be made by all to him alone (*k*), and to none others (*l*).

(*c*) 1 Kings viii. 39; Acts i. 24; Rom. viii. 27. (*d*) Psal. lxv. 2.　(*e*) Micah vii. 18.　　(*f*) Psal. cxlv. 18, 19.　　(*g*) Rom. x. 14.　　(*h*) Matt. iv. 10.　　(*i*) 1 Cor. i. 2.　　(*k*) Psal. l. 15. (*l*) Rom. x. 14.

Q. 180. What is it to pray in the name of Christ?— A. To pray in the name of Christ, is, in obedience to his command, and in confidence on his promises, to ask mercy for his sake (*m*); not by bare mentioning of his name (*n*), but by drawing our encouragement to pray, and our boldness, strength, and hope of acceptance in prayer, from Christ and his mediation (*o*).

(*m*) John xiv. 13, 14, and xvi. 24; Dan. ix. 17. (*n*) Matt. vii. 21.　　(*o*) Heb. iv. 14—16; 1 John v. 13—15.

Q. 181. Why are we to pray in the name of Christ? —A. The sinfulness of man, and his distance from God by reason thereof, being so great, as that we can have no access into his presence without a Mediator (p), and there being none in heaven or earth appointed to, or fit for that glorious work, but Christ alone (q), we are to pray in no other name but his only (r).

(p) John xiv. 6; Isai. lix. 2; Eph. iii. 12.   (q) John vi. 27; Heb. vii. 25—27; 1 Tim. ii. 5.   (r) Col. iii. 17; Heb. xiii. 15.

Q. 182. How doth the Spirit help us to pray?—A. We not knowing what to pray for as we ought, the Spirit helpeth our infirmities, by enabling us to understand both for whom and what, and how prayer is to be made; and by working and quickening in our hearts (although not in all persons, nor at all times in the same measure) those apprehensions, affections, and graces, which are requisite for the right performance of that duty (s).

(s) Rom. viii. 26, 27; Psal. x. 17; Zech. xii. 10.

Q. 183. For whom are we to pray?—A. We are to pray for the whole church of Christ upon earth (t), for magistrates (u) and ministers (w), for ourselves (x), our brethren (y), yea, our enemies (z), and for all sorts of men living (a), or that shall live hereafter (b); but not for the dead (c), nor for those that are known to have sinned the sin unto death (d).

(t) Eph. vi. 18; Psal. xxviii. 9.   (u) 1 Tim. ii. 1, 2.   (w) Col. iv. 2.   (x) Gen. xxxii. 11. (y) Jas. v. 16.   (z) Matt. v. 44.   (a) 1 Tim. ii. 1, 2.   (b) John xvii. 20; 2 Sam. vii. 29. (c) 2 Sam. xii. 21—23.   (d) 1 John v. 16.

Q. 184. For what things are we to pray?—A. We are to pray for all things tending to the glory of God (e), the welfare of the church (f), our own (g), or other's good (h), but not for any thing that is unlawful (i).

(e) Matt. vi. 9.   (f) Psal. li. 18, and cxxii. 6. (g) Matt. vii. 11.   (h) Psal. cxxv. 4.   (i) 1 John v. 14.

Q. 185. How are we to pray?—A. We are to pray, with an awful apprehension of the majesty of God (k), and deep sense of our own unworthiness (l), neces-

sities (*m*), and sins (*n*), with penitent (*o*), thankful (*p*),
and enlarged hearts (*q*) ; with understanding (*r*), faith (*s*),
sincerity (*t*), fervency (*u*), love (*w*), and perseverance (*x*)
waiting upon him (*y*), with humble submission to his
will (*z*).

(*k*) Eccles. v. 1.   (*l*) Gen. xviii. 27, and xxxii. 10.
(*m*) Luke xv. 17—19.   (*n*) Luke xviii. 13, 14.
(*o*) Psal. li. 17.   (*p*) Phil. iv. 6.   (*q*) 1 Sam.
i. 15, and ii. 1.   (*r*) 1 Cor. xiv. 15.   (*s*) Mark
xi. 24; Jas. i. 6.   (*t*) Psal. cxlv. 18, and xvii. 1.
(*u*) Jas. v. 16.   (*w*) 1 Tim. ii. 8.   (*x*) Eph.
vi. 18.   (*y*) Micah vii. 7.   (*z*) Matt. xxvi. 39.

Q. 186. What rule hath God given for our direction
in the duty of prayer?—A. The whole word of God is
of use to direct us in the duty of praying (*a*); but the
special rule of direction is that form of prayer which
our Saviour Christ taught his disciples, commonly called
" The Lord's Prayer (*b*)."

(*a*) 1 John v. 14.   (*b*) Matt. vi. 9—13; Luke
xi. 2—4.

Q. 187. How is the Lord's Prayer to be used?—
A. The Lord's Prayer is not only for direction, as a pattern according to which we are to make other prayers,
but may also be used as a prayer, so that it be done
with understanding, faith, reverence, and other graces
necessary to the right performance of the duty of
prayer (*c*).

(*c*) Matt. vi. 9, with Luke xi. 2.

Q. 188. Of how many parts doth the Lord's Prayer
consist?—A. The Lord's Prayer consists of three parts ;
a preface, petitions, and a conclusion.

Q. 189. What doth the preface of the Lord's Prayer
teach us?—A. The preface of the Lord's Prayer, contained in these words, " Our Father, which art in heaven (*d*)," teacheth us, when we pray, to draw near to
God with confidence of his fatherly goodness, and our
interest therein (*e*); with reverence, and all other child-
like dispositions (*f*), heavenly affections (*g*), and due
apprehensions of his sovereign power, majesty, and

gracious condescension (*h*); as also to pray with and for others (*i*).

(*d*) Matt. vi. 9.　　　(*e*) Luke xi. 13; Rom. viii. 15.
(*f*) Isai. lxiv. 9.　　　(*g*) Psal. cxxiii. 1; Lam.
iii. 41.　　　(*h*) Isai. lxiii. 15, 16; Neh. i. 4—6.
(*i*) Acts xii. 5.

Q. What do we pray for in the first petition?—A. In the first petition, which is, " Hallowed be thy Name(*k*)," acknowledging the utter inability and indisposition that is in ourselves and all men to honour God aright (*l*), we pray, that God would by his grace enable and incline us and others to know, to acknowledge and highly to esteem him (*m*), his titles (*n*), attributes (*o*), ordinances, word (*p*), works, and whatsoever he is pleased to make himself known by (*q*), and to glorify him in thought, word (*r*), and deed (*s*); that he would prevent and remove atheism (*t*), ignorance (*u*), idolatry (*w*), profaneness (*x*), and whatsover is dishonourable to him (*y*); and by his overruling providence, direct and dispose all things to his own glory (*z*).

(*k*) Matt. vi. 9.　　　(*l*) 2 Cor. iii. 5; Psal. li. 15.
(*m*) Psal. lxvii. 2, 3.　　　(*n*) Psal. lxxxiii. 18.
(*o*) Psal. lxxxvi. 10—13, 15.　(*p*) 2 Thess. iii. 1;
Psal. cxlvii. 19, 20, and cxxxviii. 1—3; 2 Cor. ii.
14, 15.　　　(*q*) Psal. cxlv. *throughout*, and viii.
throughout.　　　(*r*) Psal. ciii. 1, and xvi. 14.
(*s*) Phil. i. 9, 11.　　　(*t*) Psal. lxvii. 1—4.
(*u*) Eph. i. 17, 18.　(*w*) Psal. xcvii. 7.　(*x*) Psal.
lxxiv. 18, 22, 23.　　　(*y*) 2 Kings xix. 15, 16.
(*z*) 2 Chron. xx. 6, 10—12; Psal. lxxxiii. *through-out*, and cxl. 4, 8.

Q. 191. What do we pray for in the second petition? —A. In the second petition, which is, " Thy kingdom come (*a*)," acknowledging ourselves and all mankind to be by nature under the dominion of sin and Satan (*b*), we pray, that the kingdom of sin and Satan may be destroyed (*c*); the Gospel propagated throughout the world (*d*); the Jews called (*e*); the fulness of the Gentiles brought in (*f*); the church furnished with all

Gospel officers and ordinances (g), purged from corruption (h), countenanced and maintained by the civil magistrate (i); that the ordinances of Christ may be purely dispensed, and made effectual to the converting of those that are yet in their sins, and the confirming, comforting, and building up of those that are already converted (k); that Christ would rule in our hearts here (l), and hasten the time of his second coming, and our reigning with him for ever (m); and that he would be pleased so to exercise the kingdom of his power in all the world, as may best conduce to these ends (n).

(a) Matt. vi. 10.　　　(b) Eph. ii. 2, 3.　　　(c) Psal. lxviii. i. 18; Rev. xii. 10, 11.　(d) 2 Thess. iii. 1. (e) Rom. x. 1.　　　(f) John xvii. 19, 20; Rom. xi. 25, 26; Psal. lxvii. *throughout.*　　(g) Matt. ix. 38; 2 Thess. iii. 1.　　(h) Mal. i. 11; Zeph. iii. 9.　　(i) 1 Tim. ii. 1, 2.　　(k) Acts iv. 29, 30; Eph. vi. 18—20; Rom. xv. 29, 30, 32; 2 Thess. i. 11, and ii. 16, 17.　(l) Eph. iii. 14—21. (m) Rev. xxii. 20.　　　(n) Isai. lxiv. 1, 2; Rev. iv. 8—11.

Q. 192. What do we pray for in the third petition? —A. In the third petition, which is, "Thy will be done on earth as it is in heaven (o)," acknowledging, that by nature we and all men are not only utterly unable and unwilling to know and to do the will of God (p), but prone to rebel against his word (q), to repine and murmur against his providence (r), and wholly inclined to do the will of the flesh, and of the devil (s); we pray that God would by his Spirit take away from ourselves and others all blindness (t), weakness (u), indisposedness (w), and perverseness of heart (x); and by his grace make us able and willing to know, do, and submit to his will in all things (y), with the like humility (z), cheerfulness (a), faithfulness (b), diligence (c), zeal (d), sincerity (e), and constancy (f), as the angels do in heaven (g).

(o) Matt. vi. 10.　　　(p) Rom. vii. 18; Job xxi. 14; 1 Cor. ii. 14.　　(q) Matt. viii. 7.　　(r) Exod. xvii. 7; Numb. xiv. 2.　(s) Eph. ii. 2.　　(t) Eph.

i. 17, 18.   (*u*) Eph. iii. 16.   (*w*) Matt.
xxvi. 40, 41.   (*x*) Jer. xxxi. 18,19.   (*y*) Psal.
cxix. 1, 8, 5, 36; Acts xxi. 14.   (*z*) Micah vi. 8.
(*a*) Psal. c. 2 ; Job i. 21; 2 Sam. xv. 25, 26.
(*b*) Isai. xxxviii. 3.   (*c*) Psal. cxix. 4, 5.   (*d*) Rom.
xii. 1.   (*e*) Psal cxix. 80.   (*f*) Psal. cxix.
112.   (*g*) Isai. vi. 2, 3; Psal. ciii. 20, 21 ;
Matt. xviii. 10.

Q. 193. What do we pray for in the fourth petition?
—A. In the fourth petition, which is, " Give us this
day our daily bread (*h*)," acknowledging, that in Adam,
and by our sin, we have forfeited our right to all the
outward blessings of this life, and deserve to be wholly
deprived of them by God, and to have them cursed to
us in the use of them (*i*) ; and that neither they of themselves are able to sustain us (*k*), nor we to merit (*l*), or
by our own industry to procure them (*m*), but prone to
desire (*n*), get (*o*), and use them unlawfully (*p*); we
pray for ourselves and others, that both they and we,
waiting upon the providence of God from day to day,
in the use of lawful means, may, of his free gift, and
as to his fatherly wisdom shall seem best, enjoy a competent portion of them (*q*), and have the same continued
and blessed unto us in our holy and comfortable use of
them (*r*), and contentment in them (*s*), and be kept from
all things that are contrary to our temporal support and
comfort (*t*).

(*h*) Matt. vi. 11.   (*i*) Gen. ii. 17, and iii. 17; Rom.
viii. 20—22 ; Jer. v. 25; Deut. xxviii. 15, *to the
end.*   (*k*) Deut. viii. 3.   (*l*) Gen. xxxii. 10.
(*m*) Deut. viii. 17, 18.   (*n*) Jer. vi. 13 ; Mark
vii. 21, 22.   (*o*) Hos. xii. 7.   (*p*) Jas. iv. 3.
(*q*) Gen. xliii. 12—14, and xxviii. 20 ; Eph. iv. 28 ;
2 Thess. iii. 11, 12 ; Phil. iv. 6.   (*r*) 1 Tim.
iv. 3—5.   (*s*) 1 Tim. vi. 6—8.   (*t*) Prov.
xxx. 8, 9.

Q. 194. What do we pray for in the fifth petition ?—
A. In the fifth petition, which is, " Forgive us our debts

as we forgive our debtors (*u*)," acknowledging, that we and all others are guilty both of original and actual sin, and thereby become debtors to the justice of God, and that neither we nor any other creature can make the least satisfaction for that debt (*w*); we pray for ourselves and others, that God of his free grace would; through the obedience and satisfaction of Christ, apprehended and applied by faith, acquit us both from the guilt and punishment of sin (*x*), accept us in his beloved (*y*), continue his favour and grace to us (*z*), pardon our daily failings (*a*), and fill us with peace and joy, in giving us daily more and more assurance of forgiveness (*b*); which we are the rather emboldened to ask, and encouraged to expect, when we have this testimony in ourselves, that we from the heart forgive others their offences (*c*).

(*u*) Matt. vi. 12.   (*w*) Rom. iii. 9—21 ; Matt. xviii. 24, 25 ; Psal. cxxx. 3, 4.   (*x*) Rom iii. 24—26 ; Heb. ix. 22.   (*y*) Eph. i. 6, 7. (*z*) 2 Pet. i. 2, 3.   (*a*) Hosea xiv. 2 ; Jer. xiv. 7.   (*b*) Rom. xv. 13 ; Psal. li. 7—10, 12. (*c*) Luke xi. 4 ; Matt vi. 14, 15, and xviii. 35.

Q. 195. What do you pray for in the sixth petition? —A: In the sixth petition, which is, "And lead us not into temptation, but deliver us from evil (*d*)," acknowledging, that the most wise, righteous, and gracious God, for divers holy and just ends, may so order things, that we may be assaulted, foiled, and for a time led captive by temptations (*e*); that Satan (*f*), the world (*g*), and the flesh, are ready powerfully to draw us aside, and ensnare us (*h*); and that we, even after he pardon of our sins, by reason of our corruption (*i*), weakness, and want of watchfulness (*k*), are not only subject to be tempted, and forward to expose ourselves unto temptations (*l*), but also of ourselves unable and unwilling to resist them, to recover out of them, and to improve them (*m*), and worthy to be left under the power of them (*n*); we pray, that God would so overrule the world, and all in it (o), subdue the flesh (p), and restrain Satan (q), order all things (r), bestow and bless all means of grace (s), and quicken us to watch-fulness in the use of them, and we and all his people may by his providence be kept from being tempted to sin (t); or, if tempted, that by his Spirit we may be powerfully supported and enabled to stand in the hour of temptation (u); or, when fallen, raised again and re-covered out of it (w), and have a sanctified use and improvement thereof (x); that our sanctification and salvation may be perfected (y), Satan trodden under our feet (z), and we fully freed from sin, temptation, and all evil for ever (a).

(d) Matt. vi. 13. (e) 2 Chron. xxxii. 31. (f) 1 Chron xxi. 1. (g) Luke xxi. 34; Mark iv. 19. (h) Jas. i. 14. (i) Gal. v. 17. (k) Matt. xxvi. 41. (l) Matt. xxvi. 69—72; Gal. ii. 11—15; 2 Chron. xviii. 3, with xix. 2. (m) Rom. vii. 23, 24; 1 Chron. xxi. 1—4; 2 Chron. xvi. 7—10. (n) Psal. lxxxi. 11, 12. (o) John xvii. 15. (p) Psal. li 10, and cxix. 133. (q) 2 Cor. xii 7, 8. (r) 1 Cor. x. 12, 13. (s) Heb. xiii. 20, 21. (t) Matt. xxvi. 41; Psal. xix. 13. (u) Eph. iii. 14—17; 1 Thess. iii. 13; Jude 24. (w) Psal. li. 12. (x) 1 Pet. v. 8, 10. (y) 2 Cor. xiii. 7, 9. (z) Rom. xvi. 20; Zech. iii. 2; Luke xxii. 31, 32. (a) John xvii. 15; 1 Thess. v. 23.

Q. 196. What doth the conclusion of the Lord's Prayer teach us?—A. The conclusion of the Lord's Prayer, which is, " For thine is the kingdom, the power, and the glory, for ever. Amen (b)," teacheth us to enforce our petitions with arguments (c), which are to be taken, not from any worthiness in ourselves, or in any other creature, but from God (d); and with our prayers to join praises (e); ascribing to God alone eternal sovereignty, omnipotency, and glorious ex-cellency (f); in regard whereof, as he is able and willing to help us (*g*); so we by faith are emboldened to plead with him(*h*), that he would fulfil our requests(*i*). And to testify this our desire and assurance, we say, Amen (*k*).

(*b*) Matt. vi. 23.   (*c*) Rom. xv. 30.   (*d*) Dan. ix. 4, 7—9, 16—19.   (*e*) Phil. iv. 6.   (*f*) 1 Chron. xxix. 10—13.   (*g*) Eph. iii. 20, 21; Luke xi. 13.   (*h*) 2 Chron. xx. 6, 11.   (*i*) 2 Chron. xiv. 11.   (*k*) 1 Cor. xiv. 16; Rev. xxii. 20, 21.

FINIS.

Ellerton and Henderson, Printers,
Gough Square, London.

Date Due

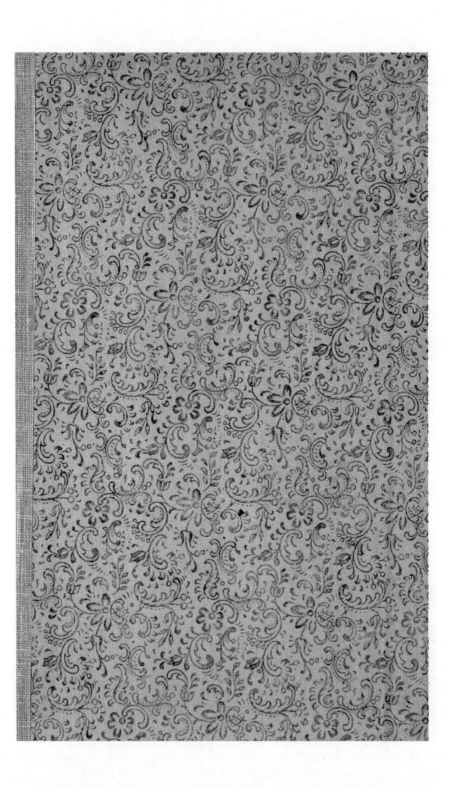

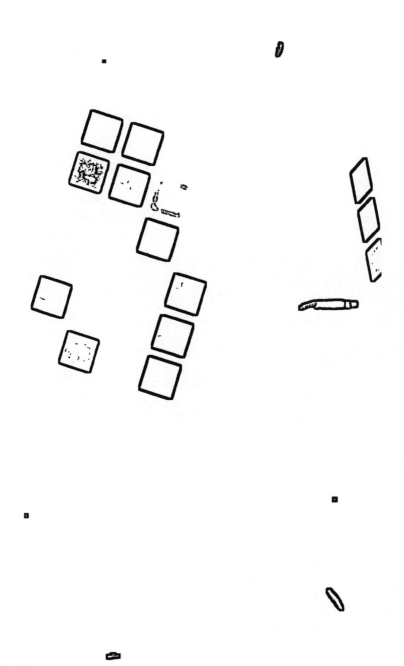